MARXISM

AND

CHRISTIANITY

MONOGRAPH SERIES
NUMBER THREE

The American Institute for Marxist Studies (AIMS) is a non-profit educational, research and bibliographical institute. Its purposes are to encourage Marxist and radical scholarship in the United States and to help bring Marxist thought into the forum of reasonable debate to produce a meaningful dialogue among Marxist and non-Marxist scholars and writers. Its policy is to avoid sectarian and dogmatic thinking. It engages in no political activity and takes no stand on political questions. It grinds no axe for any group, party, sect, organization.

To these ends it invites the support and participation of all scholars and public-spirited individuals.

IN MEMORIAM: HARRY F. WARD
(1873-1966)

Wood Engraving by Lynd Ward

MARXISM
AND
CHRISTIANITY

A SYMPOSIUM

Edited by HERBERT APTHEKER

Published for A.I.M.S. by

HUMANITIES PRESS   NEW YORK

Copyright 1968
by
Humanities Press, Inc.
New York, N. Y. 10010

Library of Congress Card Number: 68-13945

Printed in the United States of America

CONTENTS

CONTRIBUTORS

Herbert Aptheker is Director of AIMS and the author of *A Documentary History of the Negro People in the U.S., American Negro Slave Revolts, American Foreign Policy and the Cold War;* his most recent book is *The Nature of Democracy, Freedom and Revolution* (1967).

Martin J. Corbin has contributed to *Liberation, Cross Currents* and *Frères du Monde;* since 1964 he has been Managing Editor of *The Catholic Worker* and is now Co-Chairman, Catholic Peace Fellowship.

Harvey G. Cox is Associate Professor of Church and Society, The Divinity School, Harvard University, author of *The Secular City,* contributor to *Harpers, Redbook, Life* and other magazines and a Member, Editorial Board, *Christianity and Crisis.*

Richard Greenleaf has contributed to *Science & Society, Studies on the Left,* the *A.M.E. Review,* and *Religion in Life;* he has had wide experience as a newspaper reporter, especially in Florida and Indiana and is now on the staff of *The Worker.*

George H. Hampsch is Associate Professor of Philosophy at John Carroll University, a Jesuit institution in Cleveland; he is the author of *The Theory of Communism*(1965) and has contributed to professional journals.

Catherine R. Harris was an instructor in sociology for several years at Howard University; she has contributed to *Philosophy of Science* and *Philosophy & Phenomenological Research* and is currently working on a volume dealing with The Sociology of Karl Marx.

Patrick J. Hill is a teaching fellow in the Philosophy Department, Boston University; this is his first published writing.

Quentin Lauer, S.J., is Professor of Philosophy and Chairman, Department of Philosophy, Fordham University; his articles in various professional journals have centered on 19th century German philosophers, especially Hegel, Feuerbach and Marx. His books include: La *phènomènologie de Husserl* and *The Triumph of Subjectivity,* published as a Harper Torchback as, *Phenomenology: Its Genesis and Prospects.*

Richard Lichtman, formerly of the University of Missouri and the Center for the Study of Democratic Institutions, is now Professor of

Philosophy at the University of California (Berkeley). His *Toward Community: A Criticism of Contemporary Capitalism*(1965) was published by the Center; he has contributed to such journals as *Commentary, Social Research* and *Inquiry.*

Laszlo Matrai is Director, University Library, Budapest, Professor of Philosophy, University of Budapest and Secretary of the Philosophy and History Section, Hungarian Academy of Sciences. His books include: *Main Tendencies of Modern Aesthetics*(1931); *Theory of Character*(1943); and *Thought and Freedom*(1961).

Howard L. Parsons is Bernhard Professor of Philosophy and Chairman, Department of Philosophy, University of Bridgeport (Conn.). He is a former President of the Southern Society for Philosophy of Religion and of the Society for the Philosophical Study of Dialectical Materialism. His essays have appeared in many journals and in collective volumes dealing with philosophy and religion; several of his monographs have been published by AIMS.

INTRODUCTION

The present volume is the third to result from symposia sponsored by the American Institute for Marxist Studies. It was preceded by *Marxism and Democracy* and *Marxism and Alienation;* the latter was based upon lectures given at the New Hampshire summer camp of World Fellowship. *Marxism and Christianity* likewise had its roots in lectures given at that camp with the active participation of its Director, Dr. Willard Uphaus, in the summer of 1965.

The consequential nature of the three titles will be denied by no one. Though the dialogue among Christians and Marxists has become "news" only recently, it has by now a rather considerable tradition, as several of the following essays indicate. The 1930's was an especially rich period for this, as Professor Cox states; in addition to the examples he offers one may mention the series on "Christianity and Communism" that ran for weeks in 1937 in the *London Spectator* and then appeared as a small book, under that title (edited by H. Wilson Harris), and published in Oxford. Among the contributors to that effort were Dr. Ernest Barker, the Very Rev. W. R. Inge, John Strachey, Joseph Needham, and Reinhold Niebuhr. That volume had, indeed, been preceded by *Christianity and the Social Revolution,* edited by Canon Charles Raven of Cambridge; contributing an essay therein on behalf of the Marxian view was John Lewis.

In September, 1965, Dr. Lewis wrote the Editor of the present volume some lines which, with his permission, we wish here to reproduce:

> Marx never attacked religion—he saw it as an illusion which made life bearable as long as evil conditions were incapable of being removed. We must not attack those illusions, but remove the cause which makes them necessary. But does the victory of socialism remove that cause? We were over optimistic about that. So long as the threat of world war imposes wasteful sacrifices and harsh discipline, so long as the desperate need for rapid industrialization imposes hardships and iron Party rule in underdeveloped socialist countries, the freedom and fulfillment we hope for is still a distant goal. In that case religion will not disappear, nor will the moral law be the inner law of every heart.

Still the old conflict of the ideal and the real, the dream and the grim facts of life will continue—but not now without the firm hope that the forces have been set in motion and are powerfully at work even in the discipline and the sacrifices of the moment, which will most certainly achieve that long hoped for goal when the religious dream at last fades away "To be born again as the Holy Spirit of a righteous social order."

    ❖   ❖   ❖

The book must speak for itself, and each of the contributors—elsewhere identified—is well able certainly to speak for himself, or herself. It is believed that the reader does have before him a catholic volume, raising central questions, offering pertinent suggestions, not sparing in criticisms; if this is so it will contribute to the probing of two of the great schools of thought moving the hearts of hundreds of millions and shaking the globe.

It was originally hoped that this volume might be a *festschrift* for AIMS' Honorary Chairman, the late Dr. Harry F. Ward; alas, however, it must appear as a Memorial Tribute. Merely a glance at the bibliography of his writings, which concludes this book, will persuade any reader that no one better incarnated the best values of both Marxism and Christianity than he and that his life was, in essence, a striving to bring into being an effectual dialogue between them. Perhaps, then, this work is not an unworthy memorial to his life.

October, 1967

MARXISM

AND

CHRISTIANITY

THE MARXIST-CHRISTIAN DIALOGUE: WHAT NEXT?

by Harvey G. Cox

INTRODUCTION

In the spring of 1967 *Look* magazine ran a sympathetic feature about something that until recently seemed so unthinkable—a "dialogue" between Christians and Marxists. This is certainly a small sign of hope. In a world such as ours we need all the help we can get to undergird and legitimate this dialogue. The fact that it is now well enough recognized to be dealt with by a mass circulation journal is therefore something to be welcomed. We must overcome years of ingrained prejudice and instinctive suspicion on both sides—the hardened attitudes produced by the cold war. In a nuclear age we can no longer afford the lethal risks of a continuing Communist-Christian vendetta.

Still I would like to make clear at the outset that in my opinion the dialogue should not be supported merely because all of us need to live in the same world. It must have more than mere toleration and coexistence as its objective. For this reason I must take rather sharp issue with some of the ideas that have recently been voiced both within the dialogue and about the dialogue. In doing so I wish to touch on the following points:

1. The dialogue between Christian thinkers and various types of Marxists is not as new as recent reports would suggest. It goes back to the very beginning of the Marxist tradition, and the present vigorous dialogue is more a revival than a beginning. However hard it is to imagine now, future historians might chronicle the period of Pope Pius XII and Stalin as the high point in an episode of negative antagonism in what could eventually be an overall history of active and mutually valuable discussion.

2. There is no doubt that the advent of nuclear weapons has injected a note of urgency into the trite observation that we must all live together in one world. This fact does not provide, however, an adequate basis for fruitful dialogue between Communists

15

and Christians. The deeper and more significant fact is that both Christianity and Marxism have come to a stage in their respective developments in which only penetrating challenge and questioning from outside these traditions themselves will prevent atrophy and facilitate further development. In other words both traditions are beginning now to recognize the dialectical character of the truth they present and their need for each other.

3. The dialogue between Communists and Christians has sparked a lively new discussion *within* the two groups about the pre-conditions and possibilities of such a dialogue. Althought at first glance a by-product of the dialogue itself, when more closely examined this internal dialogue within the two traditions further corroborates my second point. It illustrates how authentic give and take with another and critical tradition can contribute to the health of one's own intellectual stream. Thus the questions raised by the possibility of fruitful dialogue with Christians has produced a flurry of ideological re-examination within Marxism which has spilled over into questions not directly related to religion. Likewise within Christianity the dialogue with Communists has produced a searching re-examination about the character and mission of Christianity which has also influenced thinking about areas not directly related to the dialogue itself.

4. I am not satisfied at the moment, however, with the agenda which has so far developed in the Communist-Christian conversation. So far the talk has focused mainly on comparisons of Communist and Christian views of man, society, the nature of religious phenomena, and the problems of subjectivity and transcendence. I am concerned that a dialogue which is limited to these subjects will soon reach the limits of its usefulness. Perhaps it would be better to say that since these topics are so rich and endless in their ramifications, such a dialogue could go on forever without producing any really significant results.

5. Finally there is something a bit questionable about the participants in the dialogue so far, at least in the official "dialogue" which has been so widely discussed in religious and secular newspapers and journals. Christians seem more interested in having dialogues with Communists from countries where Communists are in power and the church has been having difficulties. Communists seem more interested in having dialogue with Christians in countries where a rapproachment with Christians in some form of

popular front would strengthen their political chances. There is nothing wrong with this as far as it goes, but an enlargement of the conversation to include Christians and Marxists in quite different settings would seem to be a necessary next stage.

Now let me say something about each of these points:

I. THE PREHISTORY OF THE PRESENT DIALOGUE

The interaction of socialist thought and Christian theology is as old as socialist thought itself. If one traces the impulse toward the radical redistribution of property and privilege back to the radical sects of the 16th century, as Karl Mannheim does, then the name of the ill-fated religious reformer, Thomas Münzer, is a predominate one. Münzer, one of the leaders of the peasants' war, became what Ernst Bloch calls the first theologian of revolution. His cause failed and he was executed but not before injecting into the Western religious mentality the notion that if those who hold power do not wield it justly, then the oppressed are the ones who are designated by God to correct the injustice and to establish the Kingdom of God on earth. If we trace the impulse back to the 17th century then no history of radical ideas is complete without an account of the Levellers and the Diggers, the latter led by Gerrard Winstanley. Winstanley believed that Christianity called for a radically egalitarian society and for complete communal ownership of land.

Most historians, however, hold that modern socialism can only be understood as a response to the industrial revolution which began in the 18th century. If we accept this premise we must still deal with the very theological character of the writings of Hegel and Feuerbach, two of Karl Marx's most influential forerunners. Although Feuerbach's theological ideas were rejected by the churchly theologians of his time it is indisputable that his interest was primarily theological and it is also true that more recently some theologians are beginning to return to his analysis with a far more sympathetic regard.

Even more interesting to any history of Marxist-Christian dialogue, however, are the ideas of Claude Henri de Saint-Simon. Saint-Simon (1760-1825) saw that industry, science and technology were the forces that would shape the future of mankind and was convinced that society had to be completely restructured in order to make it livable for human beings. Significantly, his most influential book, published in 1825, is entitled *Le Nouveau Christianisme*. On an explicitly theological ground, Saint-Simon advocated a United States of Europe, a reorganization of society to facilitate brotherhood, and an economic order close to what we now call socialism. His followers later went on to call for the abolition of inheritance rights, for the emancipation of women and for public control of all the means of production. Though many of the particular ideas of the Saint-Simonists were later rejected by Marxist socialists, nonetheless they did provide much of the ferment out of which modern socialism has arisen. The interaction of Marxism and Saint-Simonism in the early years of the history of modern socialism also indicates that the dialogue between theology and Marxism did not begin last week.

Marx himself, of course, was an atheist. Still his atheism is of a peculiar and noteworthy variety. Marx rejected the notion that religion could be refuted by lampoon or argumentation. He located the religious phenomenon in the alienation of man caused by the class structure of pre-socialist society. He contended therefore that only a radical change in the sub-structure of that society through revolution could possibly rid the world of religious mystification. Marx's idea has been disputed from both wings. On the one side some Communists have argued that the mere alteration of the sub-structure does not finish religion off. It needs a shove and this shove comes about through active harassment and scientific argumentation—such as the testimony of cosmonauts who invade the heavens but encounter no angels. On the other wing there are Marxists who now argue that Marx's notion of religion can itself be understood only in the historical context of his time. They suggest that the conservative mentality of the 19th century churches and their opposition to the workers' movements evoked a misunderstanding of religion on Marx's part that would otherwise not have been the case. In March, 1963 for example, the late Palmiero Togliatti, then General Secretary of the Italian Communist Party, made a speech in which he totally rejected what he called "the ingenuous and mistaken idea" that religious beliefs will fade away under socialism. In the August 1, 1965 issue of *España Republicana* ("Republican Spain", the monthly organ of the Spanish Communist Party now published in Havana), Santiago Alvarez added the following twist to the Communist understanding

18

of religion: "In the ideas of goodness, equality, fraternity among human beings which the Christian religion also speaks of and which are reflected in the religious and sincere conscience of any believers, there are elements capable of contributing to an emancipating struggle." Alvarez says that whether or not these have their origins in religion, they are indisputably borne by religion today. He then asks himself whether ". . . these elements, instead of being a restraint to such a struggle (the emancipating class struggle), might constitute a stimulus." He answers his own question this way: "Our response is positive . . . religion is an encouraging idea where the religious movements support the social transformations and socialism". We shall return to this discussion in a moment.

But even this position is hardly a new one. In April, 1936, Maurice Thorez published a famous appeal to Catholic workers to participate and cooperate with Communists in the common workers' struggle in France. This was, of course, during the time of the popular-front policy which had been clearly called for by the Seventh Communist Party Congress in 1935. One would have expected almost no response from Catholics at all and indeed the response was rather small. It did produce, however, two significant statements. The first came from a group of left-wing priests and laymen in France who edited a short-lived monthly journal called *Terre Nouvelle* (New Earth). Its cover displayed a hammer and sickle imposed on the cross. These Catholics called themselves "revolutionary Christians". They are the forerunners of the Mission de France and the Worker Priest movement which arose after World War II.

Also in response to the appeal of Thorez a group of French Christians published a book entitled *Communism and Christianity* (which appeared in English translation in 1938 with a Preface by J. S. Scanlon). In this book such French Christian thinkers as Francois Mauriac, the Dominican Pere Ducattillon and the theologian Daniel-Rops were joined by the Protestant Denis de Rougemont and the Russian emigre orthodox theologian Nicholas Berdyaev. The tone of their articles shows these men clearly intended to begin a serious "dialogue" with the Communists. However just as the Catholic workers did not take up Thorez' invitation to a common struggle, also the French Communists at this time in effect refused the Christian invitation to a dialogue.

In Italy even during the darkest days of the Spanish Civil war which deeply exacerbated the conflict between Catholics and Communists, there was never a time without some probing back and forth between the two groups. In 1936 and 1938 the Italian Communist Party Central Committee appealed to Italian Catholics to join them in the fight against Fascism. In December, 1945 the Fifth Party Congress of the PCI which had already gone on record in favor of freedom of religion and worship insisted that it was also in favor of the freedom of religious propaganda and organization. It also offered party membership to anyone without regard to race or religious faith.

Unfortunately these moves taken by Italian Communists in the direction of cooperation with Catholics were not well-received by the Vatican. During the pontificate of Pope Pius XII some of the most severe religious measures ever taken against Communists darkened the possibility of dialogue. Catholics worked actively against the communist-socialist coalition in the 1948 election, and in July, 1949, Pius XII excommunicated Communists and their supporters. Only among small groups of Italian Catholics such as among the editors of the Florentine Catholic journal, *Testimonianze*, did any continuing openness to the Communists remain.

In 1964 two documents appeared which marked a new and auspicious beginning to the Communist-Christian dialogue in Italy. The first was a book entitled *Il dialogo alla prova* (The Dialogue Put to the Test) which was published in Florence in 1964 (Editions Valechi). This book brought together ten essays, five each by Catholics and Communists, on the question of the dialogue. It was produced under the leadership of a Communist, Professor Lucio Lombardo-Radice, and a Catholic, Mario Gozzini. The book contained some ideas to which I will return in a moment. Its importance was that it legitimated for many people the existence of a dialogue even though it exhibited some of the limitations.

The other important document for the year was the so-called *Testament* of Togliatti, his memorandum from Yalta, published after his death, in the summer of 1964 while in vacation in the Soviet Union. One paragraph from Togliatti's *Testament* reads as follows:

> The old atheistic propaganda is of no use. The very problem of religious conscience, its content, its roots among the masses, and the way of overcoming it must be presented in a different

20

manner from that adopted in the past if we wish to reach the Catholic masses and be understood by them. Otherwise our outstretched hand to the Catholics would be regarded as pure expediency and almost as hypocrisy.

In 1965 two books appeared which again escalated the Marxist-Christian Dialogue into a new stage. The first by Roger Garaudy was entitled *De l'Anatheme au dialogue,* * published in Paris. The second was *Marxismus und Dialektische Theologie* by the Czech Marxist, Milan Mahovec. The latter is a German translation of a book which first appeared in the Czech language in Prague in 1961. These books were important first because of the stature of the men who produced them. Roger Garaudy is not only a philosopher but a member of the Central Committee of the French Communist Party. Milan Mahovec is a distinguished Marxist and the Professor of Ethics at the Charles University in Prague, Czechoslovakia. These books were also important, however, because they indicated a new type of interest in Christianity among Marxists. Garaudy in his book says that Marxism itself must now learn something from Christianity, especially concerning the problems of what he calls "subjectivity and transcendence." Professor Mahovec's book is a stinging criticism of the conventional Marxist critique of Christianity. It examines one movement of Protestant theology very sympathetically and goes on to suggest the value of an interchange between the two traditions. In his later writings Professor Mahovec has come close to the position of Professor Garaudy in his suggestion that Marxists must examine the questions that Christianity raises about man's subjectivity and about transcendence, even though they do not accept the traditional Chrisian answer to these questions. In other words, these two distinguished Marxist thinkers are not interested simply in recruiting Christians for Communist causes. They are concerned to facilitate a dialogue which could alter the content of both of the traditions in question.

II   THE GROUNDS FOR THE DIALOGUE

I have stated that the co-existence argument, though important, cannot sustain the Communist-Christian dialogue very long. It is my contention that *neither* Christianity nor Marxism in their

---

*This was published in New York in 1966 by Herder & Herder, as *From Anathema to Dialogue: A Marxist Challenge to the Christian Churches,* with an introduction by Leslie Dewart—ed.

"received forms" are ready to deal adequately with the most basic questions of modern man. Here of course the vexatious question of "alienation" is the principal issue. The recent lively altercation among East European Marxists on what to do about the philosophical challenge posed by the writings of Franz Kafka focuses the issue well. The continued powerful relevance of Kafka's writings to people in socialist lands suggests that human alienation may have dimensions that transcend the solutions proferred by a previous generation of Marxists. If so, will a deeper exploration of the roots of human alienation profit from an examination of the long tradition of Christian literature on the subject? Such contemporary Czech Marxists as Mahovec, Toman and Gardovski appear to believe that it will. Their interest in Christianity is not directed toward Christianity's social ethic, as it might have been a generation ago. It is directed rather toward what is sometimes called "theological anthropology", the Christian understanding of man, his self-awareness, his place in history and in the cosmos. It could well be that Marxism will be able to speak convincingly to the modern situation only if it deepens and develops these aspects of its tradition, aspects to which previous Marxist thinkers have devoted insufficient attention. Here the dialogue with Christianity might not be simply interesting; it might even be essential.

Among Christian thinkers, the possibility of a fruitful encounter with Marxism comes at a crucial point in theological history. Recent vigorous schools of Christian theology such as the neo-reformation thought of Karl Barth, the existentialist interpretations of Rudolf Bultmann and his followers, and the personalist schools of modern French and German Roman Catholics seem to have reached the end of their creative phases. The classical idea of theology as a deductive or speculative discipline has been challenged by young theologians who insist that theology should be operational and focused on praxis. The question of how one can speak at all of "God" in an age whose worldview is formed by modern science is vigorously pressed. In my own view, the question of the nature of the theological enterprise itself is the one on which Christians have most to learn from the "dialogue". Both the method and the traditional catalog of problems in theology have been determined by and large by the scholastic history of theology. Even thinkers whose content has appeared on the surface to be inventive and fresh have relied on methods of argument that question the received tradition. Although some theologians think of theology as an intellectual discipline whose function it is to guide practice, the practice they have in mind is usually preaching. Rarely does theology devote itself to the practical guidance of Christians in the secular world. This task is generally left to something called "ethics", but the divorce of the two has contributed to both the obsolescence of theology and the rigidity of ethics.

Marx once said that the philosophers had spent long enough trying to understand and explain the world; the problem was to change it. This much quoted remark is misunderstood when we hear in it merely a call to a new agenda for philosophy. What Marx meant was that real philosophical thinking must by its very nature be operational. One only perceives the world correctly when one is attempting not merely to understand it but to change it. What theology needs is not merely a different agenda. It needs a *stance,* an understanding of its own purpose which sees theology not merely as a way to understand man, God and world history, but as an attempt to move the world toward the promise of the Kingdom of God. Only theology which understands itself in this way can be delivered from self-deception and irrelevance. Increasingly the dialogue with Marxism will raise for Christians the critical issue of what theology is and what its function should be. This is a challenge that is sorely needed and highly opportune.

Even if there were no nuclear threat Christians and Communists should be conversing. We should converse not just to avoid death but to affirm life. Life is by its very nature dialogical and dialectical. This is the real reason for the dialogue.

III: THE INTERNAL DISORDERS

Let me now turn to the "internal dialogues" within Christianity and Marxism which have been sparked in part by the dialogue and comment on the significance.

The Marxist-Christian dialogue has not been without its effect on the two groups involved. Each has a wing that strongly endorses the dialogue. Each has a wing which labels those involved in dialogue as revisionists, heretics or some other form of deviant. For Marxists the questions raised are of course serious ones. Does Marx's suggestion that religion is the "opiate of the masses" refer to religion in all times or places? If not, what were the special historical conditions that led him to make such a statement? If there were such determinants, what *other* aspects of Marx's thought can now be seen as time-bound and either irrelevant or inapplicable? These questions point to the larger question of whether Marxism is now ready to examine its own sources with real historical candor and rigorous critical precision. Is it ready to apply the historical-critical method to its own documents? Is it ready (to borrow a theological term) to "demythologize" itself? Are Marxists ready to see the impulses of Marxism absorbed, if not now then sometime in the future, in a large humanism that will include insights from many different traditions? In short, are Communists mainly interested in the future of Communism or are they mainly interested in the future of man? If these are not wholly synonymous, are they willing to make the sacrifices required?

Within Christianity the internal debate touched off by the Church's dialogue with Marxism could become the hottest altercation in decades. But the questions raised are parallel. Is Christianity willing to allow its symbols and doctrines to be transformed so that they touch the hunger of contemporary man? Is the Church willing to abandon its millenium-long coalition with property and privilege and to identify completely as Jesus did with the oppressed and disinherited of the earth? Given a choice between institutional safety and the costly effort to mold a world where love and justice are more completely realized, will *it* make the requisite sacrifice? Even more painfully, will Christians, who have preached the virtue of humility for centuries, be able to humble themselves enough to accept correction from Marxists? Ernest Bloch, a Marxist, claims that Christianity introduced in the world the category of hope, the notion that real change is possible. Roger Garaudy, another Marxist, says that Christianity unlocked man from his fixed place in the cosmos and made him the agent of historical change. If these men are right we must concede such notions have gotten lost somewhere over the two millenia of Christian history. Whether or not Christians will reappropriate them remains the crucial question.

IV: THE ISSUES AND THE AGENDA

Given the immense relief we all feel at the emergence of a Christian-Marxist dialogue, to complain about the agenda at this point may seem at first like bickering. But questions must be raised nevertheless. Roger Garaudy is a good example. He wins theological friends just a bit too easily. He suggests that the dialogue should center not on class struggle or revolution but on such problems as transcendence, subjectivity, and the meaning of love. Christians find themselves all too comfortable when they hear such phrases. Isn't this just what we discuss all the time, and haven't we proved to ourselves and others that we can discuss them endlessly? Why *not* have a Christian-Marxist dialogue? The reason that Garaudy is attractive to Christians is that he is talking about *our* traditional agenda.

But this is just the problem. Garaudy's approach to the dialogue obscures the main point that Christians need to learn from Marxists, that all human thought, including theological thought, arises not out of a vacuum but out of a specific historical situation. All theological thought emerges within a society. All societies are built on some particular set of power relationships, and the Church always has some relationship to these power factors. If we think that we can simply discuss transcendence and subjectivity without noticing the power bases that either inhibit or facilitate such a conversation, we have missed the whole point. Garaudy, although he seldom says much about it, is perfectly aware of this. He is a member of a Communist party which is now doing everything possible to build a common front of opposition to Gaullism. There is nothing wrong with this, and I personally believe that such a common front should be formed. It is important to notice, however, that Garaudy is not working at the dialogue in a political vacuum but in a situation where cooperation with Christians has weighty political significance. He is certainly not unaware of the larger connotations of this dialogue, but I wonder how carefully Christians have thought about the political overtones and implications of the same matter.

I have already mentioned the book *Il Dialogo ala Provo.* It is a collection of articles by Catholics and Communists, which, as the title suggests, puts the dialogue to test. The basic question that emerges is the following one: Should Christians and Communists first achieve a certain consensus about philosophical issues which they then apply in the social realm? Or must Christians and Communists first be engaged in the same struggle for peace and justice in the world in order to arrive at a common philosophical perspective?

The Catholics in the dialogue insisted that some common philosophical basis be developed before common work in the political area could proceed. The Communists argued, on the other hand, that no common philosophical thinking can be developed until Chrisians and Marxists participate in the same struggle on the political and social level. The book suggests that the main point of contention between Christian and Communists is *not* in the first place the problem of transcendence or of subjectivity, though these issues must eventually emerge. Rather the main point at issue is the question of *how* philosophical and theological thought is related to social and political action. Here we come to the nub of what I believe Christians have to learn from the dialogue. Christians have to learn anew from Marxists that our theologizing is not exempt from the social and political role of the Church in the secular world struggle. We have often toyed with this idea in our theological epistemology but have recoiled from accepting what it might mean for our traditional notions of theological work. If Christians could see more clearly the relationship between the theological enterprise and the issues of social change and Christian involvement in the politics of change, then the whole tone and content of the articles that we write and the books that we publish would be affected. Theological education might become a different kind of enterprise. We would learn that theological cerebration that is not conscious of its social base cannot be critical of it and therefore becomes a captive of unconscious social determinants. In my opinion, theologians have never devoted sufficient attention to the theological and methodological implications of this fact.

The readiness of Christians and Marxists to enter into a dialogue about anything is a welcome opening in the polar confrontation of the Cold War. But the terms in which the dialogue has begun could do us a disservice in the long run. They may mislead us into thinking that the Christian-Communist dialogue can proceed around tables at theological seminaries and in the refined language of the philosophical and theological tradition. This sort of dialogue has its value; however, we will soon discover as we have in the ecumenical movement that once all of the issues are stated, all of the differences are uncovered, a wholly new kind of dialogue has to begin. In the Catholic-Protestant dialogue, this new ecumenicity has taken the form of mutual participation in the secular struggle. It is quick outdistancing and outdating the traditional type of ecumenical dialogue. The same thing will have to happen very soon with the Christian-Marxist dialogue.

V   THE PARTICIPANTS IN THE DIALOGUE

Who should participate in the Marxist-Christian dialogue? So far the renewed conversation has been a very clubby affair indeed. First of all it has been geographically limited. It began in Eastern Europe with young Marxist intellectuals and young theologians. It has expanded recently to include western European Marxists and Christians. Last fall Roger Garaudy visited the USA including the Harvard Divinity School. No American Marxist was present. We Americans seem to feel a little more secure with import model Marxists. But there are many people who are not yet included in the conversation. It is understandable why Christians should want to communicate with Marxists in countries where Marxists are in power. It is equally understandable that Communists should want to communicate with Christians in countries where they are attempting to reestablish a popular front. The real question is whether either party is willing to open dialogue not in places where the revolution is either past or unexpected but where the danger and sacrifice still lie ahead. Are Marxists and Christians willing to talk and work together, for example, in Latin America, where both may end up felled by police bullets as Father Camilio Torres was last spring in Colombia?

Also, how long will the dialogue persist if it remains a coffee klatch among theologians, ideologists and philosophers?

The objective of a dialogue between Christians and Communists cannot merely be the reconciliation of the theoreticians who think they speak for these two massive groups of humanity. This kind of reconciliation would be a hollow and ephemeral one. What is needed, of course, is a reconciliation among the peoples whose despairs and fears and aspirations are symbolized in the various thought systems of the world. This is in part a question of philosophy, but it is even more basically a question of politics, power and policy.

CONCLUSION

What should come next in the Marxist-Christian dialogue? The answer must include both a short term and a long term aspect. In the short run, now, we must not only talk but act to secure the conditions of dialogue and to insure the continuance of life on this

27

planet. This entails cooperation at every level to end our nation's destruction of Vietnam, to support radical social change in the hungry nations and to strive for the elemental transformation of our own society into one that nourishes human potential rather than sapping it.

At the same time, however, Christians and Marxists must talk about the so-called Big Questions, and this means ultimately about *man*. Here the Catholics in *Il Dialogo ala Provo* were also right. What is man's place in the cosmos? What is his responsibility for history? Toward what sort of future should he shape the present? As this coming great dialogue unfolds, religion will contribute insights into man the myth and symbol maker, man the dreamer of visions, man the promise maker, man the creature who alone seems able to experience mystery, wonder and phantasy. Marxism will remind us of man the maker, man the irreduceably social being, man the custodian of change. Not just as Christians and Marxists but as human beings we *must* talk about the deepest and most profound human issues, but never apart from the issues man faces in his present world.

The central theological issue has to do with *hope* and its grounds. Perhaps it could be stated this way: Does man's unfaltering hope for a more humane and just world have any grounding in reality itself? Is there reason to believe the developing universe itself *sustains* the human aspiration it seems to elicit, or is man's hope only his own wishful projection, something to which both history and the cosmos remain supremely indifferent? It is the contention of Biblical faith that there is a mystery from which man emerges, a reality that summons him to anguished freedom and joyous responsibility, a real ground for the hopes man entertains for himself and his race.

But even with both these traditions making their contributions, our picture of man will remain incomplete. We will need insights overlooked in part both by Christians and Marxists: the serene vision of the Greeks, the wisdom of the oriental religions, the discipline of science, and insights from groups and seers still unborn. The future of the dialogue between Marxists and Christians is eventually to become a part of that larger *human* dialogue which begins with man's coming to consciousness, which is expressed in the Hebrew Psalmist's query, "What is man that Thou are mindful of him?" and which will never end so long as man remains man.

* * * * *

MARXISM AND RELIGION

by HERBERT APTHEKER

We shall deal with four questions:

1) What were the views of Marx and of Engels on religion?
2) What are the most prevalent distortions of these teachings?
3) What tactical problems present themselves in the present world, vis-a-vis Marxism and Religion?
4) What is the essence of the matter of so-called reconciliation between Marxism and Religion?

I

Marxism sees the source, the root of religious *feeling* in a sense of awe, wonder, helplessness, and misery. Marxism notes two different founts feeding this source: 1) in the earliest stages of history from man's inability to comprehend and therefore to deal effectively with the forces of nature; 2) with the development of classes, an additional fount was the oppression endured and inability to comprehend the reasons for this oppression and therefore to effectively overcome it. To the degree that the conquest of nature has been incomplete and the unlocking of its mysteries far from done, under class societies both these founts have operated to swell the ocean of religious *feeling*.

Marxism sees the source of religious *institutions* in class divisions and in the consequent division of labor, the appearance of a State power and the usefulness of such institutions to the maintenance of that power.

Marxism understands religion itself to be—and the clearest and briefest definition is in Engels' *Anti-Duehring* (1878)—"the fantastic reflection in men's minds of those external forces which control their daily life, a reflection in which the terrestrial forces assume the form of supernatural forces." Insofar as religion is held to be this "fantastic reflection"—i. e., distorted, springing from and reflecting alienation—and insofar as religion holds to

29

the supernatural—that is, the antiscientific—Marxism is radically opposed to religion.

Marxism treats religion historically, as it does and must everything else, since, of course, the dialectical quality of Marxism sees all phenomena in a dynamic and not in a static manner and sees process as the essence of all reality.

Thus, most particularly as concerns Christianity, Marxism stresses the significant contrast between early and late Christianity. It will not be amiss to illustrate this fact from some of the writings. Thus, Engels, in an essay entitled "On the History of Early Christianity"—published during the last year of his life in *Die Neue Zeit*—wrote:

> The history of early Christianity has notable points of resemblance with the modern working-class movement. Like the latter, Christianity was originally a movement of oppressed people: it first appeared as the religion of slaves and emancipated slaves, of poor people deprived of all rights, of peoples subjugated or dispersed by Rome. Both Christianity and the workers' socialism preach forthcoming salvation from bondage and misery; Christianity places this in a life beyond, after death, in heaven; socialism places it in this world, in a transformation of society. Both are persecuted and baited, their adherents are despised and made the objects of exclusive laws, the former as enemies of the human race, the latter as enemies of the state, enemies of religion, the family, social order. And in spite of all persecution, nay, even spurred on by it, they forge victoriously, irresistibly ahead. Three hundred years after its appearance Christianity was the recognized state religion in the Roman World Empire, and in barely sixty years socialism has won itself a position which makes its victory absolutely certain.

In this same essay, Engels declares of the early Christian writings: " . . . they could just as well have been written by one of the prophetically minded enthusiasts of the International."

Engels, in his earlier article on "Bauer and Early Christianity" (1882) again declared that "the essential feature" of "the new religious philosophy" — he means Christianity — was that it "reverses the previous world order, seeks its disciples among the poor, the miserable, the slaves and the rejected, and despises the rich, the powerful and the privileged . . ."

In *Anti-Duehring*, the historical, developmental treatment of religion that is basic to the Marxian approach is spelled out with particular clarity. Permit a somewhat lengthy quotation:

30

In Catholicism there was first the *negative equality of all human beings before God as sinners,* and, more narrowly construed, the equality of all children of God redeemed by the grace and the blood of Christ. Both versions are grounded on the role of Christianity as the religion of slaves, the banished, the dispossessed, the persecuted, the oppressed. With the victory of Christianity this circumstance was relegated to the rear and prime importance attached next to the antithesis between believers and pagans, orthodox and heretics.

With the rise of the cities and thereby of the more or less developed elements of the bourgeoisie, as well as of the proletariat, the demand for equality as a condition of bourgeois existence was bound gradually to resurge, interlinked with the proletariat's drawing the conclusion to proceed from political to social equality. This naturally assumed a religious form, sharply expressed for the first time in the Peasant War.

The bourgeois side was first formulated by Rousseau, in trenchant terms but still on behalf of all humanity. As was the case with all demands of the bourgeoisie, so here too the proletariat cast a fateful shadow beside it and drew its own conclusions (Babeuf).

Here will be noticed Engels' point that while institutionalized religion seeks essentially to bulwark the status quo, the content of the religious affirmations—whose sources, as we have seen, are not unitary—has its own logic and may appeal to and does appeal to different classes. That is, while ruling classes may *wish* to employ religious feeling and belief as forces for the retention of their power, religion, being a mass phenomenon and transcending in that sense classes, *may* serve as the justification for and inspiration of vast popular movements that are revolutionary.

As we have seen, Marxism emphasizes the revolutionary quality of early Christianity. Marx himself as a schoolboy, wrote a paper, "Observations of a Young Man on the Choice of a Life-Work," in which he manifested his admiration for the Christ figure, and in which he then declared: "To men God gave a universal aim—to ennoble mankind and oneself." (See on this, Robert F. Fulton: *Original Marxism* (Boston, 1960). This, of course, is the pre-Marxian stage of Marx but the reverence is to be noted and the particular point that attracted Marx to Christ is significant. This recurs in the later and fully mature Marx; for example, writing in 1855 on an anti-Church demonstration in London, he excoriated the Established Church for its callousness and reactionary policy and went on to contrast that with the teachings of Christ. Marx added: "The classical saint of Christianity mortified *his* body for the salvation of the souls of the masses; the modern, educated

31

saint mortifies *the bodies of the masses* for the salvation of his own soul."

Marxism repeatedly notes the connection between religiosity and rebellion; but it is the religiosity of masses who see in their religious beliefs goads not for pie in the sky but for battle on earth. Of such mass efforts in Europe prior to the French Revolution, Engels in his work on *Feuerbach and the End of Classic German Philosophy* (1886) wrote: "The sentiments of the masses were fed with religion to the exclusion of all else; it was therefore necessary to put forward their own interests in a religious guise in order to produce a impetuous movement." And, of course, Engels' entire book, *The Peasant War in Germany* (1850) spells this out.

There are no better illustrations of this than those that saturate United States history. The motto of Thomas Jefferson was" Resistance to tyranny is obedience to God." No American was more profoundly religious than John Brown. While the masters taught the slaves only one lesson in their religious instruction—i. e., be meek and docile; accept your lot on earth as the portion given you by an ominiscient God and know that protest against this lot is blasphemy—many slaves rejected this teaching, but they did not reject religion. On the contrary, their religion was the religion of early Christianity, because like those who created that Christianity they, too, were slaves and outcasts and among the wretched of the earth. Their slave-rebellion leaders were all religious men: Nat Turner preached to his comrades that the first shall be last and the last shall be first; that God so hated slaveowners He sent fearful scourges amongst them; that He so loved the slaves He parted the seas so that they might escape and then brought the seas together again and drowned the masters' pursuing armies. And that which was true of past popular struggles in the United States, is true of them today, as everyone must know. How multifarious is religion may be indicated by the fact that both Francisco Franco and John Brown profess religion!

The classical statement of Marxism on religion—at least that most often quoted—or, better, excerpted—is of course the "opium" one. While it is true that Americans are in a great hurry—going nowhere, commented Brecht—still it is worthwhile noting that the opium phrase appears in an essay; if one does not have time to read the whole essay, perhaps he can take the time to read the two paragraphs in which the "opium" appears. At any rate, I will now take the time. This is from Marx's essay, written in 1844, entitled "Contribution to the Critique of Hegel's Philosophy of Right". The two paragraphs are:

> Religious distress is at the same time the *expression* of real distress and the *protest* against real distress. Religion is the sigh of the oppressed creature, the heart of a heartless world, just as it is the spirit of a spiritless situation. It is the *opium* of the people.
>
> The abolition of religion as the *illusory* happiness of the people is required for their real happiness. The demand to give up the illusions about its condition is the *demand to give up a condition which needs illusions.* The criticism of religion is therefore *in embryo the criticism of the vale of woe,* the *halo* of which is religion.

Dismissing this as some sort of vulgar atheism, as a cranky and mechanical rejection of religion per se, is an utter distortion. It is as though one quoted Christ as saying, "Go and sin." Of course, he did say that, but one should at least complete the sentence—that is—Christ said "Go and sin no more."

In the above two paragraphs note is to be taken of the fact that Marx emphasizes the protest potential of religion; he emphasizes its beauty, and its source of refreshment. He also insists upon its NECESSITY given oppressive, unjust, unreasonable and unknown relationships. In this sense Marx insists upon the deeply persistent quality of religion, exactly because it serves real needs. In his great work, *Capital,* Book I, he wrote, for example: "The religious reflex of the real world can, in any case, only finally vanish, when the practical relations of every-day life offer to man none but perfectly intelligible and reasonable relations with regard to his fellowmen and to nature." On religion, I would say, Marxism does not err in underestimating its lasting potential; in other areas I think Marxism did err in this direction—I mean in the direction of minimizing its potency and lasting force. I would say this is especially true as regards nationalism.

Let me hasten to add that I absolve Marxism of this error, but by no means do I absolve all Marxists of this error. Some Christians have been frank in noting the aberrations and failures of Christianity; they insist on distinguishing between Christianity and Christians. Marxists—or those calling themselves Marxists—also have not been guiltless of errors and crimes and failures. These all are explicable in terms of history and environment and the unprecedented nature of the task—to build socialism—but while they all are explicable, not all are forgivable. But none touches the reality or validity of Marxism and all in fact violated that reality and insofar as they did impeded the advance of socialism.

＊　＊　＊

Having the views which I have summarized of religion, Marxism, of course, opposes religious persecution; it opposes coercive methods aimed at religion. This, by the way, was one of the many points of conflict between Marxism and Anarchism — between Blanqui and Marx. In this sense, in the attitude towards religion, one has a good illustration of the fact that Marxism was created not only in combat with the Right— i. e., against capitalism, but also with the ultra-Left——i. e., against anarchism and Blanquism, etc.

This attack upon religious persecution recurs in the classical writings.

At the same time, Marxism always advocates a secular society and favors separation of church and state. In doing this, Marxism makes clear that it demands not simply religious toleration for that would be intolerant towards anti-religion. In his *Critique of the Gotha Program* (1875) Marx made explicit his position that there must exist not only the toleration of all religions but also of agnosticism and of atheism.

Marxism not only opposes professional atheists; it also opposes what George Lukacs once called—in an essay published sixteen years ago in *Masses and Mainstream*—religious atheists. That is, it opposes those who so vehemently and insistently attack God as to lead to the belief that they do protest too much. Where individuals have reached intellectual and ideological positions wherein God is altogether unnecessary that is their business, and when the social order reaches the stage where religious illusions will no longer be necessary they will evaporate.

Marxists will argue their historical materialist position, of course, and will seek through their work and their writings to show its validity; and socialist states will seek to educate its population in an historical materialist direction. I do not mean there is indifference in Marxism, philosophically, to religion; but I do mean that Marxism sees the multifarious sources of religion; that Marxism carefully distinguishes between religious feeling and religious institution; that Marxism knows that religious feelings may

34

and often have impelled the most magnificent and most effective progressive and revolutionary activity; that such feeling means one thing to one class and another thing to another class; that it is itself a phenomenon in process. An attitude of contempt for religion is an anti-Marxist attitude; an attitude of superiority towards religious people is not only anti-Marxist but is also contemptible.

There have been such attitudes in the past among some Marxists. There have been sectarian patterns of behavior in the past—and perhaps not only in the past—that to recall, makes one's flesh crawl. Some of this has its roots in ignorance; in psychological failings; in reaction to persecution; in the strain of the struggle. And some of this has its roots in literal and non-historic readings of certain writings by Marx and Lenin. In the latter case, for example, one can find statements to the effect that all religion always serves reaction and nothing else. This certainly is—as we have shown—un-Marxian but statements of this nature will be found in Lenin. Of course, fully rounded presentations of the Marxian view of religion are in Lenin, but the other statements occur, too. Are these contradictory? Only on the surface. Why? Because the apparently one-sided remarks of Lenin appear in personal letters written quickly and under pressure and for the moment and to influence a particular person in a particular situation. Thus, in the awful period of Stolypin reaction and repression in Czarist Russia, prior to World War I, Gorki himself was showing evidences of despair and of a rejection of the materialist view and a kind of grasping at religious solace if not explanation. Lenin then wrote to Gorki unequivocally attacking religion as ever reactionary. But if this is not placed in its place—Czarist Russia with its established, powerful and fearfully corrupted Church—and its time—a time of pogroms and fierce repression by the Czar who, of course, also was head of the Russian Church—then one is not seeking a true reading of Lenin but is seeking rather material for the House Un-American Activities Committee.

The same phenomenon occurs at times in Marx, notably in his paper ironically called, "The Communism of the Paper *Rheinischer Beobachter*" written in 1847, where Marx is polemizing with the ultra-reactionary newspaper of Cologne and with a State Councillor who had just attacked in the name of Christianity what the official called the fearful conspiracy of communism.

One of the lessons here is to bear in mind that when one is

reading the books of Marx and Engels and Lenin he is reading not sacred scripts but rather—books. To read the books of these men in any manner other than a scientific one is to manifest contempt for them, since devotion to science was their passion.

II

Having considered the content of the Marxian approach to religion and some sources of its distortion, we turn now to the question of tactics.

Pressures for change on the part of religious institutions and religiously inclined people in their attitudes towards Marxism and Socialism are numerous and great. Simultaneously, pressures dictating a change in attitude on the part of Marxists towards such institutions and such feelings also are consequential.

The great religions of Asia, the mid-East and the West face the fact that socialism exists in one-third of the globe; exists now in Asia, in Europe, in Latin-America and is being consciously sought in Africa. These religions also face the fact that additional scores of millions of peoples in countries not yet socialist adhere to a socialist perspective, more or less avowedly Marxist. This is true in Japan, in India, in France and Italy, in Brazil and Chile, in Finland and Burma.

These great religions also face the fact that movements of national liberation—often with significant socialistic overtones—are sweeping the colonial and semi-colonial world. Related is the Negro freedom movement in the United States — also carrying challenges to the structure of the social order; that movement and the responses to it have represented among the most significant challenges faced by religion and religious organizations in the United States since the pre-Civil War era.

All these globe-shaking events are ensconced within and causally connected to the great scientific, demographic and technical revolutions and innovations of the past two generations which in another way offer challenges to traditional concepts of religion.

To these challenges, the old order of capitalism responds with the threat of fascism and war. Whatever may have been the policies of concession and adjustment—or even, in some cases, support— vouchsafed fascism by religious institutions, these were normally grudging or shamefaced and more or less coerced. And perhaps it will be agreed that in any case such policies of concession and/or support are regretted in hindsight.

The unprecedented challenge of general war with thermo-nuclear weapons and with bacterial and chemical weapons—and other horrors still on the drawing boards—presenting the real possibility of the extermination of Man, also must induce reconsiderations of tactics vis-a-vis other human beings and other social orders no matter what their character. This involves not only such philosophical questions as the possibility of a just war using such weapons—and no religion condones any but a just war, whatever the excuses may be—but also such questions as the very persistence of religion itself. The impact of these considerations may be illustrated by the fact that in the Roman Catholic Church two of the post-World War II Popes—Pius XII and John XXIII—have expressed repeated and intense preoccupation with the necessity of peaceful co-existence among states having different social systems.

It is becoming increasingly clear to church men of any sensitivity and perception that persistence in opposing the world-wide demand for an end to hunger, illiteracy and indignity is suicidal. The Catholic Professor of Philosophy at St. Michael's College in Canada, Leslie Dewart, has argued this persuasively in his book *Christianity and Revolution: The Lesson of Cuba* (Herder and Herder, N. Y., 1963) particularly in his chapter, "The Theology of Counter-Revolution."

All the considerations offered above as necessarily inducing an alteration in the attitude of religious institutions and people to Marxism, also work the other way—that is, also induce changes in attitude and conduct from Marxists relative to such institutions and people. Where Socialism exists it is necessary to deal constructively and decently—not to say creatively—with the inhabitants of such lands; or better, they as inhabitants of such lands will now be building a decent and creative society. This must be done in lands having different religions—and different traditions, even if the formal religions are the same. Problems and considerations differ, that is, not only in terms of traditionally Protestant sections of Czechoslovakia as contrasted with traditionally Catholic areas of the same country, but also between the Catholic Church within Poland—where its tradition was one of an ally in a prolonged national struggle—and that Church in Hungary where its tradition

37

was one of support for an intensely chauvinistic, aggressive and anti-Semitic hierarchy.

Again, while the Church in Italy must adjust to the reality of nearly 2,000,000 Italians who choose to be Communists and one-fourth of the electorate who vote Communist, so must the Communist Party adjust to the fact that scores of thousands of its members belong to the Church and millions of its electoral supporters also adhere to the Church.

Furthermore, with the advent of fascism to power in Germany, the entire outlook of the world Communist movement shifted—as symbolized in Dimitrov's report to the VII Congress of the Communist International (1935). This outlook remains basically in effect and it is an outlook of breadth, of unity, of shunning sectarianism and narrowness. It is an outlook of unity with all who stand opposed to fascism and war—and unity with all such no matter what other differences may be present.

It was in response to this threat on the international level that the worldwide Communist movement developed the policy of collective security; again in essence this remains in effect in a new, wider and more urgent form as the necessity for peaceful co-existence among States having different social systems. This remains and is intensified because the danger of war remains and because the nature of another general war certainly will be catastrophic and may well be quite annihilating.

In the face of the dangers of fascism and of thermonuclear war those who oppose both have in that opposition more in common than anything that can possibly divide them. To permit differences to weaken—not to say vitiate—this common need is frightful and everything must be done to prevent it.

These are the essential grounds why all of us—whatever our motivations and truths—religious or scientific, spiritual or material —must act together for our great ends and must discuss our differences with dignity and with a predetermination not to aggravate them but to delimit them. This does not mean abandoning outlooks —unless one is persuaded of a superior outlook—but it does mean recognizing the mutual necessity for respect and regard.

III

Let me say something on reconciliation. I think to project reconciliation in the sense of some kind of merger of differing outlooks by shedding what may be erroneous in both and wedding what may be true in both is unreal. I think outlooks have changed and will change in accordance with changing reality. It is vital that one avoid fanaticism and that one appreciate the necessity— for the health of one's outlook, if for no other reason—that flexibility be permitted and that change and growth be assumed. Truth advances through the detection of error; error is detected through reason and through science. To one who thinks, there is no greater service than the detection of error.

Specifically, in terms of the mutual existence of Marxism and religion: Both do exist and have existed together for a century. If Marxism is correct and if the universal achievement of communism produces a world that is reasonable and controllable and therefore a world in which religion, being unnecessary will disappear, why, then, that is what will happen. If, on the other hand, this Marxian projection is wrong—and of course it may well be wrong—then religion will not and perhaps will never disappear. Very well, in either case the worst that can happen is that one of the two—the religious person or the Marxist—will have been proven in error. Then each will be wiser. Is this a calamity?

Not only will each be wiser, but both will be alive. We say, given the will one can find the way. Surely one may also say, given life, Mankind will find solutions. If some will say, not solutions— or at least that solutions in any ultimate sense are quite impossible —I will say to that, I think not but perhaps you are right. Then let us agree that given Life, Man may always *seek* solutions.

All right. Let that be the path of reconciliation. Let us compete —those who see religion as the way and those who see Marxism as the way—and all others, too, who see other ways altogether—let us all compete in seeking solutions—in creating a LIFE that is whole, fruitful, sane, fraternal and peaceful.

On this let us *begin* our Great Reconciliation.

✿   ✿   ✿

THE ATHEISM OF KARL MARX

by Quentin Lauer, S.J.

It is significant to me that we meet during these days under
the auspices of World Fellowship. We who meet here represent
opposing ideologies and they are ideologies which, in the eyes of
many are simply irreconcilable. What is more, the purpose of our
meeting is not to provide the spokesman of these ideologies with
a platform from which to advocate their own particular views and,
perhaps, to hurl invectives at their opposite numbers, but rather
to provide all of us with an opportunity to live in fellowship, despite our differences, and, perhaps, to understand those differences
in such a way that the fellowship can increase, even though the
differences do not decrease.

When I first heard of World Fellowship, however, it was as
World Fellowship for Reconciliation, and the last word in the title,
it would seem, adds an important element of significance to what
we are doing here. In fellowship we can come together, talk to
each other intelligently—even lovingly—and come to understand
each other. But, if reconciliation is our aim, then something more
is required; the fellowship in which we stand must be one in which
the differences are really bridged and a genuine unity is achieved.
Reconciliation, of course cannot mean that differences are merely
suppressed; still less can it mean that one side or the other simply
abdicates its position. Rather it means that we can come to see
difference as not necessarily an obstacle to union and that opposition can—paradoxically—be a dynamic force which unites, provided there is a genuine will to concrete unity.

We are now engaging in a symposium to discuss Marxism and
religion, and, if I understand our purpose rightly, we are concerned
with the possibility of somehow reconciling the two — without
making either cease to be what it really is. My own acquaintance
with Marxism (professionally at least) is primarily with what we
might call classic Marxism, the Marxism of Marx himself, of Engels,
and, of course, of Lenin. Though I have been very much impressed
by a kind of development in this thinking, which seems to me to

40

make the whole question of reconciliation a lot more realistic today than it would have been a century or even fifty years ago, I shall confine myself to the relationship of Marxism and religion as I find it in the thought of Karl Marx.

Before doing this, however, I should like to mention some convictions which are purely my own. (Convictions, you know, are frequently part of one's faith rather than of that for which one can marshal irrefutable evidence.)

Reconciliation

The first of these convictions is that reconciliation is a possibility. If, of course, one were to take Marxist theory and religious theory (whatever that may be) in the abstract, then the gap would seem to be unbridgeable; despite certain similar ideals they are diametrically opposed. If, however, one takes Marxist thinking and religious thinking in the concrete—and this, I think, means confronting two views of man (our real concern)—then, I think, reconciliation can come about in a growing mutual realization of what man is—or is to be. Here the two views can complement each other.

My second conviction is that, not only is this reconciliation a possibility, but it is in the process of becoming an actuality.

The third conviction—and here I am edging out on a somewhat thinner limb—is that there must be a reconciliation, or both will perish. I don't know what will destroy them—I once thought it was capitalism—but destroyed they will be, by something which is opposed to both (perhaps the deification of human selfishness).

Lastly, I am convinced that this reconciliation will be not merely the result of a process but that it is itself a process—a dialectical process. And, I must say quite frankly before this audience, I do not think that the process in question is adequately described in the Marxist theory of dialectical development. Let us say—without going into too much detail—that the process presents itself to me as being more in the nature of a Hegelian dialectic. According to this the two positions must be seen as really opposed, since it is only as opposed that they are related to each other, and it is their very opposition which reveals a kind of complementarity, in which each needs the other in order to realize itself. I might add that each—Marxist consciousness and religious consciousness—is itself in process and that the process of reconciling the two is inseparable from the process of self-realization in which each is involved. Thus though the Marxist dialectic is not inoperative in the overall process, it is not, in my view, that which will effectuate the reconciliation of the two processes.

That I say this springs from my conviction that the Marxist dialectic (historical, naturalistic, materialistic) is not a dialectic of reconciliation at all—whatever else may be its virtues. Rather it is, at least as Marx saw it, a dialectic of substitution, or even of destruction, where the force which is hatched in the bosom of a given social structure is destined to destroy and supplant the force that engendered it. According to this—and I think I can show that this is Marx's own position—a reconciliation between Marxism and religion is unthinkable, the latter must simply cede before the onward movement of the former. The Hegelian dialectic, on the other hand, is conceived by its author to be precisely a dialectic of reconciliation—though it never envisaged a reconciliation between the two forces with which we are concerned.

At this point it seems in order to say something about what I mean by dialectic process. In doing so I feel justified in taking the Hegelian dialectic as paradigmatic, since even Marx admits that his own dialectic is but a development of the Hegelian. According to this, then—and here I am talking only of the dialectical process of history, of social growth and development—any given historical stage (economic, social, political structure) can be called a position, which, since it is historical and therefore not static, engenders its own counter position (up to this point Hegel and Marx are in agreement). The engendered position is the negation of a given one. What is characteristic of the Hegelian dialectic, however, is the relation between the opposed positions; though they negate each other, they do not simply cancel each other out, since each is at least partially true. This, of course, means that each is also partially false—and a simple triumph of one over the other would mean the triumph of what is false as well as of what is true in it. The reconciliation of the two, then, is a third position which negates what is false in the two former but retains them at least partially by affirming what is true in them. In the process of history the resulting position is not a final one but in turn engenders its own opposite, thus requiring a new reconciliation—and so the process continues.

Now, as I understand the Marxist dialectic—and here I am

thinking primarily of the characteristic dialectic of class struggle —the position is one in which one class (necessarily) dominates society and by so doing (necessarily) engenders another class which is irreconcilably opposed to it. According to this dialectic the process of history inevitably brings it about that the dominated class not only negates but also destroys and supplants the dominating class. The result is not a third position which both negates and affirms the other two, but the total abolition of one class and the total triumph of the other. This, of course, is revolution, and the ultimate revolution is that in which the proletariat destroys its own class character, thus ushering in the classless society. What is to be noted, however, is that the proletariat ceases to be a class by destroying its opposite, since to be a class is to be opposed to another class, and, if there is no opposing class, there is no class at all. This result, I contend, is not a reconciliation but a substitution, a victory of one opposite over the other.

Dialectical Relationship

So much for the dialectical process in general. Marx, it is true, did not see the relationship between his own thought and religious thought as one of dialectical opposition; but, if we are to speak seriously of reconciliation, it seems to me that we must speak in terms of some such relationship (even a Marxist cannot afford to let Marx's own thinking become dogma). Obviously, then, I am here speaking from a Christian point of view—I am convinced that the Christian can see the relationship, more readily than can Marx, as a dialectical one. This means, of course, that the Christian must be able to look at the opposition positively, but it also means that the Marxist must be able to do the same (presuming that his present goal is not simply the elimination of religion). This it is, I am convinced, that Marx himself did not do. Thus, if the contemporary Marxist can do it, he will have achieved a position which is an advance over that of Marx himself. If he cannot, then, I feel, he is being unhistorical and, therefore, untrue to Marx precisely in clinging to Marx.

The theory which Marx developed began with an observation that Marx made with regard to man as he saw him in the early 19th century. What Marx saw was a state of affairs in which man had become dehumanized (the word he used was "alienated," which meant estranged from what was man's true being). The dehumanization, or "alienation," consisted in man's having become subject to something which man himself had created and which he himself should have dominated. It is alienation, precisely because man finds his true being not in himself where it belongs, but outside himself. The irony—and tragedy—of it is that the something outside himself is man's own product; thus alienation is really self-alienation (both a state of affairs and a process).

Marx sees this alienation of man manifesting itself in a triple form, each in its own way basic. The fundamental form of alienation is economic, wherein by his work (which is the only force which adds value to nature) man produces a wealth which then takes on a personality in the form of capital and dominates man. Another form of alienation is political, since the state which man has created becomes a force which suppresses him, permitting one class in society to assume political control and, thus, to impose its interests on the whole of society, using the majority class for the furtherance and perpetuation of its own minority aims. The third form of alienation, as Marx sees it, is the religious, since man's religious inclinations have created a God who then dominates man in such a way that man loses the very liberty which characterizes him as man. We must remember that for Marx liberty means self-determination and that in all three cases man has surrendered himself to being determined by another—and by another which man's own activity has created.

Each of these three forms of alienation, I have said, Marx considered to be in its own way basic. Economic alienation is the first and fundamental form, because from it all other forms spring and because it results from the most genuinely human of all activities, the activity of material production. Religious alienation is in its turn basic, because it expresses globally, so to speak, the utter alienation of man—so long as man sees human affairs determined by God, then self-determination is out of the question. Political alienation, too, is basic (and here we must remember that Marx has in mind principally 19th century Prussia), because it has solidified a state of society in which the other forms of alienation are officially consecrated.

Marx's "Science" of History

Now, in all this there is obviously contained a rather remarkable historical insight. One need not agree with Marx's materialist or naturalist presuppositions—and I certainly do not—to recognize that each of the three factors here mentioned has at one time or another worked toward the suppression of man, toward determining him against his will and against his best interests. It is not the insight, however, with which I find fault; rather it is with the so-called "science" (with its 19th century aspiration to express "necessary" laws) which Marx links to this insight. And here be it remarked that Marx's "science" does not flow from his insights, rather his insights are commanded by his insistence that the situation of man be scientifically explained. More than one of Marx's predecessors—chief among them Hegel—had sought to construct a philosophy of history, a rational discipline which would permit human thought to see why the apparently contingent events of history had come about precisely the way they had come about.

Marx, however, would go them all one better; he would outline not a philosophy but a science of history, which would be just as rigidly scientific as were the physics, chemistry, and biology of his day (the English economists had provided a good deal of the impetus for this with their now largely discredited "science" of economics). Marx, then, could not be satisfied with a theory which would explain how things actually did come about; he wanted a theory which would explain why things could not have come about in any other way. Such a theory would have the added advantage of providing the "scientific" remedy for an admittedly bad situation. (The scientific explanation of how the situation came about would at the same time supply the remedy for the situation.)

This was really new. The natural sciences, which were blossoming in Marx's day, were constantly discovering new laws of nature, which seemed not only to explain but also to control the workings of nature. The economists were discovering laws which enabled them to explain and to a certain extent control the course of economic events. Marx now came up with a theory of history which would discover the laws of society and thus enable man both to explain what had already come about and control what was to come about in the future (to the extent, of course, that the very freedom to control depended on the necessary working out of the laws of history). The theory which would explain man's self-alienation would also explain how man would reappropriate what had been alienated—and the reappropriation would be as inevitable (scientific) as was the alienation.

In the spirit of the late 18th and early 19th centuries there was no question of meaning one thing by science when applying it to the events of nature and another when applying it to the events of history or of human society. I mentioned before that Marx began with a naturalist presupposition. Strictly speaking it was not a presupposition at all; it was a decision. It is a decision to be scientific, of course, but beyond that it is the decision that the only way to be scientific is to accept only a natural explanation of what takes place. This sort of decision had proved to be quite successful in physics, why not in history? It would not require the disproving of other historical explanations; given the scientific explanation, all other explanations simply fall apart and are abandoned. The point is that no proof is needed that the natural explanation is the only acceptable explanation—nor is any proof possible —it is simply a decision as to what will count as explanation; if it is not natural it is not an explanation. In this connection it is interesting to note that Marx, who is the mortal enemy of all metaphysics, has here adopted a metaphysical position—not merely that what is not a natural explanation is not an explanation but, that what is not a natural explanation is not true.

If, then, there is to be a science of history, it must discover the "laws" which explain why the human situation is the way it is, why man is essentially alienated. By the same token, if history is to be history, it must be a process in which going backwards can never provide a remedy for what has taken place. The real task of history, then, is to explain scientifically the only possible way in which man is to reappropriate what has been alienated. On the individual level man has not only lost whatever self-determination may have been his (there is serious question whether, in Marx's mind, man ever had this), but there is no possible way of regaining it on the individual level—that would be going backwards. If, then, man is to reappropriate what has been alienated—or if he is to appropriate what he never really had—this must take place on the collective level (incidentally, "must" here means that this inevitably will take place).

An Examination of Conscience

Here I should like to digress for a moment or, if you will, return to the theme of reconciliation. There is little question in my mind that, from the scientific point of view, what Marx says here makes little sense (it is not based on the kind of evidence one can call "scientific"). This is not science, but it is a kind of vision, let us say, prophetic vision. The movement of human consciousness has been and continues to be away from individual and towards social consciousness. Salvation—whether this-worldly or other-worldly—is becoming more and more a social matter, and human, self-realization is becoming more and more a social task. If, then, the reconciliation of which we have been speaking is to become a reality (I will not say, as the result of a necessary dialectical process), then there must be a growth in social consciousness on both sides, and for each to recognize the partial truth of the opposite position will mean that each will have to realize the partial falsity of his own position. If nothing else, this will mean the reexamination of certain emphases which in the past have made for division rather than conciliation.

In this I leave the Marxist examination of conscience to the Marxist (though make it he must), and I merely suggest what a religious—and here I mean specifically Christian—reexamination might involve. Christianity should ask itself whether its orientation to the hereafter has caused it to neglect the realities of the here and now and thus to falsify to some extent concrete living. Catholic Christianity, incidentally, might ask itself if its structure is not basically medieval and, therefore, very much in need of updating if it is to be viable in the twentieth century. Finally, in the hypothesis at least that a classless society is on its way, Christianity might reexamine all its structures and find out to what extent they postulate a class society. Frankly, I do not think that Christianity will have to fear for its life if it asks these questions, but it cannot simply refuse to face them.

Perhaps all this can be reduced to one basic question which the Christian must ask when he confronts Marxism: does Marxism, precisely as a philosophy of history make a greater effort to come to terms with the changing world in which we live than any so-called Christian philosophy? The answer to this will, I think, be that a philosophy today cannot even call itself Christian if it is unable to synthesize the insights and methods which Marxism has provided.

This does not mean that the Christian should become a Marxist. Still less does it mean that Christianity should take over Marxism. It does mean that an honest confrontation is necessary, that a failure to confront Marxism honestly is simply unchristian. And this, in a somewhat roundabout way, brings us back to the original theme of Karl Marx's atheism—which, I think, can legitimately prescind from the question as to whether certain dialectical developments within Marxism itself alter the problematic. I am speaking of Karl Marx himself, and of him it can be said that not only was he an atheist but he recognized thought as legitimate only if it excluded any reference to God. No attempt to come to terms with Marx or with Marxist thought can afford to ignore that.

The Atheistic Postulate

Marx's thought, then, is atheistic, and this atheism has two outstanding characteristics. First of all, it is utterly radical; it is impossible to be more atheistic than was Marx. For him God is not an unproved hypothesis which can be rejected for lack of proof; he refuses even the hypothesis; for him it simply contradicts reason. The second characteristic of Marx's atheism is that it is integral; there is no private cranny of life, so to speak, of any life, that can dispense with atheism. Unlike most atheists whom history has known, Marx does not war against a popular or even a current theological conception of God; there is no conceivable god that would be acceptable to him; any being in any way superior to man is simply inconceivable.

There were many reasons for this. Marx's main target, as we shall see, was not God but religion, and chiefly Christian religion which, he felt, was an obstacle to man's self-realization. At the root of it all, however, was what I consider to be a rather understandable disappointment. Like most young German liberals of his generation—and particularly of the generation preceding his— Marx manifested great enthusiasm for the French Revolution. As he put it—and as Hegel before him had put it—here for the first time in history reason had constructed its own revolution. In other words, reason had formed a concept of man's true dignity and had then gone to work to realize what it had conceived. The disappointment came when Marx—as one of the first—realized that it had turned into not a popular but merely a bourgeois revolution.

Now, out of the French Revolution, or out of the Enlightenment which was its source, had come a new religion known as Deism. This, its followers held, was to be the religion of reason, it was to deify reason itself, and it was to supplant all other religions, particularly Christianity. It paid very vague honor to a very vague deity, but above all it enthroned human reason (whose rationality, incidentally, was also very vague). It turned out, however, that this exalted religion was, in the minds of the Deists, quite compatible with ignoring the very real social evils under which man lived. If even the religion of reason could do this, thought Marx, then reason simply had no use for religion at all; religion was non-reason (the logic is faulty, but the passionate concern for man is commendable).

The most important part of deist theory, however, was its conviction of man's essential freedom, and this it proclaimed loudly and vigorously. Marx very rightly saw that there is no point in proclaiming the liberty of man, if one does nothing to bring about the exercise of this liberty. Marx, then, took the opposite approach and proclaimed that man is not free—until by his own work he has made himself free. Here, then, we have what I think is the most important point in all of Marx's teaching: the task of destroying man's alienation is not a task of restoring man's liberty—that liberty has never yet existed—it is the task of bringing about a not-yet-existent freedom. Man's work (that which characterizes him as man) is to make man become what he is not yet. In this view the laws of history had up to Marx's time worked as laws of nature and had succeeded only in producing a being who was capable of becoming free. These laws were to take on a different character only when man would consciously intervene in their operation and thus make himself free, realize his potential freedom.

In this context Marx sees religion as an obstacle, the greatest obstacle to freedom; it condemns man to accept what he is, thus blocking the impulse to become what he is not yet. It is for this reason—among others—that he denies that religion can be a private affair (even where, as in the famous "opium of the people" passage, he recognizes that religion is a constant in human consciousness, he does so with the utmost regret). One does not have to agree with Marx to recognize his perspicacity here; along with Hegel he sees that religion affects the whole of man's behavior. If he were to admit freedom of religion—even privately—he would be contradicting his own position. Whatever may be the position of Marxists today, freedom of religion is absolutely inadmissible to Marx; in any form whatever it is essentially antithetical to real freedom.

49

As we said before, the very essence of alienation is, according to Marx, expressed in religion. Like the alienation expressed in the institution of private property it cannot be permitted to exist. Freedom of religion is simply an irresolvable contradiction. By the same token, separation of church and state is, in Marx's thinking, a non-entity, inconceivable; it would allow the basic contradiction which is religion to subsist.

This is Marx's anti-religion, and from it, of course, follows his atheism. Quite consistently, if religion is an evil, then God is a nothing. This, however, was not a position at which Marx arrived as a result of losing his faith; he never had a faith to lose. Unlike Engels, who as a young man had almost fanatical religious leanings, Marx never went through a religious crisis. In this area he never experienced even a philosophical crisis. The metaphysical question as to why anything exists at all he simply never asked; in fact he considered it a thoroughly invalid question. He was concerned with explaining how things came to be the way they are, not with explaining how they came to be at all. That the world is possible needed no explanation; it was simply there. That and that alone, however, could be accepted as given; all else was process, and to know the process was to effect its transformation by work. Along with this went the fact that he did not see his own explanation of development in terms of need and fulfillment as needing any further explanation—it was itself all the explanation that was needed. It is true, of course, that he read the constant proof of this dialectical development in history, but the section of history which he actually examined in so doing was extremely brief, and from that he extrapolated to the whole of history.

Still, there is in all this a peculiar paradox. As Feuerbach had pointed out, man's belief in God is the fulfillment of a very human need, the need to make sense out of history, out of human events. Marx dismissed this need of God very summarily by calling it an illegitimate need, and yet his own "science" is an answer to the very same need, the need to make sense, scientific sense, out of history. Thus the need which has been the source of so much religious thinking was a need that Marx felt, too. The difference is that, for him, the need to make sense out of history was coupled with a decision to refuse any transcendent sense of history; it was a decision to find sense in man and only in man. It was for this reason, too, that he never asked himself the question whether his opposition to religion was opposition to a perverted manifestation of it. In the spirit of the Enlightenment he was quite convinced that he knew the essence of religion, and that his opposition was to religion as such, not to any particular manifestations of it (another reason why a dialogue such as ours here is indispensable).

Religion and Process

Because for Marx religion was simply an invalid form of consciousness, there could be no question of recognizing in religion itself a dialectical development; dialectical development is rational development, and reason simply cannot coexist with unreason. Like morality—or philosophy, or legal systems—religion belongs to the famous category of the superstructure, and it rests on the economic base which molds society. Whatever is superstructural is the product of a particular form of society and as such has only a temporary value—or validity. There is, however, a great difference. For other superstructural forms Marx will recognize a validity corresponding to the structure of the society which has produced them, and, by the same token, he could recognize the validity of similar superstructures on a new base, even on the final base of the classless society. But, for religion he will recognize no validity of any kind; it was an illegitimate superstructure from the beginning and, therefore, though it is a social product it could never be an acceptable social product—in any form of society.

The reasons for this inconsistency are not entirely clear, but the ground would seem to be pragmatic rather than historical. Because Marx saw only one possible ultimate motive of human action, i.e. self-interest (individual self-interest in pre-class society, class interest in a class society, and the interest of man as such in a classless society), he could not tolerate any force or institution which would look beyond and above man for its motivation. In no conceivable social structure would such an institution be legitimate.

It is for this reason, too, that the prime concrete target of Marx's anti-religious polemic is Christianity, both because it was the dominant religion in the society which he knew and because, along with Hegel, he considered it as the absolute religion which synthesized in itself all the religious tendencies which the history of man had manifested. Marx will not say, as Nietzsche said later, that Christianity is immoral; for Marx Christianity is immorality itself. Nor need any other religion be refuted; by accomplishing

51

the rejection of Christianity he feels that he has rejected religion as such. The only other religion that comes in for any mention at all is the Jewish religion, and this in a pamphlet which is political rather than religious, entitled "The Jewish Question." In it the question is that of the inferior status which has always been assigned to Jews in a Christian society. The solution, says Marx, is quite simple: since the only difference separating Jews from anyone else is a difference of religion and since religion itself is illegitimate, the whole problem can be solved by simply doing away with religion. (We who have lived through the '30's and '40's know that Marx missed the boat on this.)

Criticism of Christianity

To get back, then, to Marx's criticism of Christianity, it can be summed up in the declaration that Christianity is the "transcendent justification of social injustice." Christianity is, he says, in fact absurd and needs no refutation, since with the advent of true reason it will simply disappear. In the meantime, however, he sees fit to level some very sharp criticisms against it; and here one must recognize some very keen and, to a certain extent, valid insights. Christianity, he says, is so interested in the kingdom of heaven that it blinds men to the values of earth; it represents the absolute break between man and reality. Though Marx did not possess Nietzsche's poetic genius, I am sure he could have agreed with the latter when he called Christianity "earth-slandering." Now, Marx sees no possibility of reconciling the values of the heavenly kingdom with those of the earthly kingdom; they are in total opposition to each other and simply cancel each other out—no dialectical opposition here. Christianity, he says, stands for the *"Jenseitigkeit der Wahrheit"* (the otherworldliness of truth), whereas what man must see is the *"Wahrheit des Diesseits"* (the truth of this world). This is, as we can see, a valid criticism of a certain kind of Christianity, and as such it must give us pause.

Another criticism—which is leveled chiefly at the rational religion of the Deists, but which also has its application to Christianity—is that by merely declaring the equality of men (without working to produce it) religion is in fact consecrating the inequalities which exist. If, in a society built on inequality, you give to each a so-called "equality of opportunity," you are really assuring the stronger of greater opportunity; on the individual level equality between the president of a huge corporation and a factory worker is meaningless.

Furthermore, Marx condemns the Christian substitution of charity for justice—which, I think, any Christian must also do. The real Christian task is not that of helping the poor with charity (though only in Utopia will the necessity of this disappear entirely); rather it is to insure for the poor the exercise of those rights whereby they can cease to be poor. Marx concretizes this criticism by once more referring to the "Jewish Question." In the eighteen centuries of Christian domination, he says, whatever has been granted to the Jews has been given grudgingly and by way of concession, never as a recognition of their rights as human beings. Although one could question the overall historical accuracy of this statement, there is enough truth to it to make us blush (modern society has taken over the idea with its utterly degrading concept of "tolerance").

Another criticism—which resembles the first—is that Christianity has taught men to be satisfied with a future reward in heaven, thus dulling their consciousness of the miseries of life on earth (the "opium of the people" theme). By emphasizing the Christian doctrine of "original sin," he says, one makes of human misery a punishment to be accepted meekly (one is reminded of the pious mouthings of the wealthy leaders of the industrial revolution).

Christianity, then, is absurd, and it will perish of its own absurdities. In any case it is utterly incompatible with communism, the classless society which reason is ushering in. Just as the notion of divine providence is incompatible with a (naturalistic) science of history, so a supernatural religion is incompatible with a scientific society. That Marx's criticisms here are based on a confidence in science which science itself can today scarcely share and upon an unwarranted conviction that his own endeavor is thoroughly scientific does not take away from the force these criticisms should have to make Christians rethink their own beliefs—in my opinion, to question whether they are genuinely Christian. I do not think it is true that religion—Christianity in particular—makes men cowardly and irresponsible in the face of human problems; but it is true that in the concrete many a Christian has found in his religion an excuse for not bothering with "mundane" problems. If Marx can awaken such unchristian Christians from their "dogmatic slumber," more power to him!

Integral Humanism

In view of all this there is a sense in which we must say that Marx was not even an atheist, that he was opposed to atheism too. To speak positively, Marx was an integral humanist, who saw supreme value in man, and only in man. Atheists, he feels, give God far too much importance; denying Him isn't even worth the effort (one is reminded of the mental gymnastics that a Jean-Paul Sartre must go through in order to "prove" that there is no God). Marx is not out to get rid of God; he is out to free man—not to free him from God but from himself and from his enslavement to religion, which is his own creation. It is not God but the belief in God which must go, if man is to be free. Thus, theoretically at least, he does not see the destruction of religion as an important aim. The disappearance of religion will be the normal outcome of rational thinking and rational living. Marx's atheism, then (and we can call it that) is but the logical corollary of his theory of human liberty. Man's ultimate task as he sees it, is self-creation, which man accomplishes by creating a world. The world which man thus creates is so rich that there is no room left in it for belief in anything but man himself and his world. Quite simply, then, Marx does not feel it important to deny God; his aim is to affirm man, and he finds that the affirmation of man is incompatible with an affirmation of God.

One result of all this—in my opinion—is that Marx, and the Marxists, have never really touched the question of the validity of religion as such. The real question is the total validity of Marx's own theory. If the theory is valid—and I'm afraid I find the very notion of a totally valid theory meaningless—then religion is invalid. To say this, however, is to bypass religon, not to refute it. One could, for the sake of the argument, concede that belief in God is a social product—or at least that successive stages of social development have left their mark on the way men believe in God. To admit this, however, is not to admit that belief itself is an illusion—no more than to trace the social origin of any idea is to demonstrate the invalidity of the idea (unless, of course, one subscribes to a theory which states that successive stages in history invalidate all the ideas which were proper to previous stages). If belief in God is incompatible with belief in man, then, of course, one cancels out the other. But, by showing that certain characteristics of a certain kind of belief in God are incompatible with a kind of belief in man which a certain scientific theory (itself a social product) postulates, one does not show any basic incompatibility at all. It may be, too, that belief in God as manifested in a hypothetical classless society would have other characteristics than those which it manifests in a class society, but this, too, does not affect the basic validity of the belief.

There is another paradox which grows out of Marx's theory of belief as a social product, which is probably even more difficult to resolve. Marx himself was—as was Engels—the product of a bourgeois social structure. That he should grow out of this in a process of social change which he helped to inaugurate and advance may be understandable; but, that he should have from the beginning refused a belief which was the inevitable product of that social structure is not so easily understandable on his own principles. We can look back and say that Marx's personal liberty transcended his social conditioning. It is doubtful, however, that Marx himself could consistently admit this—unless, of course, he could consistently admit that everyone else's personal liberty could also transcend his social conditioning. If he were to admit this latter, then, it would seem, he would also have to admit that belief, just as well as unbelief, could be the exercise of personal liberty and not merely the product of social conditioning.

Once again, then, we are back to the theme of reconciliation. Having read Marx very carefully over a period of many years I seriously doubt whether he could ever have accepted the possibility of reconciliation between Marxism and religion. In his view religion must eventually abdicate before reason. That he should so think, however, is due to a certain inconsistency in his own thinking. It is not inconceivable, therefore, that a Marxist could be more consistent than Marx himself and not only recognize but even welcome the possibility of such a reconciliation. It can come; I believe it will come; but it is going to demand much honesty on both sides.

ATHEISM AND THE AFFECTIVE LIFE*

by Laszlo Matrai

It is not only those directly concerned with atheist propaganda but also many progressive educators in more general fields who are often brought face to face with a problem which, though rarely formulated or discussed, is nonetheless quite real: Does not the emotional life of a man liberated from the belief in God and religion become impoverished by being cut off from the loving memories of childhood, the lofty sentiment of fearing God? Progressive people agree that religious ideas, fallacious in their very foundations, have no place in the 20th-century conception of the world in which truths, rational and demonstrable, have the last word. This unanimity ends, however, and answers become more hesitant, the moment ones poses the question: Would it not be better to encourage some part of the religious experience for the children of the 20th century—our children? Could it not be looked upon as "the poetry of tradition," with the quality of charming, popular or pathetic childlike belief—a sublimation of problems unsolvable by the mind, the "positive" sentiments of man meditating on the great problems of existence?

At first glance, the question may seem "merely" a practical problem for daily instruction and propaganda. If we examine it more closely, however, we perceive that the most primitive strains of human history are caught up in it. For it is only within the last few decades that people, at least a certain number of them, have reacted to atheists with a more-or-less indulgent shrug. By and large, however, the interpenetration between the ideology of class society and religion still exists, making its effects felt up to our own time and in our own society. Although somewhat dislocated by science, it is still maintained in the emotional realm, out of which it acts and reacts ceaselessly on the ideological evolution of scientific thought, particularly under the conditions of capitalism.

---

*This essay was submitted in French; it has been translated for this volume by Nan Braymer.

The history of human thought only too fully confirms this state of affairs. Did not Plato say that atheism is a malady of the soul? This aphorism became the classic formulation of an erroneous philosophical concept which has become the favorite slogan of religious apologists of all periods including our own. Moreover, the present official doctrine of the Church declares: "Subjectively, atheism always signifies a grave moral aberration." (*Lexicon für Theologie und Kirche,* 2 völlig. neubearb. Aufl. Freiburg, 1957. 1. Bd. colonne 993.) This reflects an even more backward position— what was only a malady of the soul to Plato is considered by the present-day Church as a moral stigma.

Here it would be instructive to consider the history of official and literary judgments brought to bear on atheism. Obviously, it would be difficult to go into this in full detail—from Plato to Jaspers, or from Bellarmine to Wetter. Even a cursory examination, however, will suffice to demonstrate that long centuries of exclusive ideological domination by the Church have succeeded in rooting in public opinion—and even in literary and artistic opinion —the fallacious idea that atheism is a negative thing, a kind of blight, a deformation of mental life.

It is not only lesser writers who thus depict the atheist but also, for example, a writer like Rousseau (progressive even when compared to other great precursors of the French Revolution). In his "Nouvelle Héloise" he depicts Holbach in the guise of a personage (Wolmar) who is extremely sympathetic and of an elevated morality *despite* his "very lamentable," i.e., atheist, ideas, which his devoted wife never ceased to deplore. Jóseph Szinnyei, who, if he is not a "Hungarian Rousseau," is nevertheless a reputable and tireless bibliographer of the history of Hungarian culture, says basically the same thing about János Horárik, calling him the "Hungarian Rousseau, in that he was an eccentric and a disturber of the peace in theory." Szinnyei goes on to say, "He was, nevertheless, innocent, tolerant and amiable in his personal life." Which amounts to saying that the courageous author—faithfully mirroring public opinion—is amazed to have to admit that a spokesman for atheism and "disturbing" theories is not a villain, is not intolerant or misanthropic as a human being.

But even without recourse to innumerable examples of history and literary history, one can explain, by means of nothing but simple logic, why so great a number of people have considered, and still consider, atheists as invalids suffering from an emotional lesion, from a malady of the soul. In fact, the affective world of man is linked in multiple relationships and by many psychological functions to his moral sentiments. Inversely, a considerable part of his moral experience is simultaneously emotional. The two domains cannot be dissociated categorically without falsifying the facts in a metaphysical fashion. If, up until the time when we arrived at the threshold of socialism, the evolution of ethics has, of necessity, given the hegemony to religious morality, the only deduction to be made was: To be ethical is equivalent to being religious, to believing in God; and, conversely, atheism, the negation of God, must be paired with immorality; therefore, when a decent atheist appears, it is a rare and amazing phenomenon. And if a moral taint is an emotional taint (and this has become an exact formulation) we can see clearly the logical structure of the false concept we are trying to analyze.

These historical and logical connections help us to resolve, on the level of our daily experience, the actual, psychological problem of how to present the rich emotional content of atheism.

Regrettably, but understandably, scientific psychology advances only with considerable difficulty in its investigations of the emotional life of man. And this in spite of the fact that sentiments, emotions, passions have been matters of intense interest to thinkers, even in an epoch when autonomic psychology as a special science was not yet in existence; when it was the philosophers who, among other preoccupations, concerned themselves with psychological problems. In spite of these early beginnings, the psychology of the emotions is a territory less explored than, for example, the psychological problems of perception, of reflection, or even those of the personality.

This lag is primarily explainable by the fact that it is only quite recently that we have begun to discover the physiological bases of emotional life—that is to say, a system of stable correlations analyzable in an exact manner. Without this, a scientific, materialist psychology cannot exist; without this, the analysis of emotions is forced—in spite of the best will in the world—to content itself with abstract philosophical speculation—already an outworn phase. As to the physiological bases of the emotions, the psychologists have believed for some years now that only the "negative" emotions—those linked to the sensation of pain—possess such bases (i.e., the simple transmission of excitations familiar to the physiologists), and that "positive" emotions (joy, for example) do not have demonstrable physiological correlations. This surprising "discovery," while bringing water to the idealistic mill, also accords unmistakably with the thinking of certain pessimistic ancient philosophers who maintained that "joy is nothing other than the absence of pain."

But if the hypothesis of emotions without physiological bases seemed possible and logically justifiable, it was because psychologists studied the neuro-biological mechanism of the genesis of emotions by posing an analogy with the already well-known processes of perception and cognition, taking into account the interaction that exists between the nerves linking sensory organs to the cerebral cortex and nerve centers. But in these regions they could not find anything but the genesis of pain sensations to serve effectively as a basis for the physiology of emotions. Only the most recent physiological investigations, and the deductions that materialist psychology has been able to draw from them, enable us to finally find the description and the scientific explication of the affective life. These recent advances show that the psychological liaison between the external world and the individual (his psychological life), the interaction between the sensory organs and the cortex, can arise not only by the single path followed by the psychologists, but also by a second "path". This path is, in fact, a "detour," in the sense that it passes through the subcortical regions of the cerebro-spinal system. It has been known for some time now that one of the subcortical regions, the thalamus, plays an important role in the life of the emotions, and that it is in direct contact with the hypothalamus, which, in turn, is the directive organ, the "orchestra conductor" of the entire neuro-endocrine system, and, like this system, has a vital importance.

What can we deduce from all this evidence on the psychology of the emotions?

In the first place, the affective, emotional functions cannot be detached from the total psychological functioning of the individual, since they are the organic constituent elements, necessarily present, of an individual's connection with both his outer and inner world; they are, in the case of a normal individual, the inevitable corollaries of the reflection of reality by the psychological mechanism. This amounts to saying that reflection cannot be separated from sentiments in a mechanical or metaphysical way—as if reflection and sentiments were the automatic "spiritual faculties" of the individual. In truth, we are linked to reality by both thoughts and feelings, and the difference between these two phenomena is not of the same genre as that existing between two autonomic functions; they differ particularly in that objects appear in our thoughts in accordance with our previous knowledge of a given object, while our feelings indicate, or—to use a more adequate expression—guide, our reactions to the object. These reactions, moreover, are determined by our biophysical condition at the moment.

Complicated as is this parallel, double system—on the psychological plane as well as on the plane of the individual man's personality—it is certain that, just as there is no perception of an object without the emotional reaction that accompanies it, no emotion can exist, in the usual sense, without an object, without a content that belongs to it. This in no way signifies that we deny the relative autonomy of intellectual and emotional functions; on the contrary, it means that their total dissociation does not correspond to physiological facts, and therefore leads us to psychological fictions, to erroneous psychological conceptions. "Great emotions allied to paltry thoughts," or "profound thoughts accompanied by paltry emotions" are formulations which are supposed to be accurate, but they are unreal in that they describe conditions that are nonexistent in life. Quite to the contrary, psychological reality—the relationship truly demonstrable by experience between the intellect and the emotions, between thought and feeling—reveals correspondence to a far greater degree than disproportion or contradiction in the contemplation of a common object.

And so, having arrived at this point, we come back to the problem of atheism and the emotions, which we have illustrated by historic examples of the characters, the personalities of Holbach and Horárik. We can justly claim that the contradiction between their "unprincipled" thoughts and their "principled" characters belongs in the category of psychological fiction, of distorted portraiture. The true reality, the psychological verity authenticated by history, is that Rousseau, permeated by petit-bourgeois religious feelings, and Szinnyei, financial bourgeois, were totally unaware of the richness of militant atheism's content. They could only recognize the admirable emotions, the nobility of character that they honestly attribute to Holbach and Horárik; they could not know

that these traits were not inconsistent with, but actually inseparable from, their richness of thought. This human virtue, recognized by all, this appealing humanism, this superior morality
(which, incidentally, Cicero discovers with equal surprise in Epi-
curus), far from being characteristics that accidentally or con-
tradictorily accompany Holbach's or Horárik's atheism, are direct,
logical and inevitable consequences of the inner and outer social
and ethical struggles they had to wage against the society of their
time, and, no less, against their own education and their own
doubts. In truth, it is the man who is recovering from the effects
of his own errors who is intolerant of erroneous *conceptions* (because he knows how burdensome errors can be), but is tolerant
toward *men* who deceive themselves (because he understands from
his own experience how errors arise.) Courage, in theory and
practice, in the inner as well as the outer life, is a quality that, by
the very nature of things, atheists of all time have had to possess;
this courage is a positive quality that indicates *a priori* (again a
psychological argument) that the high moral character of atheists
need not be interpreted as a surprising antithesis to their ideas but
rather as their direct, logical, inevitable emotional equivalent.

The development of our theme thus far may make both theistic
and atheistic readers feel we are analyzing the relations between
atheism and the affective life in a defensive manner, seeking
"excuses," as it were; tacitly admitting the negative aspect of these
relations because they need to be defended. This is not so. It may
seem so because we have deliberately made an abstraction (insofar
as abstraction is possible) of the weightiest arguments against faith
and religion, the social arguments, in order, first and foremost, to
try to analyze, however briefly, the psychological aspects of the
question. Nevertheless, even conceding this deliberate methodological limitation, even putting aside the most decisive social arguments, the problem has one psychological aspect that can be considered decisive in the quarrel between atheism and theism. This
aspect concerns one of the major problems of atheism as well as
of the psychology of the emotions. I refer to the emotion and
sentiment of fear.

Fear, historically as well as psychologically, engenders its own
gods. "It is fear that gives birth to the gods" can be considered
a classic statement. This thesis was broadly exploited by the
bourgeois atheists of the 18th century; they developed it by putting

the emphasis, even more strongly than their predecessors, on ignorance as the cause of fear. But, obviously, to make ignorance the sole and everlasting cause of fear is, from the psychological standpoint, quite erroneous. As modern psychology rightly teaches, a certain amount of mental activity always accompanies fear, so that it is not necessarily the outcome of deficient understanding or ignorance; rather, fear and ignorance are the combined effects of the nature of the relations between the individual and his environment, his outer world.

It is precisely at this point that society and history enter into the problem presented by the genesis of fear and of the gods; it is here that the historical and psychological effects of the narrowness of the bourgeois atheist's view appear clearly: Fear gives birth to the gods, ignorance engenders fear—they say this and they rest on this. They could not, in their own interests, pose the question that remained to be posed, the decisive question: Who is it that engenders ignorance? They could not pose it because the answers would have been social answers, prejudicial not only to the interests of the feudal class in power but also to those of the rising bourgeoisie. In other words, bourgeois atheism, because of its class limitations, left open the question of the relation between fear and religion in its social aspects. As to the psychological aspect, it could not, in any case, resolve this, because of the rudimentary state of physiology in their day. So it's up to us to attempt a forward step.

Although the physiological processes of fear and pain are sensibly different—the first being an emotion and the second a sensation—their psychological function is, in more than one way, analogous: Both signal the "necessity" of a change in the relation between the exterior and interior worlds. Illimitable possibilities and tasks await material psychology when it sets out to explore all the laws that control fear. This exploration is even more imperatively required by the needs of socialist society, and, at the same time, it is precisely the kind of task that can be resolved by socialist society in a truly scientific manner. One thing, however, becomes ever clearer to the physiologists, the physicians, the psychologists, the teachers and the philosophers of Marxism: In the struggle against pain and fear, the political objectives of the class struggle, led by the proletariat, correspond on a broad front with ethical objectives of socialist, humanist and communist morality. At the same time, this correspondence is in line with the trend of socialist education

62

and Marxist-Leninist psychology, as it is with the ideological results of their most recent developments. If we were to seek to evaluate the degree of societal development of men liberated from exploitation, using psychological criteria and projections, we could not do it except by evaluating the degree to which we conquer pain and fear in the lives of actual men, considered as individuals.

And this is the point at which religion loses the battle, simultaneously on the social and psychological fronts. Modern psychology is far from considering fear as a negative phenomenon, and, still less, as a useless one; in fact, fear, in the view of modern psychology, is precisely the vitally important instrumentality by which we may escape at times from the dangers that menace us. (At a certain age, particularly at an early age, when it can become one of the basic incentives for the acquisition of knowledge, fear can play an even more pervasive role—it can be positive from the viewpoint of cognition as well.) But it is from this angle that the general psychological form of fear differs essentially from its special variety—the fear of God.

While fear, in its generalized sense, leads to its own elimination in the process of helping us to determine whether to destroy its object, avoid it, or resolve it by knowledge, the fear of God leads in a diametrically opposite direction: It signifies a psychological impass because it leads to the intensive retention of the cult of the object, denying in advance the possibility of resolving fear by comprehension. Such a conservation of fear leads religious emotions into a physiological and psychological impasse. It is for this reason that religion is utilized for the political objective of historical impasses: to crush the aims of the class struggle or to retard their realization.

What we have briefly said of the emotional aspects of atheism and the critique of religious sentiments may appear too complicated and too abstract to the propagandist working at the hub of daily problems. Nevertheless, we believe that the teachers, the medical-pedagogical instructor, the psychologist, the writer, and the political man, who cultivate the "tree of practice," will agree with us when we say that the time has come when we can no longer content ourselves with demonstrating the negative role of religion: We must undertake to compose a vast, rich, detailed and attractive picture of the positive role of atheism.

The splendid qualities of atheism, the appeal of the high morality shown by men who have learned to conquer fear and to help others to conquer their fears—here we have a great arena in which, thanks to results already acquired, theoretical and practical analysis have become attainable in our society and by our science. This is not to say that henceforth we will neglect to refute erroneous ideas—among them, religious ideas. To refute bad thinking is the natural duty of all who are devoted to scientific conceptions of the world. But we can, and we should, devote much more time to the task of transcending the irrationalism and idealism of religion, as well as the rationalism and vulgar materialism of bourgeois atheism, in a veritable flood of monographs and articles and series of psychological and sociological analyses. We must move ahead to utilize the riches of atheism and of socialist humanism.

THE MARXIAN CRITIQUE OF CHRISTIANITY

by RICHARD LICHTMAN

The intention of this essay is to introduce the reader to the views which Marx and Engels held about the nature and social significance of Christianity. We are not interested in what follows in the writings of other Marxists, for in many instances their views conflict with those of Marx and Engels, whether they recognize this fact or not. Furthermore, the essay shall be presented in the form of a legal brief in that it will attempt to present the Marxian position in the most favorable possible light and will neither note nor evaluate the many criticisms which may obviously be directed against it.

There is a procedural, an epistemological and a political reason for so limiting the scope of the essay. First, a careful evaluation of the claims and counterclaims in this case is worthy of a treatment too lengthy for the limits of this essay. Second, the first act of the understanding ought always to be the sympathetic comprehension of the position of the author, a comprehension which alone can justify further criticism. And finally, the political climate of our own time is such that it may readily be assumed that a critical environment already exists in regard to the Marxian position, so that the presentation of the case in favor of the position becomes all the more imperative. I shall first outline briefly the Marxian position, and then in the second part of the paper offer some evidence from Christian literature and non-Marxist scholarship in favor of the thesis.

- I -

1. Marx's theory of the nature of religion can only be understood against the background of his general view of the nature and dynamics of society as a whole, that is, in the context of the economic interpretation of history. In the best known summary of the position, Marx described it in the following way:

In the social production which men carry on they enter into definite relations that are indispensable and independent of their will; these relations of production correspond to a definite stage of development of their material powers of production. The sum total of these relations of production constitutes the economic structure of society—the real foundation, on which rise legal and political superstructures and to which correspond definite forms of social consciousness. The mode of production in material life determines the general character of the social, political and spiritual processes of life. It is not the consciousness of men that determines their existences; but, on the contrary, their social existence determines their consciousness.

After describing briefly how the property relations of a society eventually come to frustrate the continued growth of productive forces, thereby forcing a change in the fundamental economic structure and eventually in the entirety of the social system, Marx continues:

In considering such transformations the distinction should always be made between the material transformation of the economic conditions of production, which can be determined with the precision of natural science, and the legal, political, religious, esthetic or philosophic—in short, ideological—forms in which men become conscious of the conflict and fight it out. Just as our opinion of an individual is not based on what he thinks of himself, so we cannot judge such a period of transformation by its own consciousness; on the contrary, this consciousness must be explained from the contradictions of material life, from the existing conflict between the social forces of production and the relations of production.[1]

Or as Engels put the matter very briefly in *Socialism: Utopian and Scientific*:

The materialist conception of history starts from the proposition that the production of the means to support human life, and next to production the exchange of things produced, is the basis of all social structure; that in every society that has appeared in history, the manner in which wealth is distributed and society divided into classes or orders is dependent upon what is produced, how it is produced, and how the products are exchanged. From this point of view, the final cause of all social changes and political revolutions are to be sought not in men's brains, not in man's better insight into eternal truth and justice, but in changes in the modes of production and exchange. They are to be sought not in *philosophy*, but in the *economics* of each particular epoch.[2] (Italics in the original.)

66

There is obviously a good deal in these passages that is far from clear, particularly the meaning of such terms as "material powers of production," "relations of production," "mode of production," and "social forces of production." Even more confusing is the relationship which these concepts bear to each other. But for the purpose of understanding Marx's view of religion, the general structure of the position emerges clearly enough. It is maintained that the economic institutions of society form the basis upon which all other institutions are formed; that the economic institutions are independent variables to a very large extent and the remaining institutions reflections of these dominant social forces. Law, politics, religion, philosophy and art all manifest the vital imprint of the social relations of production. When the economic system undergoes a basic change the remaining institutions will be changed in corresponding ways, not merely in the sense that they will be structured in accordance with ultimate economic characteristics, but in the additional sense that they will rationalize the nature of this system by justifying it in law, protecting it in politics, rooting it in philosophy, and idealizing it in art.

But if the social relations of production determine the life of society, the most important fact about these social relations themselves is the division of classes which they embody. The rules which define, protect and justify the ownership and control of productive property are merely the legal expression of the fact that a given class has come to dominate the economic power of the social system, or what is the same thing, that it has come to oppress other classes of men whose labor it has been able to use for its own ends. At different moments in history we find different classes standing in various relations to the fundamental economic power of their time.

In the earlier epochs of history we find almost everywhere a complicated arrangement of society into various orders, a manifold gradation of social ranks. In ancient Rome we have patricians, knights, plebians, slaves; in all the Middle Ages, feudal lords, vassals, guild masters, journeymen, apprentices, serfs. . .

Our epoch, the epoch of the bourgeoisie, possesses, however, this distinctive feature: it has simplified the class antagonisms. Society as a whole is more and more splitting up into two great hostile camps, into two great classes directly facing each other: bourgeoisie and proletariat.[3]

But if, as we have seen, it is the social existence of men that determines their consciousness, then the specific class existence of men will further determine their particular mode of consciousness. This is precisely what we discover in 18th and 19th century Europe. As the remnants of the old feudal aristocracy, the conservatives continue to manifest a devotion to such ideas as fealty, honor, organic solidarity, social rank, hierarchical subordination, and the whole system of thought grounded in its fixed, landed wealth. But the mentality of the rising bourgeoisie was fixed upon fluid capital and its supporting ideological structure of private property, social contract, laissez-faire, and ascetic free enterprise; in short, the ideational structure of capitalism. It is no surprise to learn that socialism grew from the economic class position of the proletariat, and that its insistence upon the abolition of private property in production, the initiation of a genuine equality and brotherhood, and the demand for the destruction of class structure itself, were the reflections in political consciousness of the dynamic of its economic existence.

This tendency must be balanced, however, by another upon which Marx and Engels placed great emphasis—the tendency of the ideas of the ruling class to become the dominant ideas of the society as a whole:

> The class which has the means of material production at its disposal, has control at the same time over the means of mental production, so that in consequence, the ideas of those who lack the means of mental production are, in general, subject to it. The dominant ideas are nothing more than the ideal expression of the dominant material relationships, and dominant material relationships grasped as ideas, and thus of the relationships which make one class the ruling one; they are consequently the ideas of its dominance.[4]

Of course, the ruling ideology tends to be the reflection of the ruling class in and through the very process by which it acts to distort the nature of social reality. For the mental superstructure of the ruling class is the "ideal expression" of its dominant class position, and the function of this superstructure is to glorify the existence of the dominant class and discredit other aspirants to its power. If we examine the bourgeois conception of justice we will find it a perfect justification for the system of unequal power and reward which obtains under the social form of capitalism. But

68

all class mentality bears a tortuous relationship to the actual material conditions under which it is produced. So Marx and Engels note that:

> If, in all ideology, men and their circumstances appear upside down as in a *camera obscura*, this phenomenon arises from their material life process just as the inversion of objects on the retina does from their physical life-process.
>
> We begin with real, active men, and from their real life-process, show the development of the ideological reflexes and echoes of this life-process. The phantoms of the human brain also are necessary sublimates of men's material life-process . . .[5]

It is striking how similar these reflections of Marx, with their insistence on mental "reflexes" and "sublimates", are to the otherwise radically divergent thoughts of Freud. For both these seminal thinkers, conscious thought is most often a mask, a cloak under whose darkness exist forms of irrationality and avarice, too painful to be observed by oneself or disclosed to another. Whether it is the seething passion of libido or the exploitative power of class, both Marx and Freud could concur that the general mentality of man lies on a distorted surface of "false consciousness," beneath which pressing forces threaten to disrupt.

This is the background in Marxian thought against which specific interpretations of the nature of religion must be understood. But two specific clarifications must be introduced into the theory as stated, before we can pass to a detailed analysis of religion. First, it must be noted that what Marx is concerned with is the function of classes of men, that is, of men as they are similar to each other and organized into more or less cohesive and unified groups. Marx does not pretend to account for the activity or thought of every specific individual who has lived and died on this planet. What he does care to explain is the movement of large social forces, and the manner in which basic patterns of social existence have evolved. He cannot be refuted, then, by noting the existence of exceptional individuals who fail to conform to a general social pattern, unless it can be successfully maintained that such individuals significantly alter the movements of history, a contention which Marx would vigorously deny.

Secondly, it must be noted that the economic interpretation of history grants a dominant role to economic forces, but in no way maintains that such factors are the sole historical agency. Engels made this point quite clearly in a letter to Joseph Bloch:

> . . . According to the materialist conception of history, the *ultimately* determining element in history is the production and reproduction in real life. More than this neither Marx nor I ever asserted. . . The economic situation is the basis, but the various elements of the superstructure-political forms of the class struggle and its results, to wit: constitutions established by the victorious class after a successful battle, etc., juridical forms, and even the reflexes of all these actual struggles in the brains of the participants . . . also exercise their influence upon the course of the historical struggles and in many cases preponderate in determining their *forms*.[6] (Italics in original).

We may well wonder when we read such commentary how we would determine the 'ultimate' causal factor or compare the degrees of influence which specific aspects of the situation contributed to the whole. But we cannot doubt that other factors than merely economic forces play their role, and that the explanation of the structure of any given system requires a careful analysis of many variables, rather than the simplistic application of a simple formula.

2. So much for the fundamental background of Marx's thought. It is necessary now to say something of those immediate predecessors who influenced his reflections on the nature of religion.

The first of these was David Friedrich Strauss, who in 1835 published a truly crucial work in the history and theory of Christianity—*The Life of Jesus* (Das Leben Jesu). Strauss, as befits a pupil of Hegel, treated the two prominent contemporary accounts of the Gospels, those of the supernatural school and of the rationalists, as two extreme and mistaken positions whose synthesis might establish a viable position. The Biblical account of Jesus was intelligible neither as the result of divine imposition in the course of history, nor as an essentially naturalistic though symbolised description of quite literal events. The raising of the dead was due neither to the exercise of a miraculous power nor to advanced medical techniques. It was largely a legend flowing from the mythical capacity of the human mind.

What Strauss produced in elaborate and painstaking detail was an account of the Gospel narratives which made abundantly clear their inherent historical inaccuracy, narrative absurdity and self-contradiction. But if this were in fact the case, how could one account for the existence of these narratives? They were for Strauss, in large part, the result of man's need to construct and entertain myth, a need which was to fulfill itself progressively in the future elaboration of belief, symbol, doctrine, dogma, and the eventual freeing of the ideal spirit of religion from its rigid material form.

But though the effect of his work was to introduce into the discussion of Christianity a skepticism from which it would never free itself, it was far from Strauss' intention to deny the existence of an historical Jesus. He was perfectly willing to accept some aspects of the Biblical account as far less marred by myth-making than others—the whole eschatological tendency of the Gospels is taken as inherently authentic—and he was unwilling to let his belief in the validity of the Christian "idea" depend upon the accuracy of particular accounts of the life of the unique God-man of that religion. It was for Strauss the fact that the critical idea of "God-manhood" had been introduced into history by the person of Jesus, that was of ultimate significance, and not the perfection with which Jesus himself embodied, or failed to embody, the ideal. It was, in fact, precisely because Strauss regarded the ideal of a synthesis of divinity and humanity as beyond historical criticism that he permitted himself to proceed so critically with the historical material itself.

But established religion was to receive even more vigorous criticism from the pen of Bruno Bauer, whose three-volume *Criticism of the Gospel History of the Synoptics* appeared in 1841. This work carried the Biblical criticism of Strauss to a much higher point of critical accuracy, and to a conclusion as radically beyond Strauss as was the latter beyond the tradition of his time. For Strauss had not engaged in a searching criticism of the relative validity of the four Gospel accounts of the life of Jesus, though he did conclude that the Johanine narrative was inferior to the synoptic version. Bauer proceeded to a detailed analysis of the relative credibility of Mark, Matthew and Luke, the initial result of which was to pronounce the former a model upon which the remaining authors constructed their elaborations.

But if the whole Biblical account now depended upon Mark, the foundation of this monumental structure had been considerably weakened. And if additional criticism could be successfully directed against that last remaining source of credibility, the whole

71

edifice could be reduced to rubble. This is precisely what Bauer accomplished, and he performed the task by the simple device of extending the insights of his contemporaries to their ultimate conclusions. Once the idea had been introduced that the narrative of a Gospel author might have a purely literary origin, it became possible to elaborate this thought to the point at which it cut away the entire Gospel narrative, root and branch. And though Bauer first took the existence of a unique historical Personality as fact, he was led finally to a thorough-going skepticism: "In the prophecy as well as in the fulfillment, the Messiah was only the ideal product of religious consciousness. As an actually given individual he never existed."[7] The conclusion of Bauer's later work remains the same—there is no reason to believe that an historical Jesus ever existed.

But more important than the historical skepticism engendered by Bauer's work was his total rejection of the Christian ideal. Strauss, though he had questioned the actual temporal nature of Jesus, remained a firm advocate of the profundity of the Christian world view. Its monumental truth for Strauss lay in its denial of dualism, for in the person of Jesus it embodied a doctrine of the fundamental unity of the human and the divine. What impressed Strauss in this conception was not the humanity of God, but the divinity of man, and the adoration traditionally reserved for the transcendent power of the creator was transferred by Strauss to the species of humanity. "Is not the idea of unity of the divine and human natures a real one in a far higher sense, when I regard the whole race of man as its realization, than when I single out one man as such a realization?"[8] There was a social implication in this view of which Strauss himself was not unaware:

> The earth is no longer a vale of tears through which we journey towards a goal existing in a future heaven. The treasures of divine life are to be realised here and now, for every moment of our earthly life pulses within the womb of the divine.[9]

But if Strauss was arguing for the fulfillment of the Christian ideal, Bauer was advocating its destruction. For in his later works (which foretell the position of Nietzsche), Bauer maintained that Christianity developed from the demoralized slave mentality of the dissolution of the Roman world, and that by idealizing its own brutality it fastened man to suffering and a denial of the natural humanity of his being. Christianity achieved separation from the world, but it was an abortive victory, for instead of acting from its transcendence to humanize the world, it merely fixed in a violent and destructive opposition, the realms of nature and of man. Something of the spirit of Bauer's vehement criticism can be sensed in these lines on the nature of miracle:

> Spirit does not fume and bluster, and rage and rave against Nature, as it is supposed to do in miracle, for that would be the denial of its inner law, but quietly works its way through the antithesis. In short, the death of Nature implied in the conscious realisation of personality is the resurrection of Nature in a nobler form, not the maltreatment, mockery, and insult which it would be exposed to by miracle.[10]

It was Ludwig Feuerbach's *The Essence of Christianity* (1841), however, that developed most thoroughly and profoundly the charge that man had corrupted his own being in religion, and it was from this work that Marx's interpretation directly followed. For Feuerbach, religion was neither the creature of myth nor of literary indulgence. "Religion is the dream of the human mind"[11] —that is the root of his position. The secret of religion is man himself, but man fantastically projected into a transcendent realm which is then mistakenly regarded as objective and even autonomous. Religion is merely the externalization of man himself, his self-alienation fixed in eternal dogma and the rigidity of the church. *The Essence of Christianity* is devoted to a defense of this contention; it proceeds in the first part by arguing that the attributes of God are identical with the attributes of man, and that the two natures are consequently one, and in the second part, by affirming that any attempt to separate the theological and human predicates must lead to contradiction. The result of both analyses is the same—"Theology is Anthropology":

> Man—this is the mystery of religion—projects his being into objectivity, and then again makes himself an object to this projected image of himself thus converted into a subject. . .
> God is the highest subjectivity of man abstracted from himself . . . because God is, *per se*, his relinquished self . . . As the action of the arteries drives the blood into the extremities, and the action of the veins brings it back again, as life in general consists of a perpetual systole and diastole; so it is in religion. In the religious systole man propels his own nature from himself, he throws himself outward; in the religious diastole he receives the rejected nature into his heart again.[12]

Religion is the self-consciousness of man, but it is self-consciousness in a peculiarly distorted and illusory form, for ". . . ignorance . . . is fundamental to the peculiar nature of religion."[13] Religion is the earliest form of man's awareness of himself, and religion everywhere precedes philosophy historically. Man first sees his own nature in the external natural world about him. "Religion is the childlike condition of humanity; but the child sees his nature-man-out of himself. . . ."[14] So the progress of religion consists in the continual discovery that what was previously accorded objective status is in reality subjective only, ". . . . what was formerly contemplated and worshipped as God is now perceived to be something *human*."[15] Religion is a perpetual struggle against idolatry because in each later stage of development man discovers that he has in fact been worshipping his own nature. His religious development consists in the progressive realization that he has been unknowingly objectifying himself in his prior religious experience. But however far one may carry this process, and however many deceptions one religion may have uncovered in its rivals, the alienation of man in an illusory projection is the essence of all religion and cannot be cured unless one comprehends the religious consciousness at its root—as a form of anthropology. This will make possible man's recovery from himself in the discovery that religion is only a repressive distortion of his true divinity, the final liberating end which Feuerbach conceived of as the function of his work.

> And it is our task to show that the antithesis of divine and human is altogether illusory, that it is nothing else than the antithesis between the human nature in general and the human individual. . .
> Religion, at least the Christian, is the relation of man to himself . . . but a relation to it, viewed as a nature apart from his own. The divine being is nothing else than the human being, or, rather, the human nature purified, freed from the limits of the individual man, made objective.[16]

It is crucial to understand that the unmasking of religion is the purification of man. For when Feuerbach is accused of atheism, he responds that atheism is the secret of religion, not in the sense in which religion intends its own significance, but in the sense that the moment of truth which is distorted in religion is the "truth and divinity of human nature."[17]

74

Feuerbach's "reduction" of religion to anthropology must not be misunderstood; the reduction is logical in structure in that the material of one domain is replaced by another. But morally, the process is one of exaltation for the intention is not to lower God or religion to *mere* anthropology, but to raise man to the level of the divine.

This is the radical humanism of Feuerbach's position which so much impressed Marx—that the critical analysis which reveals the human source of the illusion of a transcendent realm of God, and so annihilates the ostensive remoteness of man from what is sacred and divine, is the same act which heals the wound of alienation and returns man to himself. Religion is not merely an error, though it is that. It is a distinct deception which is concomitantly, a distinct self-perversion. For religion is a compensatory illusion, in which man completes in his imagination what the illusion itself has prevented him from achieving in his actual existence:

> The monks made a vow of chastity to God; they mortified the sexual passions in themselves, but therefore they had in heaven, the Virgin Mary, the image of woman—an image of love. . . The more the sensual tendencies are renounced, the more sensual is the God to whom they are sacrificed.[18]

The enrichment of God and the impoverishment of man are but a single fact. "The more empty life is, the fuller, the more concrete is God."[19] The early Christians and the Catholic Church rejected in their own persons natural love and the sexual union of the family. They regarded this physical love as an unholy and unheavenly thing. But in compensation they were satisfied by an unearthly Father, Son and Mother of God:

> Only he who has no earthly parents needs heavenly ones. The triune God is the God of Catholicism; he has a profound, heartfelt, necessary, truly religious significance, only in antithesis to the negation of all substantial bounds. . . The triune God has a substantial meaning only where there is an abstraction from the substance of real life.[20]

Nor are the values which ground human existence in any way dependent upon a transcendent divinity. Love, wisdom and justice have an intrinsic and independent validity. It is only when the illusion of God is destroyed that man can grasp this fact and re-

75

alize the autonomy and dignity of his own moral being. For, as Feuerbach notes, ". . . The belief that God is the necessary condition of virtue is the belief in the nothingness of virtue itself."[21] When the intrinsic moral significance of man and the inherent validity of those norms which define his being are both denied autonomy, and are forced beyond themselves into an illusory place remote from their proper ground and nature, the result can only be the dislocation and consequent perversion of human existence.

> Religion is the relation of man to his own nature . . . but to his nature not recognised as his own, but regarded an another nature, separate, nay, contradistinguished from his own: herein lies its untruth, its limitation, its contradiction to reason and morality; herein lies the noxious source of religious fanaticism . . . of all the atrocities . . . in the tragedy of religious history.[22]
>
> Only when we abandon a philosophy of religion, or a theology, which is distinct from psychology and anthropology, and recognise anthropology as itself theology, do we attain to a true, self-satisfying identity of the divine and human being, the identity of the human being with itself . . . every theory of the identity of the divine and human which is not true identity is . . . a perversion, a distortion; which, however, the more perverted and false it is, all the more appears to be profound.[23]

3.   Marx and Engels were deeply impressed by Feuerbach's analysis and never denied that their own interpretation was heavily dependent upon it. But they did not believe it had gone far enough in its dissection of the motive of the religious projection or in its comprehension of the particular social circumstances from which that projection derived. Feuerbach had traced religion to anthropology, but his anthropology was too abstract, and had itself to be rooted in a detailed sociology. In particular, Marx did not believe that Feuerbach had penetrated the source of human dependency from which the compensatory illusion of religion sprang. As Marx wrote in his *Theses on Feuerbach*:

> Feuerbach starts out from the fact of religious self-alienation, the duplication of the world into a religious, imaginary world and a real one. His work consists in the dissolution of the religious world into its secular bases . . . the chief thing still remains to be done. For the fact that the secular foundation detaches itself from itself and establishes itself in the clouds as an independent realm is really to be explained only by the self-cleavage and self-contradictoriness of this secular basis. . . .

Feuerbach, consequently, does not see that the "religious sentiment" is itself a *social product,* and that the abstract individual whom
he analyzes belongs in reality to a particular form of society.[24]

Marx was unwilling to accept any pure religious sentiment
operating in an abstract human nature. It should be clear that the
materialist theory of history and the particular theory of ideology
demand this conclusion. For the forms of consciousness are reflections of the social relations of production existing in a given
society at a specific moment in time. It is consequently to social
structure that we must turn to reach the roots of religious ideology.
The heart of Marx's position is contained in the following passage,
which deserves to be quoted at some length because of its crucial
importance to the theory as a whole, and because it is not possible
to do justice to it in paraphrase:

> For Germany the criticism of religion is in the main complete, and
> criticism of religion is the premise of all criticism.
>
> The profane existence of error is discredited after its heavenly
> *oratio pro aris et focis* (speech for the altars and hearths) has been
> rejected. Man, who looked for a superman in the fantastic reality of
> heaven and found nothing there but the reflexion of himself, will no
> longer be disposed to find but the semblance of himself, the non-
> human (unmensch) where he seeks and must seek his true reality.
>
> The basis of irreligious criticism is: Man makes religion, religion
> does not make man. In other words, religion is the self-consciousness
> and self-feeling of man who has either not yet found himself or has
> already lost himself again. But man is no abstract being squatting
> outside the world. Man is the world of man, the state, society. This
> state, this society, produce religion, a reversed world-consciousness,
> because they are a reversed world. Religion is the general theory of
> that world, . . . its universal ground for consolation and justification.
> It is the fantastic realization of the human essence because the human
> essence has no true reality. The true struggle against religion is there-
> fore mediately the fight against the other world, of which religion is
> the spiritual aroma.
>
> Religious distress is at the same time the expression of real distress
> and the protest against real distress. Religion is the sigh of the op-
> pressed creature, the heart of a heartless world, just as it is the spirit
> of a spiritless situation. It is the opium of the people.
>
> The abolition of religion as the illusory happiness of the people is
> required for their real happiness. The demand to give up the illusions
> about its condition is the demand to give up a condition which needs
> illusions. The criticism of religion is therefore in embryo the criticism
> of the vale of woe, the halo of which is religion.

Criticism has plucked the imaginary flowers from the chain not so that man will wear the chain without any fantasy or consolation but so that he will shake off the chain and cull the living flower. . . . Religion is only the illusory sun which revolves round man as long as he does not revolve around himself.

The task of history, therefore, once the world beyond the truth has disappeared, is to establish the truth of this world. The immediate task of philosophy, which is at the service of history, once the saintly form of human self-alienation has been unmasked, is to unmask self-alienation in its unholy forms. Thus the criticism of heaven turns into the criticism of the earth, the criticism of religion into the criticism of right and the criticism of theology into the criticism of politics.[25]

In the context of Marx's large system, this very dense and brilliant passage can be viewed as affirming the following important propositions:

1. Feuerbach has completed the criticism of religion itself, and established it as distorted projection of man's being.

2. Religion is either the expression of a society too primitive to grant man an awareness of his independence from nature, or too corrupt to permit him autonomous control of his own being.

3. Religion is the reversal of the world in the sense that the corruption of social existence finds its purported validation in religious doctrine.

4. Religion is a consolation for misery—an opiate. It is a cry against real degradation, but an expression of human impotence which confirms and enhances the very distress against which it arises.

5. If man is to grow in dignity, the narcotic of religious illusion must be wrenched from him. But this is only the beginning of man's task. It is subsequently necessary to discover the perversion in man's social being that led him to find this crippling distortion attractive.

6. It is finally necessary to eradicate the source of this perversion, an act that can only be fulfilled by a revolutionary restructuring of the human society.

This is the essential thrust of Marx's position; it remains now to fill in its outline and draw the implications it entails. We must first locate more concretely the nature of the social corruption which forms the basis of religious projection. We may best begin by contrasting present religiosity with its primitive varieties. All religion reflects the fact that man's life is controlled by external power over which he has no control; but in primitive society it was the power of nature which so constrained man, while in the modern world, it is the force of the social system which exercises this external dominance. So Engels wrote in an interesting passage in *Anti-Dühring*:

> . . . it was not long before, side by side with the forces of nature, social forces begin to be active—forces which confront man as equally alien and at first equally inexplicable dominating him with the same apparent natural necessity as the forces of nature themselves. The fantastic figures, which at first only reflected the mysterious forces of nature, at this point acquire social attributes, become representative of the forces of history.[26]

The "fetishism of commodities" comes to replace the original fetishism of nature.

The root source of religion is alienation and the illusory attempt to overcome it. For the primitive the dominating external force is in nature, while for developing man it lies in society itself; this is the dialectical foundation of human history for its means that man is the source of his own disfigurement and the vehicle of his own restoration. It is man himself whom man must overcome in the process of his transformation. The hand that inflicts the wound is the hand that cures it. This contention is at the heart of everything that Marx and Engels wrote, and is not, as has recently been maintained, a youthful enthusiasm of Marx which he came with maturity to abandon.

But how is it possible for human activity to confront man as "an alien power opposed to him, which enslaves him instead of being controlled by him?"[27] In a word, the answer for Marx is that human society is not a free, conscious, purposefully-planned product of human cooperation, but a class divided, antagonistic and therefore, irrational form of existence. In this latter circumstance, the decisions of multitudes of men combine to establish a realm in which they cannot achieve mutual realization. In this Marxian vision, the invisible hand of Adam Smith is stood on its head, for while Smith viewed social reason as the result of the interplay of individually reasonable acts (defining "reasonable" as "efficiently egoistic") Marx viewed social irrationality as the medium in which individual rationality was necessarily aborted:

> This crystallization of social activity, this consolidation of what we ourselves produce into an objective power above us, growing out of our control, thwarting our expectations, bringing to naught our calculations, is one of the chief factors in historical development up to now. . . .The social power, i.e., the multiplied productive force, which arises through the cooperation of different individuals as it is determined within the division of labor, appears to these individuals, since their cooperation is not voluntary but natural, not as their own united power, but as an alien force existing outside them, of the origin and end of which they are ignorant, which they thus cannot control, which, on the contrary, passes through a peculiar series of phases and stages independent of the will and action of man, nay even being the prime governor of these.[28]

In alienated society the product of human labor confronts man as natural, not voluntary, that is, as imposed upon him as an unalterable fact, rather than as chosen by him in response to human requirements. At first sight, society is qualitatively different from nature, for in the natural realm, nothing at all occurs as the result of conscious intention. But with closer inspection the difference begins to disappear, and we discover that while the agents of history work deliberately for the satisfaction of conscious goals, it is not the case that the joint effort of their individual purposes can prove satisfactory to them as purposeful men. For within any society characterized by class division "a cleavage exists between the particular and the common interest,"[29] and the course of history, though it is the resultant, in some sense, of the intentions of human beings, is in no sense the resultant at which any of those conscious agents aimed. History is therefore, the outcome of human intention while it is simultaneously, the negation of human intention:

> That which is willed happens but rarely; in the majority of instances the numerous desired ends cross and conflict with one another, or these ends themselves are from the outset incapable of realization, or the means of attaining them insufficient. Thus the conflicts of innumerable individual wills and individual actions in the domain of history produce a state of affairs entirely analogous to that prevailing in the realm of unconscious nature . . . Historical events thus appear on

the whole to be likewise governed by chance. But where on the surface accident holds sway, there actually it is always governed by inner, hidden laws, and it is only a matter of discovering these laws.[30]

These last lines point in the direction of genuine human liberation. For if society is like nature in the fact that its accidental facade masks a realm of law, it is also like nature in that the understanding of law makes man the potential master of the forces which have previously oppressed him. To the primitive, with overwhelming effect, and to historical man in continually diminishing effect, nature is destructive precisely because it cannot be understood and mastered for human ends. The understanding of nature brings with it power over natural forces. The same is true of social existence, for once we understand the forces active in society

> when once we grasp their action, their direction, their effects, it depends only upon ourselves to subject them more and more to our own will, and by means of them to reach our own ends. And this holds quite especially of the mighty productive forces of today.[31]

With the socialization of the productive forces of society it becomes possible for man to overcome his alienation. At this moment he emerges fully from the realm of mere nature, for his existence is now in his own control, and whatever suffering and defeat he experiences in this new life will bear the characteristics of tragedy rather than farce. His objectified activity will no longer constrict him of necessity in an alien mold, but will constitute the free environment in which he manifests his essential humanity. In this circumstance he will achieve mastery over history, and in Engels' markedly Kantian words "pass from the kingdom of necessity to the kingdom of freedom."[32]

It is of the greatest significance, however, to note that this overcoming of alienation is not achieved in thought, but in action. For, as we recall, it is not thought that determines social existence, but social existence that determines thought:

> Mere knowledge . . . is not enough to bring social forces under the domination of society. What is above all necessary for this is a social act. And when this act has been accomplished, when society, by taking possession of all means of production and using them on a planned basis, has freed itself and all its members from the bondage in which they themselves have produced but which confront them as

an irresistible alien force . . . only then will the last alien force which is still reflected in religion vanish; and with it will also vanish the religious reflection itself, for the simple reason that then there will be nothing left to reflect.[33]

So long as man remains under the control of alien forces, religion will persist. So long as economic power continues to confront man as an inexorable destiny which he is helpless to oppose, rendering him thereby incapable of eradicating the social evils which afflict him, or even of understanding the crucial fact that human degradation is the work of man, the result of institutions which he himself has created and which he is equally capable of remaking for his own fulfillment, so long will the need for illusory compensation remain. The only redemption open to man is that which he will render through his own labor. He must make himself autonomous. When he does so he will realize that the ideals which are rooted in his nature need no longer be projected beyond society and history into an unearthly realm, dependent for fruition upon the mysterious intervention of some heavenly savior. Man will come to realize that he has been the source and agency of his own corruption, and that he possesses the power to establish the conditions of his own dignity. To hold that the evil of this world will be redeemed by an agency beyond man and time is to destroy the motive for secular transformation. But significantly, to accomplish the needed social transformation is to destroy the foundation upon which religious illusion flourishes. The religious illusion is ingredient in a corrupt superstructure which will wither of itself with the revolution in man's social existence.

The obvious implication of this position is that religion will disappear independently of any external pressure. Here, again, the similarity with Freud is interesting. For just as a psychoanalyst could never advocate the destruction of a patient's illusion through violence or terror, neither can an intelligent disciple of Marx. Social illusion will disappear as an individual hysterical symptom disappears, with the cure of its cause. Nor is it irrelevant that for both these great traditions the cure is effected by extending the rational autonomy of man. Man's object for Marx ought to be the transformation of his social existence; those who repress religion only assure its martyrdom and its prolongation. Those who understand religion can affort to await its natural death.

What has been said thus far, consitutes the basic tendency in the views of Marx and Engels; but there is a countertendency which appears late in the works of Engels which should also be noted. In an essay in which Engels is discussing the role of labor in the evolution of mankind he makes the following observation:

> Let us not flatter ourselves overmuch on account of our human conquest over nature. For each such *conquest takes its revenge on us.* Each of them, it is true, has in the first place the consequences on which we counted, but in the second and third places it has quite different, unforeseen effects which only too often cancel out the first. The people who, in Mesopotamia, Greece, Asia Minor, and elsewhere, destroyed the forests to obtain cultivable land, never dreamed that they were laying the basis for the present devastated condition of these countries, by removing along with the forests the collecting centers and reservoirs of moisture. (emphasis added)
> But if it has already required the labor of thousands of years for us to learn to some extent to calculate the more remote *natural* consequences of our actions aiming at production, it has been still more difficult in regard to the more remote *social* consequences of these actions. (emphasis in the original.) [34]

Engels does not deny that there has been steady progress in discovering the remote effects of social behavior, but he underscores too, the laboriousness of the effort. If it has taken thousands of years to learn of the more remote natural consequences of our actions and if the situation is still more difficult in regard to the social consequences of our actions, there cannot be any realistic prospect of an early mastery of social existence. It will apparently continue to be true for a very long time, and even under a system of socialism, that the indirect consequences of our social actions will remain unknown to us. But if that be the case, alienation will continue into a quite distant future and can hardly be expected to disappear even with the advent of socialism. For alienation results essentially from the fact that human labor produces a world opaque to man and destructive of his purpose.

If the remote consequences of his acts cannot be predicted, then some element of opacity is built into man's social existence in the foreseeable future, and if his social world is opaque, it will only be some happy miracle that will prevent some of the unforeseen results of his actions from returning to man in a destructive form. But in so far as alienation is the fundamental cause of religion, man's inability to master the remote effects of his social

83

actions will produce a tendency toward religion in any society, socialist or otherwise, which man can realistically envision in the course of history. It is, in fact, not even clear that the notion of a thoroughly transparent social existence is even intelligible, since it would seem to imply that all of men's future actions are predictable, while the implication of this consequence is that I can predict my own future action, a conception which seems to invalidate any meaningful notion of what human action is.

4. It is now possible to turn to the specific character of Christianity. And the first thing we must note about the Christian religion is that it made its original appeal to the miserable, oppressed and rejected orders of men that languished in despair as the Roman Empire sank into oblivion. Christianity promised an other-worldly compensation to those who suffered most from the evils of earthly existence. Christianity bears the essential imprint of that populace of the slaves, the subjugated, the poor and the impotent to whom it made its original appeal. So, when Professor Anton Menger wondered why with the enormous concentration of ownership and widespread misery of the oppressed that existed at the time of Rome's decline, socialism did not follow, Engels answered that:

> . . . this "socialism" did in fact, as far as it was possible at the time, exist and even become dominant—in Christianity. Only this Christianity, as was bound to be the case in the historic conditions, did not want to accomplish the social transformation in this world, but beyond it, in heaven, in eternal life after death, in the impending "millennium."[35]

Christianity appealed to an alienated agglomeration of men for whom a truly human existence was impossible in this world, and who were therefore seduced by the projection of a fantasied fulfillment. The fact of worldly degradation is masked by the dream of eternal beatitude. For all the varied components in the mass who embraced the Christian dream, earthly salvation was a thing of the past:

> for the ruined free men it was the former polis, the town and the state at the same time, of which their forefathers had been free citizens; for the war-captive slaves the time of freedom before their subjugation and captivity; for the small peasants the abolished gentile social system and communal landownership . . . Where was the way out, salvation, for the enslaved, oppressed and impoverished, a way out

common to all these groups of people whose interests were mutually alien or even opposed? And yet it had to be found if a great revolutionary movement was to embrace them all.

This way out was found. But not in this world. In the state in which things were it could only be a religious way out. Then a new world was disclosed. The continued life of the soul after the death of the body had gradually become a recognized article of faith throughout the Roman world . . . Then came Christianity, which took recompense and punishment in the world beyond seriously and created heaven and hell, and a way out was found which would lead the laboring and burdened from this vale of woe to eternal paradise.[36]

Crucial to their interpretation is the view of Marx and Engels that Christianity is grounded not in a political, but in an eschatological vision. The thrust of Christianity is toward escape, not transformation, and the end of history — the second coming of Christ and the establishment of the Kingdom of God—was something which Jesus and his earthly disciples fully expected to be realized quickly, within the lifetime of their own generation. Engels refers in some detail to John's vision of the Apocalypse to support his contention that the whole meaning of Christian preparation is for a vision which negates the life of earthly man, a vision which is immanent, and soon to occur.

But if Christianity is preparation for eternity rather than secular change, it is not surprising that it contains no ethic upon which human society can be established. The function of the teaching of Jesus was to prepare men for the second coming, and not to root them in an existence whose nature, no matter how improved by secular means, was an essential corruption to be radically cancelled by the redemption of the divine kingdom. The root of Christian morality is the denial of this world for the sake of another, and the negation of human society for a beatific community. If the suggestions which the Gospels contain for the transition to a realm beyond secular history were mistakenly applied within history the result could only be chaotic. Marx seems thoroughly to enjoy the point when he asks:

Do you offer your right cheek when you are struck upon the left, or do you not institute proceedings for assault? Yet the Gospel forbids that. . . .

Are not most of your court proceedings and the majority of civil laws concerned with property? But you have been told that your treasure is not in this world.[37]

It followed that when the paradise failed to materialize, Christianity was left to accommodate itself to earthly existence without an intrinsic criterion in terms of which it might discriminate among the social systems of men. So, Marx contends, Christians find themselves living in states with radically different governments and constitutions accepting their given lot in the conviction that one is to render under Caesar what is his own, and submitting to authority since it is "ordained by God."[38] But as a result of its normative vacuousness and its willingness to comply with any secular authority which would protect its own religious practice, Christianity ended by accommodating itself through history to everything vile and degrading in man's social existence.

> The social principles of Christianity justified the slavery of Antiquity, glorified the serfdom of the Middle Ages and equally know when necessary, how to defend the oppression of the proletariat, although they make a pitiful face over it.
>
> The social principles of Christianity preach the necessity of a ruling and an oppressed class, and all they have for the latter is the pious wish the former will be charitable.
>
> The social principles of Christianity transfer the . . . adjustment of all infamies to heaven and thus justify the further existence of those infamies on earth.
>
> The social principles of Christianity declare all vile acts of the oppressors against the oppressed to be either the just punishment of original sin and other sins or trials that the Lord in his infinite wisdom imposes on those redeemed.
>
> The social principles of Christianity preach cowardice, self-contempt, abasement, submission, dejection, in a word all the qualities of the canaille; and the proletariat, not wishing to be treated as canaille, needs its courage, its self-feeling, its pride and its sense of independence more than its bread.[39]

There is one additional consequence of the origin of Christian ethics that must be noted; the inherent hypocrisy of Christian ideals. For if the original counsels, admonishments and preachings of Jesus were designed to prepare men for a release from their worldly existence, and if in fact that monumental expectation was never realised, what could become of the ideals originally proposed? One might argue that they should have been discarded and replaced by other standards pertinent to the mundane life of men. But in fact, given the ostensive nature of Jesus and his relation to the institutionalized Church that followed him, this was impossible. Some pretense had to be made of adopting the eschatological vision of the founder to the wholly unforeseen and disparate conditions which actually prevailed. But those conditions, man's continued historical existence, were incompatible with the profession vision. The result could only have been an internal disruption and falsification of the ideal itself. Some variant of the original ideal was professed, but one so opposed to its original intention, that the norm was reconstituted as a denial of itself. It is against such a process that the following contention of Engels acquires full meaning:

> . . . Christianity knew only *one* point in which all men were equal: that all were equally born in original sin—which corresponded perfectly to its character as the religion of the slaves and the oppressed. Apart from this it recognized, at most, the equality of the elect, which however was only stressed at the very beginning. The traces of common ownership which are also found in the early stages of the new religion can be ascribed to solidarity among the proscribed rather than to real equalitarian ideals. Within a very short time the establishment of the distinction between priests and laymen put an end even to this incipient Christian equality.[40]

But while actual equality disappears under the development of Christianity, one continues to hear innumerable sermons about God's equal love for all of men.

Marx and Engels never tire of noting the baseness of organized religion and the extent of its hypocrisy. Whatever the pretentious piety in which religion dresses the justification of its enslavement of man through the illusion of impotence and compensatory solace, its historical place has been at the side of the oppressor. Marx rarely misses the opportunity to vent his sarcasm at the self-seeking of this institution, as when he notes in *Capital* that the "English Established Church will more readily pardon an attack on 38 of its 39 articles than 1/39 of its income."[41] The same sneer is carried in the following passage and in the whole thrust of Marx's work:

> In England even now occasionally in rural districts a laborer is condemned to imprisonment for desecrating the Sabbath by working in his front garden. The same laborer is punished for breach of contract if he remains away from his metal, paper, or glass works on the Sun-

day, even if it be from a religious whim. The orthodox Parliament will hear nothing of Sabbath-breaking if it occurs in the process of expanding capital.[42]

5. It is now possible to say something about the development of specific Christian churches and doctrines, that is, about Christianity and the economic system of which it was a reflection. Here, the role of class plays a very large part, for if the economic interpretation of history and the theory of ideology are correct, religion has no independent history, and its internal conflicts must finally express more ultimate conflicts, among economic interests, that is, among the rising and falling economic classes in society.

> Even the so-called religious wars of the sixteenth century involved primarily positive material class interests; those were class wars, too, just as the later internal collisions in England and France were. Although the class struggles of that day were carried on under religious shibboleths, and though the interests, requirements, and demands of the various classes were concealed behind a religious screen, this changed nothing in the matter and is easily explained by the conditions of the time.[43]

When Christianity is examined in the Middle Ages it is readily seen to be an institution bearing the heavy imprint of class power and prestige. This fact was born at the time of Constantine when Christianity was made the official religion of the State. The Church grew as "the most general synthesis and sanction of the existing feudal domination."[44] The clergy obtained a monopoly on learning and education, both of which became essentially theological. Politics and jurisprudence bore the same mark. In time the Church passed from a persecuted minority to a powerful oppressor of the dissenting beliefs of others. It had "partaken of the fruits of slavery in the Roman empire for centuries, and later did nothing to prevent the slave trade of Christians, either of the Germans in the North, or of the Venetians on the Mediterranean . ."[45] It came to mirror exactly the practice of the nobles, requiring the small farmer to transfer to its growing power the title to his land and his independence. In this way it helped to reduce the free farmer to a serf. In these circumstances, "all the generally voiced attacks against feudalism were above all attacks against the Church, and all social and political, revolutionary doctrines were necessarily at the same time and mainly theological heresies."[46]

Since the Church stood as the ideological sanction of the feudal system, it was necessary to de-mythologize that system before it could be directly destroyed. It was in the context of this need that the Protestant Reformation occurred.

Vigorous opposition to the system of feudalism existed throughout the Middle Ages in the form of mysticism, heresy or actual insurrection. Some of these heresies were the expression of patriarchal shepherds resisting the spread of feudalism, but these were of minor importance. Much more significant was the opposition to feudalism that developed in the towns that had already outgrown it, and among the plebeians that stood outside it. In this bifurcated opposition one can see the roots of the fundamental antagonism between bourgeoisie-burgher and peasant-plebian opposition that was to break out again at the time of the Peasant War.

The original form of heresy, that of the Albigenses in France, appeared in the 12th century as an expression of the interest of town burghers in a "cheap church." Its demands included the revival of simple early Christianity and the abolition of exclusive priesthood, a demand not unlike that of later bourgeoisie for simple and cheap government. But this heresy was paralleled by another which, while it shared burgher interest in the elimination of Church authority, went much further.

> It demanded the restoration of early Christian equality among members of the community and the recognition of this equality as a prescript for the burgher world as well. From "equality of the children of God" it inferred civil equality, and partly even equality of property. Equality of nobleman and peasant, of patrician, privileged burgher and plebeian, abolition of the corvee, ground-rents, taxes, privileges, and at least the most crying differences in property . . .[47]

At first these different strands were not clearly distinguished from each other, but by the 14th and 15th century their distinctive forms were more clearly marked. So John Ball stood alongside the Wycliffe movement and the Taborites beside the Calixtines in Bohemia. What was appearing, of course, was the incipient class structure which would in times emerge in full reality in the distinction between bourgeoisie and proletariat. And just as the process was to repeat itself later, so it was the burgher class itself that brought forth "an appendage of propertyless urban plebeians, day laborers and servants of all kinds, belonging to no recognized social Estate . . ."[48] These were the ranks that stood outside of official feudal society, without privilege or property, without rights, burdened by heavy taxes, the most obvious manifestation of the breakdown of feudal society. It was understandable that a group so thoroughly exploited and miserable and without real historical hope should produce the chiliastic vision of common ownership, absolute equality and elimination of authority, which derived its violent fantasy from the impossibility of its aspiration. But this plebeian element was also to give rise to the movement of Thomas Munzer and the Anabaptists, the precursors of the later prole-tariat, and to merge with the free peasants, serfs and bondsmen, all of whom sought the overthrow of the feudal system. At the time of the Reformation, then, Engels saw society as divided among three significant classes:

> While the first of the three large camps, the *conservative Catholic camp*, embraced all the elements interested in maintaining the exist-ing conditions, i.e., the imperial authorities, the ecclesiastical and a section of the lay princes, the richer nobility, the prelates and the city patricians, the camp of the *burgher-like moderate Lutheran* reforms, attracted all the propertied elements of the opposition, the bulk of the lesser nobility, the burghers, and even a portion of the lay princes who hoped to enrich themselves through confiscation of church estates and wanted to seize the opportunity of gaining greater independence from the Empire. As to the peasants and plebeians, they united in a *revolu-tionary* party whose demands and doctrines were most clearly ex-pressed by Munzer.[49] (Italics in original).

The rising commercial class had to direct its attack against the conservative Catholic establishment and it did so first in Germany under the banner of the Lutheran Reformation. It must be under-stood at this point that the religious revolution which goes by the name of the Protestant Reformation was a reflection of underlying economic forces. We have already alluded to this fact but it is important enough to underline. For though its form was religious, and it was undoubtedly understood as a religious movement by most of those who were caught up in its passion, the Reformation can for a Marxist have no ultimate foundation in religiosity for the simple reason that religion is a part of the social superstructure and is therefore primarily an effect, rather than a cause, of social action. To put the matter crudely, what is progressive in religion does not, for Marx, derive from some inherent virtue in the religious mode of consciousness, but rather, from the fact that the economic forces which are the ultimate causes of the religious mentality, are entering a progressive stage. There often have been in history humane religious movements directed at the reform of established religious institutions, but by and large these do not derive from any logic inherent in the spirit of religion itself, but from more basic social causes. This view is often stated by Marx and Engels but one or two references will have to suffice for our purposes:

> The new world religion, Christianity, had already quietly come into being, out of a mixture of generalized Oriental, particularly Jewish, theology, and vulgarized Greek, particularly Stoic, philosophy . . . The fact that after no more than 250 years it became the state religion suffices to show that it was the religion corresponding to the conditions of the time. In the Middle Ages, in the same measure as feudalism developed, Christianity grew into the religious counterpart to it, with a corresponding feudal hierarchy. And when the burghers began to thrive, there developed, in opposition to feudal Catholicism, the Protestant heresy...The Middle Ages had attached to theology all the other forms of ideology—philosophy, politics, jurisprudence—and made them subdivisions of theology. *It thereby constrained every social and political movement to take a theological form. The sentiments of the masses were fed with religion to the exclusion of all else; it was therefore necessary to put forward their own interests in a religious guise in order to produce an impetuous movement.*[50] (emphasis added)

The same fundamental observation is made by Engels in the course of an analysis of the devoloping role of Thomas Munzer. In tracing the growing boldness of Munzer's position, Engels notes that his

> philosophico-theological doctrine attacked all the main points not only of Catholicism, but of Christianity generally. *Under the cloak of Christian forms he preached a kind of pantheism* . . .[51] (emphasis added)

The nature of this pantheism was to exalt reason over faith, secular existence over some supposedly future heaven, and a communistic egalitarianism over the propertied hierarchy of the feudal church. But Munzer's protest was nevertheless "cloaked" in Christian phraseology.

In its early stages Luther's revolt was not yet definite in

character; it had to rely on the unified opposition of a variety of elements. And it was violent in its demands, as in the following passage which Engels quotes from Luther:

> Since we punish thieves with the halter, murderers with the sword, and heretics with fire, why do we not turn on all those evil teachers of perdition, those popes, cardinals and bishops, and the entire swarm of the Roman Sodom *with arms in hand and wash our hands in their blood?*[52] (Italics in original.)

But Luther's revolutionary posture soon collapsed. From among the peasants, plebeians, burghers, lesser nobility, and lay princes who originally supported him, Luther had eventually to choose. "He dropped the popular elements of the movement, and took the side of the burghers, the nobility, and the princes. His appeals for a war of extermination against Rome were heard no more."[53] As he identified himself with burgher sentiment he came to rely more heavily upon peaceful change, moderate progress and political activity within the bounds of law. But the separation of Lutheranism from plebeian and peasant factions brought it more and more completely under the influence of the reformed princes. This regressive tendency finally culminated in Luther's reactionary violence in the face of the Peasant War, for when the princes and lords of Protestant regions were attacked by the peasants, Luther acted against them with unbridled vehemence:

> They must be knocked to pieces, strangled and stabbed, covertly and overtly, by everyone who can, just as one must kill a mad dog. Therefore, dear sirs, help here, save there, stab, knock, strangle them everyone who can, and should you lose your life, bless you, no better death can you ever attain.[54]

The result of the Lutheran movement was not only the destruction of the peasant revolt, but of the burgher aspirations as well, so that it was the secular princes who benefited, thereby removing Germany "for three centuries from the ranks of countries playing an independent active part in history."[55]

But while the bourgeois thrust of the Reformation was defeated in Germany it made much better progress under the influence of Calvin. In Geneva, Holland, Scotland and England it forced important changes in existing social institutions, playing, in the latter country, so important a part that it was largely incorporated in the restored Established Church of England. And although the Calvinists were suppressed in France in 1685 they led to a liberation of free thought which manifested itself in an expanding, secular, commercial class.

Marx clearly regarded Protestantism as the perfect religious expression of capitalism. In his view even the Calvinist notion of predestination was rooted in economic fact—that in capitalist competition, success or failure depended not on personal effort, but on economic factors that were beyond understanding or control. He even notes, in a striking passage, the affinity between Protestant asceticism and capitalism that was to form a later theme in the writings of Max Weber:

> The money cult implies its own asceticism, its own self denial, its own self-sacrifice—parsimony and frugality, a contempt for worldly, temporal, and transient satisfactions: it implies the striving for *everlasting* treasure. Hence the connection of English puritanism, but also of Dutch Protestantism, with money making.[56] (Italics in original)

Nor was Protestantism without its effect upon the development of capitalism. Marx notes that the process of "forcible expropriation" of property in the 16th century received "a new and frightful impulse from the Reformation, and from the consequent colossal spoliation of the church property."[57] The inhabitants of the monasteries were hurled into the proletariat and the subtenants of the church's estates had their land confiscated as they were themselves forcefully removed. Again, Protestantism supported the genesis of capital by "changing almost all the traditional holidays into work days."[58] But of course, in these and numerous other ways, Protestantism was merely carrying out the underlying thrust of the growing tendency of capitalism itself.

The great moral fact of Protestantism remains its alliance with the propertied oppressor against the proletariat. Colonialism and the institution of slavery are obvious instances of capitalist rapacity. Marx quotes from William Howitt's *Colonisation and Christianity*, the following passages:

> The barbarities and desperate outrages of the so-called Christian race, throughout every region of the world, and upon every people they have been able to subdue, are not to be paralleled by those of any other race, however fierce, however untaught, and however reckless of mercy and shame, in any age of the earth.[59]

Nor is the domestic situation any better. The " 'holy ones' . . . show their Christianity by the humility with which they bear the overwork, the privations and the hunger of others."[60] In another passage Marx refers to the Venetian monk, Ortes, who in the 18th century maintained that the antagonism between great riches and widespread privation was a natural law of social wealth. He contrasts with Ortes the view of the Protestant, Townsend, who in 1786 wrote in praise of the hunger of the poor, that it acted as a "natural motive to industry," served to assure that the most sordid and disgusting tasks of society would be fulfilled, freed the most delicate from drudgery, and concluded finally that the Poor Laws tend to "destroy the harmony and beauty, the symmetry and order of that system which God and Nature have established in the world." On the contrast between Ortes and Townsend, Marx then makes the following comment:

> If the Venetian monk found in the fatal destiny that makes misery eternal, the raison d'etre of Christian charity, celibacy, monasteries and holy houses, the Protestant prebendary finds in it a pretext for condemning the laws in virtue of which the poor possessed a right to a miserable relief.[61]

The bourgeoisie realized the importance of "the evangelization of the lower orders" as a means for anchoring them more securely to their oppression. For religion represents as much the spiritual force of oppression as the state represents its physical force. Religion is the opiate through which the proletariat is rendered incapable of protesting its own exploitation. "The mortgage the peasant has on heavenly goods gives guaranty to the mortgage the bourgeoisie has on the peasant's earthly goods."[62]

- II -

Marx's portrait of Christianity is provocative and brilliant, but in general it is more the outline of a position complemented by occasionally vivid elaborations, than it is a finished work. This is not to say that the theory cannot be completed, and in this section we shall make an extremely brief attempt to indicate how that task might be accomplished. To this end we need to turn to the New Testament itself and to writings of some of the widely recognized historians of Christianity, such as Ernst Troeltsch.

The Marxian Critique of Christianity

1. The view that Christianity is essentially based on an eschatological vision has come to be more thoroughly accepted today than it was at the time of Marx and Engels, whose argument in favor of the view was based on an inadequate understanding of biblical sources. "Repent ye: for the kingdom of heaven is at hand"; "This generation shall not pass till all these things be done."[63] It is phrases such as these that, to a great deal of current scholarship, embody the essential thrust of the Christian position.

Albert Schweitzer credits Johannes Weiss with first correctly grasping the significance of the eschatological question. He paraphrases Weiss' position briefly in the following passage:

> The general conception of the Kingdom was first rightly grasped by Johannes Weiss. All modern ideas, he insists . . . must be eliminated from it; when this is done, we arrive at a Kingdom of God which is wholly future. Being still to come, it is at present purely supramundane.
>
> With political expectations this Kingdom has nothing whatever to do. "To hope for the Kingdom of God in the transcendental sense which Jesus attaches to it, and to raise a revolution, are two things as different as fire and water." The transcendental character of the expectation consists precisely in this, that the State and all earthly institutions, conditions, and benefits, as belonging to the present age, shall either not exist at all in the coming Kingdom, or shall exist only in a sublimated form. *Hence Jesus cannot preach to men a special ethic of the Kingdom of God, but only an ethic which in this world makes men free from the world and prepared to enter unimpeded into the Kingdom. That is why His ethic is of so completely negative a character; it is, in fact, not so much an ethic as a penitential discipline.*[64] (Italics added.)

A parallel point is noted by Walter Rauschenbusch in regard to the teaching of Paul:

> Paul expected an immediate spiritualization of the entire Cosmos. The dead would be raised in a spiritual body; the living would be transformed into the same kind of body; for flesh and blood in the nature of things could not share in that spiritual kingdom. Death would cease. Nature would be glorified, and the long travail of all creation would end when the children of God would be manifested in their glory. *In Paul's program of the future there is no room for a millennium of happiness on this present earth. . . . His outlook is almost devoid of social elements.* To him the spirit was all. This material world could be saved only by ceasing to exist.[65] (Italics added.)

95

It is impossible to stress the importance of this insight too much, for it completely undercuts the interminable historical debate about the social significance of the Christian gospel by indicating that the whole question is spurious. The teachings of the founders of Christianity, as distinct from any particular practices in which Christians may have engaged, is neither progressive nor reactionary, socialist nor capitalist, Right nor Left: it is an attempt to escape these categories altogether by transcending the entire realm of existence in which they are at all meaningful. As Troeltsch notes:

> . . . there is no hint of any formulation of the "Social" question; the central problem is always purely religious . . . Early Christian apologetic contains no arguments dealing either with hopes of improving the existing social situation, or with any attempt to heal social ills . . .[66]

These representative quotations tend firmly to support the contention of Engels which we have already discussed, that the social transformation which concerned Christianity was not "in this world, but beyond it, in heaven, in eternal life after death . . ." From this fact there follows a conclusion, which, while often adumbrated by Marx and Engels, can be made still clearer in the following proposition: *it was precisely the social vacuousness of the original teachings of Christianity which so simplified the process of adapting them to any conceivable status quo: in other words, it was because the religious motive of total transcendence was so radical in Christianity that it lent itself so readily to the politically conservative function of accepting or sanctioning any existing social order.*

The Marxian position also receives modern support for its contention that the original appeal of Christianity was to the oppressed segments of the Roman empire, for whom it exercised the attraction of a compensatory dream. Troeltsch states the matter forcefully in an extremely detailed argument from which we may glean the following summary:

> The fact, however, remains that Jesus addressed Himself primarily to the oppressed, and to the "little ones" of the human family, that He considered wealth a danger to the soul, that He opposed the Jewish priestly aristocracy which represented the dominant ecclesiastical forces of His day. It is also clear that the Early Church sought and won her new adherents chiefly among the lower classes in the cities, that members of the well-to-do, educated upper classes only began

to enter the Church in the second century, and then only very gradually; and we are aware that this change did not take place without a good deal of opposition on the part of the educated and wealthy sections of Society.[67]

We may also conclude, that the disastrous effect of the great social conflicts which lasted for centuries, and the indescribable misery which they caused, opened the minds of men to thoughts of religious redemption. Further, the renunciation of individual activity in social matters, and submission to the world domination of the Empire, drove the individual into his own inner life, and forced him to concentrate his energies on the effort to elevate private and personal morality; it also gave social ideals a transcendent turn; meanwhile both individuals and groups composed of individuals on a voluntary basis, *found comfort in religious exaltation as a compensation for the hopelessness of the temporal outlook.*[68] (Italics added.)

The tendency of the observations of this great non-Marxist scholar, culminating in the italicized passage, might well have come from the writings of Marx himself. Nor is there anything here which ought to surprise us, since both the old and new Testaments are rich in supporting examples. If we consider Jewish history we are struck with the fact that reference to an afterlife comes to play an important role for this people only after the humiliation of its Babylonian exile. Nor is the compensatory factor any less striking in the Sermon on the Mount, where Jesus appeals to the meek, the mourners, the persecuted, the poor in spirit, and the seekers after righteousness.

As a corollary of this compensatory appeal we must note another fact which Troeltsch calls to our attention:

It was also quite natural that Christianity should primarily seek and find its disciples among those who were feeling the weight of this oppression most acutely . . . thus for a long time, in the main, it found most acceptance among the lower orders; *in its apologetic, therefore, it turned this necessity into a virtue.*[69] (Italics added)

The inversion through which the impotence of the lower classes is redeemed by Christian teaching is not difficult to locate. That passage in Luke (16: 19-31) in which the rich man suffers in hell while his poor counterpart is comforted in heaven may be one of the more striking instances, but the same process is behind the basic emphasis on social quietism which marks the gospel narratives. Jesus admonishes his followers, "I send you forth as sheep,

97

therefore be quiet as doves";[70] "resist not evil (M 5: 39-41); "take no thought of your life, what ye shall eat or what ye shall drink, nor yet for your body" (M 6: 25-34); "put up again thy sword into his place, for all they that take the sword shall perish with the sword." (M 26: 52). The oppressed are incapable of political revolution, and it is this necessity which is turned into their virtue. The mechanism is most clearly manifested in Jesus' counsel to "render unto Caesar the things that are Caesar's; and unto God the things that are God's." (M 22:21)

It is this last command to the faithful that is so vividly elaborated by Paul. It may be remembered that Marx had condemned Christianity for justifying oppression and the tyranny of governments; it would be difficult to find a more striking confirmation of this criticism than the letters of Paul.

> Let every soul be subject unto the higher powers. For there is no power but of God; the powers that be are ordained of God.
> Whosoever therefore resisteth the power, resisteth the ordinance of God: and they that resist shall receive to themselves damnation. . . .
> Render therefore to all their dues: tribute to whom tribute is due; custom to whom custom; fear to whom fear; honor to whom honor. (Romans 13: 1-7)

It is not difficult to understand or possible to deny the vehement criticism Marx directed against a social institution which in the midst of enormous evil, could threaten resistance with damnation, and prescribe to the oppressed that they abide in that calling wherein they are called. (I Corinthians 7:21)

Nor does this criticism exhaust the ultimate Marxian ground for the rejection of the Christian ethic. At the heart of Christian moral corruption is its heteronomy, its subjugation of moral experience to a source of validity and a sanction which is foreign to its proper autonomy. Christianity is an ethic of salvation and at every turn it counsels or admonishes virtue not for its own sake, but the sake of the personal salvation which God would confer upon the religious. But Marx surely subscribed to the remark of Feuerbach which we have already quoted: ". . . the belief that God is the necessary condition of virtue is the belief in the nothingness of virtue itself." The wellspring of Marxian morality is its contention that man's dignity and fulfillment are possible only under conditions which he rationally and freely imposes upon himself,

98

for his own end, and under canons which are intrinsic to his nature. The overwhelming importance of autonomy in the Marxian ethic is clear in the following passage in which Engels comments on the nature of man under socialism:

> The laws of his own social action, hitherto standing face to face with man as laws of nature foreign to, and dominating him, will then be used with full understanding, and so mastered by him. Man's own social organization, hitherto confronting him as a necessity imposed by nature and history, now becomes the result of his own free action . . . Only from that time will man himself, with full consciousness, make his own history . . .[71]

Everywhere Christianity is marked by a denigration of man's rational autonomy, e.g., the reliance on Jesus' miracles—and the dependence on external reward for the motivation of virtue. When we turn to the beatitudes, for example, we discover that what the oppressed are offered is not a call to virtue for its own sake, but the promise that they shall be comforted, shall inherit the earth, be filled, obtain mercy and enter the kingdom of heaven. Blessed are those who are reviled for the sake of God, for their reward in heaven shall be great. (M5: 110-12) In the tale of the good Samaritan (Luke 10: 30-37) or the parable of the rich man in Luke 18, the promise that virtue will be rewarded with salvation—"thou shalt have treasures in heaven"—is never absent. One ought not to display alms before men, to be seen by them, "otherwise ye have no reward of your Father which is in heaven." (M 6: 1) Pray in secret, for "thy Father which seeth in secret shall reward thee openly." (M 6: 6) The whole attitude is summed up in one of its basest instances:

> For if ye forgive men their trespasses, your heavenly Father will also forgive you.
> But if ye forgive not men, neither will your Father forgive your trespasses. (M 6:14-15)

What has happened to the "Christian" virtue of forgiving one's enemies?

This feature of Christianity is neither accidental nor unimportant, but rooted in the nature of its early appeal. To the oppressed it promised salvation and the release from earthly torment, and it is in no way surprising, then, that its attraction was grounded in this promise. Rauschenbusch catches the essence of the matter in the following passage:

> Nearly all the early Fathers wrote on the resurrection . . . *The Nicene Council was not merely the triumph of a cristological formula, but of that conception of Christianity which made it primarily redemption from death and impartation of immortality.* The prayers for the dead and to the dead, the festivals of the martyrs and saints, the poetic speculation on heaven and hell and purgatory, the desire for a blessed death with all "the consolations of religion" the apparatus presented in the sacraments of the Church *to attain security from hell and early release from Purgatory,* the churchyards crowding up to the churches and into them—all these testify to the place which the future world held in the thoughts of ancient and medieval Christianity.[72] (Italics added)

This fundamental tendency in Christianity to concentrate upon individual salvation through the satisfaction of God's will, and to reduce moral and social existence to means to this salvation, had a disastrous effect on man's estimate of his own worth and his conception of the nature of human community. The ground of man's value was located not in himself, but in the God who had given birth to him. This is moral heteronomy and alienation of the most debilitating sort, for in drawing man's significance out of his intrinsic being and reifying it in a transcendent projection, man is left without any internal nature worthy of respect. It is not surprising that the result of this interpretation is the sinfulness and insignificance of man. Troeltsch puts the matter very clearly, when after remarking that it is "only fellowship with God which gives value to the individual," he goes on to note that:

> . . . the emphasis falls not only on the individual's sense of his dignity in being united with God, but also on his sinful weakness and creaturely infirmity, the sense of the need for trust in God and the help of God, and the confidence in *His mercy as the source of all that is good.* . . . The individual, in spite of his sense of personal worth, still remains an "unprofitable servant," needing forgiveness, and in expectation of a settlement of accounts with God, must in brotherly love destroy all human debit accounts, all calculations between man and man.[73] (Italics added)

This is merely an acute illustration of the baseness of that religious projection and consequent alienation which had been dissected

100

by Feuerbach and then by Marx. In sucking the value of man out of the intrinsic characteristics of his human nature one cannot help but leave that nature a desiccated void. Since some sense of worth is essential to life man fills that void again, but in abject reliance upon an alien source of value. The compensation cannot fully succeed, however, and one is never finally free from the sense of impotence and wickedness. Engels' contention that men were in Christianity equal in original sin is not without foundation.

The sense of human community is equally distorted, because the foundation of Christian fellowship is equally alienated—established in a source beyond the nature of man himself. The source of Christian fellowship is not the intrinsic needs and obligations of men, but the fact that they are held to be equally the children of a common father. Their love for each other is grounded not in the contribution which love makes to the fullness of human life but in its contribution to individual salvation in the being of God. Troeltsch sums up the matter in one sentence: "love is desired for the sake of God and not for the sake of man."[74] Two great consequences follow from this interpretation. First, the motive of social amelioration is totally absent. To this matter we will shortly return. Second, the problem of love for the anti-Christian is raised in an acute form:

> It is not simply kindness and gentleness in general, but the union of those who are united in God, and the revelation and awakening of the understanding of the real values of life through the manifestation of love, the melting down of earthly smallness and worldliness in the Fire of the Divine Love, which nothing worldly can resist. But this fellowship only extends as far as the religious message is known. Where this is so it is absolute; where it is absent it seeks and woos; but the way to salvation is narrow, and few there be that find it, and amongst those few those who suffer enter most easily. *There is no thought here of a humanitarian ideal in itself.*[75] (Italics added)

But the implication is even more striking than Troeltsch himself concludes. For if fellowship is derived from unity in God, what shall be the fate of those who explicitly reject the very claim to this source of identity? It is in fact their absolute rejection by Christianity and their consignment to hell and damnation. This is an aspect of Christianity around which a great deal of sentimental self-deceit has arisen. Christianity is credited with discovering the value of love toward the non-Christian (although the idea is already present in Leviticus 24:22) and the brutal vindictiveness of the religion is simply ignored. But it is Jesus who threatened the gnashing of teeth and unquenchable fire and who admonished those who rejected his precepts "Depart from me, ye cursed, into everlasting fire" (M 25: 41-46) and "Whoever shall deny me before men, him will I deny before my Father which is in heaven." (M 10: 32-33) Nor are we engaged in gratuitous quotation, as other passages amply indicate.[76]

The great historian G. G. Coulton noted in commenting on Book XXI of Augustine's *City of God*:

> To Augustine, it was 'very absurd' that Christians, from sentimentality, should hope for any end to the agonies of the damned, so long as they believed in the eternal happiness of the blessed . . . The saints do not pray for the damned, since these are not the saints' enemies but the enemies of God; nor can we believe that Christ, when he spoke of *'eternal fire,'* was threatening what he did not mean.[77] (Italics in original)

In fact, the tendency in Christianity to identify salvation with appropriate belief was responsible for loosing upon the world the first mass 'ideological' warfare, and led directly to the Inquisition as its logical conclusion. Everything in liberal culture which derives its value from the notion that men may regulate their public behavior so long as they continue to respect ultimate diversity in belief is totally negated in the Christian contention that ultimate dissent is a denial of God which threatens the salvation of the dissenter and empowers the Church to 'redeem' him on his own behalf, regardless of how little he shares of the Church's estimate of his condition.

2. It is very difficult to escape the current myth which grounds culture, democracy, freedom, social obligation and the dignity of man in Christianity. Nor is the pressure of the Cold War likely to permit a serious popular re-evaluation of this position. Nevertheless it is a view without foundation. Troeltsch is once again much closer to the truth:

> In sum: the egalitarian-socialist-democratic conceptions of natural and divine law, and of Christian liberty founded on such law, never issue from the dialectic of the pure Christian idea, but are brought about in all instances only by political and social revolutions; and even then they are related only to those elements in Patristic ethics which

are not derived from the development of Christian ideas. Wherever these ideas are to be realized by force, and a revolution is to be given a Christian basis, it is always, here also, the old Testament must help out.[78]

Or as the same author put the matter in another place, "with the New Testament alone, no social teachings at all can be generated."[79] From this point it follows, of course, that no social criticism can be generated. This is in fact the case whether we consider the Early or the Medieval Church.

It is not difficult to understand this denial of concern with the world in the original eschatological period of Christian development. For the early Christian vision combined the ideas of ultimate equality in God, the insignificance of worldly existence— "Hunger can have no terror for him who is ready to die with Christ" —(Tertullian), the explanation of secular evil as the result of sin and the continued assurance that "the Lord will provide." Nor does the external position of the Church change in the Medieval period despite the fact that the motive for its social quietism has undergone an important revision.

> While the Early Church accepted the social order of the Ancient World as something fixed and incapable of being reformed, and learnt to tolerate it as the sinful corruption of the orders of Natural Law, while it strove to heal its harmful effects by works of charity, the Medieval Church, on the other hand, believed firmly in the Divinely appointed harmony of Nature and Grace, and regarded the relative approximation of actual social institutions to the ideals of the Church as the natural, necessary, logical world-order, which, to be secured, only needed the authority of the Church, and a constant renewal of the vitality of its religious principles . . . so far as economic life and social life in the narrower sense were concerned all was left to the Law of Nature . . . The concentration of Christianity upon the inward, personal and religious aspects of life was still predominant . . . there was still no idea of the need for a systematic transformation of the social order, subduing and moulding the natural basis for life.[80]

But if this be the case, what shall we say of those Christian values which are widely held to have deeply influenced the historical existence of the West? We can only permit ourselves the briefest of replies and to that end we may take cognizance of the examples of Christian charity and equality. The main source of reference, once again, will be the account of Troeltsch.

Christian charity was deeply influenced from the beginning by the fact that Christianity was rooted in the existing social order. The church then, was concerned to ameliorate the worldly evils which originated in institutions beyond the Church's active concern. But under the eschatological thrust of Christianity this act was directed not to man's worldly perfection, but to his preparation for divine existence.

> The aims of this charity was not the healing of social wrongs, nor the endeavor to remove poverty, but the revelation and awakening of the spirit of love, of that love which Christ imparts and in which He makes known to us the attitude of God Himself . . . The relief of distress which she actually achieves is the result of this spirit, not her first intention. . . .[81]

It must be clearly understood that under this interpretation poverty continued to be highly prized, and was in fact often voluntarily induced as a means for attaining proximity to God. Whatever relief of distress was intended was directed at "securing the minimum of existence," for the worldly restraint of religion was never to be violated. But under circumstances in which poverty was honored and charity regarded as a means of personal redemption, this virtue very soon

> . . . as the earlier ethic of love shrank into one of "good works" . . . was able to merge itself in ascetic achievements, *whose aim was no longer the welfare of others but the salvation of one's own soul.*[82] (Italics added)

When the position of the Church changed from that of a persecuted minority to an institution permeating the whole of society, the love which was originally embodied in small, intimate communities, now had to become coextensive with the entire social structure. But this was something that Christianity, with its emphasis on the individual, personal and internal aspects of love, and lacking any vehicle for the institutional embodiment of that value, could not accomplish. It dissipated and corrupted itself in the face of the challenge of the total social structure.

> In this atmosphere the whole practice of charity was changed from being a means of help to others into a practice of ascetic self-denial, into "good works" which acquire merit for oneself and for others, into penances for sin, and into a means of mitigating the fires of purgatory.[83]

104

The history of Christian equality does not fare any better, as a very brief reference to Paul will help to make clear. Of course, the Pauline ethic is grounded in a very definite conception of equality, but as the root of this conception is the identity of men before God, the idea of identity is actually limited to the religious realm. It is an equality which exists solely from the point of view in God, not of men. There is no intention whatsoever to grant men an equal claim upon God, for as Engels noted, the particular locus of equality is negative, the fact that all "have sinned and come short of the glory of God." Men are equal in their common need for redemption, so that the leading principle of the missionary message is the insignificance of worldly differences among men in view of their equal distance from the being of God.

The construction of human despair is, however, only a prelude to salvation. It is through the awareness of their own corruption that men are prepared for the salvation which is mediated by the Church and its sacraments. Those who receive grace are equally its recipients, and there is no hierarchical order among them. But this fact bears two important consequences: first, the equality of salvation which comes to men through God's grace is perfectly consistent with the most unequal relationships among men in their social life. The point of identity among men is the institution of the Church and the right of equal participation in its sacraments. Within the religious service the slave and the emperor are equal. But just so, their social inequality is maintained without objection.

In fact, the phrase "without objection" is misleading for it is far too negative. Christianity did not merely fail to protest against slavery, its effect was to condone and legitimate the relationship. For in the Pauline ethic individual differences were made the basis for the view of fellowship and of organic interdependence among social elements. Just as the natural organism contains a mutually beneficial interrelationship among nobler and baser parts, so it is with the social life of man. The inequalities among men become the occasion for their virtue—for the loving concern of the strong and the obedience of the weak. Troeltsch speaks to this point when he notes that Christianity did not merely accept slavery, but

> . . . by its moral guarantees it really strengthened it. This applies very clearly to slave laborers, whose lot, however, was already being humanized in the natural course of events by the merging of slavery into

105

the colonate of serfdom. In the opinion of Christian thinkers this right to possess slaves was due, like all law, to the Fall, and since then it has been an institution which God has permitted to exist. . . .

Thus the Christians changed nothing whatever in the laws affecting slaves. . . . As a legal institution . . . even with all its barbarous penalties, slavery still existed. The Christian Church allowed it to endure, without question, right on into the Middle Ages—*it was only largely modified by the process of economic evolution*. . . .[84] (Italics added)

Second, and more important, since the positive fulfillment of men is the gift of God's grace, it is necessary to ask whether all men are equally to receive this divine gift? Are all men equally destined to move from the negative equality of sin to positive redemption in God? And if God's grace is not equally distributed, is this due to the acts of men or to the unfathomable will of God? With the answer to these questions the Pauline conception of equality takes a completely different turn, but one that is rooted in essence, in the Christian view of God as an infinite being, whose power, knowledge and goodness transcended the limits of human comprehension. The being of God must always remain opaque to man under this conception, and the love of mercy which God displays will consequently defy any merely human attempt to comprehend it. This aspect of Christianity is, if anything, emphasized by Paul, whose position Troeltsch summarizes in the following way:

> God's goodness is grace and fathomless mercy, equally in creation and in redemption. Therefore there can be no claim of the creature for an equal share for all in salvation; it is God's own affair to call one and not to call another, and to leave some longer in error than others. In this the predestinarian Will of God is expressed . . . The idea of predestination cuts the nerve of the absolute and abstract idea of equality, the equal vocation of all to the ultimate values, the right of all to the highest goal. In spite of the equality of all in their sinful unworthiness and in their possession of grace, however, the real equality in itself, the equal claim of all to an equal share in the highest life-value through equal working out of vocation and destiny, is invalidated.[85]

Rooting man's equality in an incomprehensible source can only lead to an incomprehensible idea of what it is to be equal. True to the Marxist notion of the inversion of value under alienation, what begins under the impulse of equality, ends in the notion of the theological aristocracy of the elect. How different is this conception, and how invidious in its social consequences, when compared, for example, with the Stoic view of the equality of men as common creatures of reason.

When we pass from the Early Church to Medieval Catholicism the most notable change we can discover in regard to equality can be found to occur within the Church itself. The early Christian communities often embodied the ideal of communistic fellowship described in *The Acts of the Apostles*:

> No one regarded as being his what belonged to him; everything was in common. Those who possessed lands or houses, after having sold them, brought the proceeds and laid them at the feet of the Apostles. And to each was distributed according to his needs. (IV: 32, 34, 35)

But by the fourth century the situation is very different. We can infer the change from the admonition of Churchmen like St. John Chrysostom, patriarch of Constantinople, who in his XI Homily on the Acts of the Apostles wrote:

> And there was a great charity among them (the Apostles); none was poor among them. None considered as being his what belonged to him, all their riches were in common . . . a great charity was in all of them . . . They did not divide their fortunes into two parts, giving one and keeping the other back; they gave what they had . . . What they gave was not passed from the hand of the giver to that of the recipient; their gifts were without ostentation; they brought their goods to the feet of the apostles who became the controllers and masters of them and who used them from then on as the goods of the community and no longer as the property of individuals . . . Ah! Why have these traditions been lost?[86]

But the pronouncements of isolated figures could not stem the growing tide. In time the custom of common meals and common property disappeared. Goods were no longer offered to the community, but a part of them were distributed to the poor as alms. So a difference between rich and poor began and grew within the Christian community itself. In the beginning, too, no separate clergy existed. The religious community elected a member of itself to conduct services, and every member was eligible to become a religious leader in the community. As the religion grew in membership the function of leadership became a full-time occupation, and those who assumed its burden came to be paid by the members.

> Parallel with the inequality between rich and poor, there arose another inequality, that between the clergy and the people. The ecclesiastics, at first elected among equals with a view to performing a temporary function, soon raised themselves to form a castle which ruled over the people.[87]

By the sixth century, Gregory the Great had rescinded the provisions which permitted the slave to hold office in the Church.

In this way the hierarchical structure within the Church was intensified as was the general role which the Church played in the society as a whole. In the beginning, wealth belonged to the whole religious community, but by the fifth century the revenue of the Church was divided into four parts, with only one part going to the needy. More striking still, was the reversal which occurred when the Church demanded the offering of gifts to itself by the poor as well as the rich. The tithe imposed by the Church upon the people weighed upon many as an oppressive burden. In this way the Church came more and more to ally itself with the nobility and the other exploiting elements in fedual society, and became in time the largest owner of wealth in the whole medieval structure. Its treatment of its own serfs was often more brutal than that of the nobility, and Coulton has noted:

> So great was the oppression of its serfs by the Chapter of Notre Dame de Paris in the reign of St. Louis that Queen Blanche remonstrated 'in all humility' whereto the monks replied that 'they might starve their serfs as they pleased.'[88]

It is not to be expected that under these circumstances the Church would suddenly reverse its historical position and speak for equality. It merely developed the original patriarchal and organistic ideas of Paul into a full social philosophy. The notion of organism justified the conception of a system whose internal differences contributed to a common end. The stratification of these differences into fixed classes occurred both within Medieval society as a whole, and of course, within the Church, with its distinctions among priests, monks and laymen. All personal relationships were organized around mutual duties and obligations, the charity of the powerful and the obedience of the less fortunate. But the character of this organic ranking was made far more oppressive, fixed and incomprehensible through the influence of the patriarchal view which grounds ultimate authority in the inscrutable will of God. Its clearest social instance is probably the family, in which the dominance of the husband over all the members of the household was accepted as both a natural fact and the source of social virtue. Authority and subordination, however tempered by devotion and love, were essential features of the most personal human relationships. It is true in theory that privilege carried with it the opportunity and obligation for great service, but in the social context in which that theory was applied, privilege also came to carry with it the opportunity for great exploitation and indifference.

Troeltsch's account of Medieval Catholicism shows very clearly that while the organic conception was responsible for introducing into Christianity the elements of "communism," social activism, and the criticism of despotic rule, the patriarchal position moved the Church into the direction of conservatism, class rigidity and authoritarianism. And though in theory the Christian could never abdicate the right in conscience to disobey despotic rule, in fact, the history of Christian protest is centered on those instances in which secular authority interferes with religious practice itself. Despotism remains a punishment for sin, the implication being that actual rulers have been chosen through the will of God — i.e., the Divine Rights of Kings. The whole matter is summed up by Troeltsch in the following passage:

> To sum up these "irrational" elements which lead to a passive acceptance of the inequalities appointed by God: in the Family the ruling element is a male domination, which extends to the complete absorption of the wife's property by her husband, and the dominance of the male includes an extensive right of discipline; this state of affairs must be patiently endured as the result of the curse of sin. Again, the masses of the serfs have been bound to serve their masters since the Fall, and actual slavery persists throughout the Middle Ages, for as a result of the Fall, labor has become punishment and pain; it is laid as an obligation upon different classes and callings, though in very different ways, for the claims in life are strongly differentiated according to class and position, so that, on the one hand, more freedom is permitted to those in the higher ranks of Society, while, on the other, no man may try to rise beyond the limits of his class, nor forsake the position or the calling which he inherits from his father.[89]

109

3.   It remains to say a few words about the Marxian view of the development of Protestantism. So much of such importance has been written about the relationship between Capitalism and Protestantism that nothing more can be attempted in this section than the briefest indication of the possibilities of interpretation and a hint or two at an argument favorable to the Marxian position. A full discussion of the question of whether it is Capitalism or Protestantism which is the cause of the other's appearance has already engaged the efforts of scholars as significant as Weber, Sombart, Kautsky, Tawney, Brentano, Robertson and Parsons. In view of the complexity of the problem and the compelling arguments possible on either side, it is best perhaps to suggest a different consideration.

Let us bracket the question of whether Marx was correct in believing that Protestantism was the result of economic developments, or whether the positions of Weber and Sombart, which attributed final importance to the mentality or spirit of the age were ultimately more sound. That debate is beyond our scope. Let us rather construct the incredible hypothesis that at the time of their origin, the two movements were causally independent of each other, and let us consider merely the problem of which tradition has been more thoroughly influenced by the other. From this perspective a good deal can be said on the side of the materialist conception of history, for capitalism seems to have developed much more thoroughly in accordance with its own internal tendencies than have any of the great Protestant religious movements. In many significant instances they have had their original position seriously altered in accordance with capitalist values. In the case of the Lutheran Church and even more particularly for Calvinism, the transformation seems unmistakable.

It is perfectly true that Calvinism was in very profound accordance with the spirit of early Capitalism, but it is equally true that Calvin never had any intention of permitting the purely secular aim of Capitalism to achieve its own dominance. Troeltsch notes this point very persuasively in the following passage:

> The Christian element in this Calvinistic justification of Capitalism would, however, be greatly misunderstood if one did not at the same time remember the limits with which the real Christian idea of love here also surrounds the ethic of industry, and which have continued to exert a beneficent influence right down to the present day,

wherever, in all capitalistic labor, the main Calvinistic ideas have remained vitally alive. Labor is asceticism, an asceticism which is absolutely necessary. Profit is the sign of the blessing of God on the faithful exercise of one's calling. But labor and profit are never intended for purely personal interest. The capitalist is always a steward of the gifts of God, whose duty it is to increase his capital and utilize if for the good of society as a whole, retaining for himself only that amount which is necessary to provide for his own needs.[90]

That Calvin had a particular vision of the purpose of the accumulation of wealth cannot be denied, nor can it be seriously doubted that the religious view which guided Calvin had to be imposed on a system that was clearly developing in a very different direction. But Troeltsch's account seems more governed by sentiment than reason when he suggests that the Christian idea of love has continued to play a significant role in the operation of contemporary capitalism. How far any contemporary capitalist of note regards himself as 'God's steward' utilizing his capital for the general welfare and retaining only "that amount which is necessary to provide for his own needs" is a matter which can be left to the reader to decide. Some reflection on the contrast between early American Puritanism and modern economic institutions may facilitate that judgment. Consider in this regard the account by Governor John Winthrop of the Bay Colony of one Robert Keanne who, in 1639, aroused the greatest contempt of the citizens of Boston and was

> . . . charged with many particulars; in some, for taking above sixpence in the shilling profit, in some above eightpence; and in some small things, above two for one . . . After the Court had censured him, the church of Boston called him also into question, where (as before he had done in court) he did with tears, acknowledge and bewail his covetous heart . . . These things gave occasion to Mr. Cotton, in his publick exercise the next lecture day, to lay open the error of such false principles, and to give some rules of direction in the case.
> Some false principles were these:
> 1. That a man might sell as dear as he can, and buy as cheap as he can.
> 2. That if a man lose by casualty of sea, &c. in some of his commodities, he may raise the price of the rest.
> 3. That he may sell as he bought, though he paid too dear . . . and though the commodity be fallen. . .
> 4. That, as a man may take advantage of his own skill or ability, so he may of another's ignorance or necessity.

5. Where one gives time for payment, he is to take like recompense of one as of another.

Some of the correct rules for trading were the following:

1. A man may not sell above the current price, i.e., such a price as is usual in the time and place, and as another (who knows the worth of the commodity) would give for it. . .
2. When a man loseth in his commodity for want of skill, &c. he must look at it as his own fault or cross, and therefore must not lay it upon another. . .
3. A man may not ask more for his commodity than his selling price, as Ephron to Abraham, the land is worth this much.[91]

This passage is worth quoting at length because it shows very clearly the total dominance exercised over the motive of private gain and material accumulation by the prevailing Calvinist ethic of justice and self-restraint. It goes without saying that the system which Governor Winthrop recorded bears only the faintest ancestoral relation to our own. In this radical transformation it is surely Capitalism which has reshaped the original Calvinist concern. It seems clear too that it has accomplished that task by dichotomizing what was inseparably united in the Calvinist ethic —the emphasis on the "calling" of labor with its concomitant accumulation of capital, and the rigid control of that capital by a religious elite, for Christian ends. Under the pressure of commercial expansion in the sixteenth and seventeenth centuries the second element weakened and finally disappeared as a significant social force. As Tawney has observed:

> The separation of economic from ethical interests, which was the note of all this movement, was in sharp opposition to religious tradition, and it did not establish itself without a struggle. Even in the very capital of European commerce and finance, a bitter controversy was occasioned by the refusal to admit usurers to communion or to confer degrees upon them; it was only after a storm of pamphleteering, in which the theological faculty of the University of Utrecht performed prodigies of zeal and ingenuity, that the States of Holland and West Friesland closed the agitation by declaring that the Church had no concern with questions of banking. In the French Calvinist Churches, the decline of discipline had caused lamentations a generation earlier. In America, the theocracy of Massachusetts, merciless alike to religious liberty and to economic license, was about to be undermined by the rise of new States like Rhode Island and Pennsylvania, whose tolerant, individualist and utilitarian temper was destined to find its greatest representative in the golden common sense of Benjamin Franklin.[92]

Tawney's comments are particularly valuable in suggesting how very extensive was the decline of the Church as a dominant social institution. It passed from the prestige and power which it exercised as the central determiner of the whole life of its time, to an institution which gained protection in its religious privacy at the price of its social impotence before the growing secular state. Eventually it lost the will to dispute with secular, commercial power as its own aims became increasingly indistinguishable from that growing force it had once opposed. This reconstitution of Calvinism by capitalist power is clear in all its aspects.

The original structure of Calvinism was heavily authoritarian and in Tawney's words, "savored more of a collectivist dictatorship than of individualism."[93] The proper unit of society was never, in Calvin's view, the individual, but the city-community which governed with rigorous discipline. It was not only that the Consistory was able to regulate the economic behavior of the populace; it controlled every aspect of man's activity — religious devotion, dress, drink, artistic expression, the naming of children, proper style of a woman's hair, setting of the family table and every large and small element in the whole range of human behavior. Class inequality was accepted as fixed and permanent, and opposition to religious or secular authority was expressly forbidden. Obedience to magistrates was a religious duty as secular authority was constituted the viceregent of God. No private individual was ever justified therefore in resisting civil authority. Some of the autocratic flavor of the Calvinist system can be gleaned from these brief passages from the *Institute of the Christian Religion*:

> The spiritual kingdom of Christ and civil government are things very widely separated. Seeing, therefore, it is a Jewish vanity to seek and include the Kingdom of Christ under the elements of this world, let us, considering, as scripture clearly teaches, that the blessings which we derive are spiritual, remember to confine the liberty which is promised and offered to us in Him within its proper limits. For why is it that the . . . . apostle . . . . forbids slaves to be solicitous about their state (I Corinthian 7:21), unless it be that spiritual liberty is perfectly compatible with civil servitude?
>
> We cannot resist the magistrate without resisting God . . . Under this obedience I comprehend attempting anything at all of a public nature.
>
> Those who domineer unjustly and tyrannically are raised up by him to punish the people for their iniquity . . . Even an individual of

the worst character, one most unworthy of all honor, if invested with public authority, receives that illustrious divine power. . . In so far as public obedience is concerned, he is to be held in the same honor and reverence as the best of kings.[94]

Of course these passages are reminiscent of the words with which Luther had already replied to the demands of the peasants for the abolition of serfdom in 1525.

This means Christian freedom would be quite carnal—did not Abraham and other patriarchs and prophets also have bondmen? Read St. Paul and what he teaches about the servants who in his time were all slaves! Therefore, this article is clean against the Gospel and sheer robbery, for every man who considers his body thus his own has stolen it from his master. For a serf can, indeed, be a Christian and have Christian freedom; this article wishes to make all men equal and make the spiritual Kingdom of Christ into a secular external kingdom which is impossible. For a secular kingdom cannot exist without personal inequality where some are free and some are bound, some are lords and others are subjects.[95]

Whatever the specific form of this Protestant autocracy and subservience to class division, whether grounded in agrarian patriarchial life with Luther or in a growing commercial class as in Geneva, the whole fixed, hierarchal structure of its domination was inimical to the expanding powers of capitalist production and to the interests of that class who were its appropriators. Capitalism might well instigate a system of unequal privilege and class domination of its own, but it certainly could not accept the grounding of economic and political power in the elected, righteous few whose superiority was established through the choice of God. Nor could it bind itself to the denial of civil dissent and revolution when these were necessary to overthrow the persisting vestiges of feudal structure and to free itself from the restraints of aristocratic codes and royal monopolies. In the seventeenth century in England and again in the eighteenth century in France, the repression exercised by the remnants of medieval power upon the development of capitalist enterprise had to be denied by force. A limited capitalist democracy was much better suited to the needs of the rising middle class.

Therefore, under the impact of an expanding capitalism, Protestantism came to be significantly transformed. The system

114

of Calvin, for example, was built firmly upon the notion of God's total power and man's inherent sinfulness. In his sovereignty, God willed whatever occurred in human history, and so depraved was man that unless he could rely upon God's grace and the wisdom of the Holy Writ, he would be led by his own corruption into eternal anguish. All of us are corrupt, but God visits his grace upon those whom He inscrutably elects. Thus some are "preordained to eternal life, others to eternal damnation," and in the whole matter of his salvation man is thoroughly impotent. So, the original position of Calvinism and its inherent opposition to the capitalist spirit. However, the rising commercial classes were not impressed by their own impotence or the need for their resignation in the face of divine power, but rather by the wholly contrary sense of the value of active manipulation of nature and man and the attainment of position on the basis of labor and industrial merit. In the capitalist ethos, as against the Calvinist, good works *were* the means to salvation. In this context Engel's suggestion that "predestination" was merely the reflection in religion of the underlying impotence of the rising middle class in its personal commercial transactions seems far too simple an application of the materialist conception of history. The growing middle class had not yet the sense of alienation that was more thoroughly to characterize it on later occasions, and the pervasive activism and optimism under which it originally flourished were not at all compatible with the rigidity of Calvin's theology. The following brief summation by H. Richard Niebuhr seems much closer to the point:

> There is truth in the statement that Calvin, in the doctrine of predestination, "did for the bourgeoisie of the sixteenth century what Marx did for the proletariat of the nineteenth" by giving "assurance that the forces of the universe are on the side of the elect"; but, on the whole, this element derived by Calvin from purely religious sources was hard to reconcile with the native interests of the bourgeois mind and *suffered an early eclipse wherever the trading class was dominant.*[26] (Italics)

A parallel transformation affected the very notion of work, which was changed from an ascetic "calling" devoted to God, into a hedonistic pursuit aiming at the possession of goods, satisfaction and power. The early thrust of the religious motive for the accumulation of capital was largely in accordance with the needs of the capitalist system itself, and under these conditions there was more mutual support than antagonism between the economic and religious aspects of life. But in time, under an assortment of pressures, the overwhelming need for capital accumulation declined before the growing importance of consumption, and in this new situation, Keynes was eventually to emerge as far more compelling than Calvin.

But this crucial reconstruction of capitalism on a hedonistic rather than an ascetic base was already inherent in the system of Adam Smith and in all the later work of the classical economists. Under this shifting emphasis the whole life of Western man was transfigured, so that to take but one instance, the school which was originally dominated by the Church for religious ends came more and more to reflect the needs of rational and scientific manipulation of nature which were of significance to the commercial and industrial elements of society. There is probably no better summary of this transformation of Protestantism under the influence of capitalism than the following passage from Niebuhr, the brilliance of which may excuse its being quoted at length:

> A single line of development leads from Jonathan Edwards and his great system of God-centered faith through the Arminianism of the Evangelical revival, the Unitarianism of Channing and Parker, and the humanism of transcendental philosophy, to the man-centered, this-worldly, lift-yourself-by-your-own-bootstraps doctrine of New Thought and Christian Science. *The common strand that runs through these various movements is the adaptation of the early faith to the changing attitudes of the bourgeoisie. . .* Here the gospel of self-help has excluded all remnants of that belief in fatality which formed the foundation of Puritan heroism. Here the comfortable circumstances of an established economic class have simplified out of existence the problem of evil and have made possible the substitution for the mysterious will of the Sovereign of life and death and sin and salvation, the sweet benevolence of a Father-Mother God or the vague goodness of the All. Here the concern for self has been secularized to its last degree; the conflicts of sick souls have been replaced by the struggles of sick minds and bodies; the Puritan passion for perfection has become a seeking after the kingdom of health and mental peace and its comforts. This is not the religion of that middle class which struggled with kings and popes in the defense of its economic and religious liberties but the religion of a bourgeoisie whose conflicts are over and which has passed in the quiet waters of assured income and established social standing.[27] (Italics added)

It would seem then in conclusion, that the example of Protestantism may be reasonably interpreted in accordance with the general Marxian view of the relationship between economic institutions and religious consciousness. For if we bracket the basic argument between Marx and Weber over the original causal dominance of economic or religious factors, we are still faced with the imposing transformation which the development of capitalism seems to have effected in the nature of Protestantism. This would lend some credence to the position which Engels outlined in his letter to Bloch according to which economic factors were the "ultimately" significant causal agencies in social transformation. Of course, if Weber's argument is correct, then Marx is fundamentally mistaken. But that is a matter we have not attempted to determine, and around which there exists an already voluminous literature.

4. The basic Marxian contentions in regard to religion generally, and Christianity in particular, are: that religion is the expression of alienated man, that the fundamental source of this alienation is the tyrannical control exercised over the humanity by the class-divided economic system upon which he is dependent, that religious institutions are rooted in this exploitative domination and participate accordingly in the defense of that class which exercises social control, and specifically, that Christianity made its original appeal to the dispossessed masses to whom it promised salvation beyond the confines of ordinary history. No attempt has been made to offer anything like a significant defense of these propositions; rather, a suggestion has been made as to how the argument might be constructed.

It is unlikely that some of these propositions could be fully tested by anything less than a significant social revolution—for example, we would require instances in which economic alienation as defined by Marx had been transcended by a genuinely communistic society to confirm or disconfirm the claim that religion is dependent upon such economic subjugation. But some evidence has been adduced in defense of the contention that the Marxian position is serious, significant and worthy of careful consideration. It is a view uncongenial to large numbers of people, but no less compelling in the face of that fact.

Nor can it be said that while the analysis makes some sense when applied to medieval Catholocism or some aspects of the Ref-

117

ormation it has been bypassed by contemporary events. The conservative and oft-times reactionary role of the Christian churches in the 20th century, for example, is as painful a spectacle as anything which has occurred before it. The part played by the churches in the rise of European Fascism can hardly be condemned too seriously. It was the Catholic Church under Pacelli, Pius XII, that reshaped the Catholic Center Party, replacing the trade unionist Stegerwald with the monarchist reactionaries Kaas and Bruening; that dissolved the Catholic "Populari" party under the liberal Don Sturzo, thereby paving the way for Mussolini; that signed a concordat with Hitler which, for the promise of Church freedom, granted the Nazi regime its first respectable acknowledgement; and that blessed Mussolini's arms in Ethiopia and the volunteers who helped to bring down the Spanish Republic. "Hardly a Catholic or Protestant took a stand against Hitler until Hitler, in defiance of explicit promises that he had made to them, began to meddle in Church affairs."[98] This is a contention that can be supported by the works of Gordon Zahn, Guenter Lewy, and Hochhuth's play *The Deputy*.

The only astounding thing about the criticism recently voiced against the Church's role as an accomplice of Nazi brutality is in the sense of total shock with which some of these critics propound it. But the Church had played a powerful role in the creation and maintenance of anti-Semitism for centuries. It was St. Ambrose who referred to the Jewish synagogue as "a house of impiety, a receptacle of folly, which God himself has condemned," (99) and in the fourth century it was St. Gregory who wrote of the Jews:

> Slayers of the Lord, murderers of the prophets, adversaries of God, haters of God, men who show contempt for the law, foes of grace, enemies of their father's faith, advocates of the devil brood of vipers, slanderers, scoffers, men whose minds are in darkness, leaven of the Pharisees, assembly of demons, sinners, wicked men, stoners, and haters of righteousness.[100]

Nor is the following passage from the *Sixth Homily Against the Jews* by St. John Chrysostom any less significant for the absence of its introduction at Nuremberg:

> So, whenever the Jew tells you: It was men who made war on us, it was men who plotted against us, say to him: Men would certainly not have made war unless God had permitted them.[101]

118

It is necessary to note, too, in closing, that whether popular dependence on religion has been decreasing or not, certain very grave doubts seem to have affected the theological defense of the foundations of religious belief. The traditional Catholic arguments for the existence of God do not satisfy reason, and the Protestant metaphysics of such theologians as Tillich end in notions like "being-itself," which are opaque to the attempts of any ultimate rational concern. The present age is characterized by nothing so much as the sense of mass helplessness and longing and the incapacity of institutionalized religion to satisfy the need. It is affluence rather than any Church which provides whatever solace the mass of Western men enjoy. But the affluence is rooted in those conditions of human helplessness which Marx's analysis of alienation was designed to expose. The proper human reconstitution of man by man remains as yet the great unfinished task of humanity. "The death of God" so much spoken of today may express man's incipient awareness of the uselessness and harmfulness of the supports upon which he has traditionally depended. Marx may well have been right in his central contention that the death of God and the birth of autonomous man are but the corresponding facets of a single transformation. The present age seems increasingly disquieted by the power of the claim.

NOTES

1. Feuer Pp 43-44 Marx and Engels—*Basic Writings on Politics and Philosophy.* Ed. By Lewis Feuer, Anchor Books, N.Y. 1959.
2. Ibid P. 90
3. Ibid P. 7
4. B and R, P. 78 Karl Marx, *Selected writings in Sociology and Social Philosophy.* Ed. by T. B. Bottomore and Maximilian Rubel, McGraw-Hill Paperback, New York, 1964.
5. P. 75
6. Feuer P. 397
7. Quoted in Randall—P. 363 *The Career of Philosophy* Vol. II John Herman Randall, Columbia University Press, 1965.
8. Quoted in *From Hegel to Marx*—Sidney Hook, Ann Arbor Paperbacks, The University of Michigan Press, 1962—P. 86.
9. Ibid P. 87
10. Quoted in Schweitzer—*The Quest for the Historical Jesus*—Albert Schweitzer, Macmillan Paperbacks, N. Y. 1962—P. 154.
11. *The essence of Christianity*—Ludwig Feuerbach, Harper Torchbooks, New York, 1957 P. XXXIX.
12. Ibid Pp. 29-31
13. Ibid P. 13.

14. Ibid
15. Ibid
16. Ibid P. 14
17. Ibid XXXVI
18. Ibid 26
19. Ibid 73
20. Ibid 73
21. Ibid 202
22. Ibid 197
23. Ibid 231
24. Feuer, 244-245
25. *On Religion*—Karl Marx and Frederich Engels—Foreign Languages Publishing House, Moscow, 1955. Pp. 41-42.
26. Ibid. Pp. 147-148
27. Feuer, 254
28. Feuer, 254-256
29. Feuer, 254
30. Feuer, 230
31. Feuer, 105
32. Feuer, 109
33. *On Religion* op. cit. P. 149
34. *The Dialectics of Nature*—New World Paperback—Pp. 291-292.
35. *On Religion* op. cit. P. 316-317.
36. Ibid Pp. 334-336.
37. Ibid P. 35
39. Ibid Pp. 83-84
39. Ibid P. 145
40. Ibid P. 145
41. *Capital*—Karl Marx—The Modern Library, New York. P. 15.
42. Ibid P. 291 note
43. Ibid P. 98
44. Ibid P. 99
45. *The Origin of the Family, Private Property and the State*—Engels—Foreign Languages Publishing House, Moscow. P. 247.
46. *On Religion*, P. 99
47. *On Religion*, P. 101
48. *On Religion*, P. 264-265
49. *On Religion*, P. 103
50. *On Religion*, P. 264
51. On Religion, P. 111
52. Ibid P. 105
53. Ibid P. 105
54. Quoted by Engels on P. 107 of *On Religion*
55. On Religion, P. 265
56. *Quoted in The Political Economy of Growth*, Paul Baran, Prometheus Books, 1960 P. 49.
57. *Capital*—Marx—Modern Library Edition. P. 792.
58. Ibid P. 303 note
59. Ibid P. 824
60. Ibid P. 291 note
61. Ibid P. 701-710
62. Quoted in Bober P. 156 Op. Cit.

63. See M3-2, 4:17, 10:7, 10:23, Mk 9:1, 13:30-33.
64. *The Quest for the Historical Jesus*—Albert Schweitzer, Macmillan, N.Y. 1926, Pp. 239-240 Op. Cit.
65. *Christianity and the Social Crisis*—Walter Rauschenbusch, Harper Torchbooks 1964; Pp 104-105.
66. *The Social Teaching of the Christian Churches*—Ernst Troeltsch, Harper Torchbooks, N.Y. 1960, Pp 39-40.
67. Ibid P. 39
68. Ibid Pp 46-47
69. Ibid P. 49
70. Matthew, 10:16-18, See also M. 5:25, 12:15-16, 6:20.
71. Feuer, Pp 108-109
72. Rauschenbusch Op. Cit. Pp 161-162
73. Troeltsch Op. Cit. Pp. 57-58
74. Ibid P. 173
75. Ibid P. 56
76. See Mark 3:29, 6:11, 9:43-48; Matthew 3:12, 5:22 5:29, 6:14-15, 6:18, 23:33, 24:51, 25:46; Luke 12:8, 12:30-31 13:12, and John 3:5, 3:18, 14:6.
77. *Five Centuries of Religion*, Volume I, G. G. Coulton, Cambridge, at the University Press, 1923, P. 27 f.
78. Quoted in *The Faith of a Heretic* by Walter Kaufman, Anchor Books, N.Y. 1963 P. 246.
79. Ibid
80. Troeltsch—Op. Cit. P. 303
81. Troeltsch—P. 134
82. Troeltsch—P. 135
83. Troeltsch—P. 136
84. Troeltsch—P. 132-133
85. Troeltsch—P. 74-75
86. *Jean Chrysostom*, Abbe Bareille, Paris 1869, Vol. VII P. 599-603.
87. *Socialism and the Churches*, Rosa Luxemburg, a Young Socialist Publication, Nov. 1964, Ceylon, P. 13.
88. Quoted in *An Economic and Social History of the Middle Ages*, by J. W. Thompson, The Century Company, N.Y. 1928, P. 652.
89. Troeltsch Op. cit. Pp 295-296
90. Ibid P. 648
91. Winthrop, John *The History of New England from 1630 to 1649.* James Savage, ed., Boston, 1853 Pp 313-317.
92. *Religion and the Rise of Capitalism*, R. H. Tawney, Penguin Books, Inc., New York, 1947, P. 198.
93. Ibid P. 100
94. *Institutes of the Christian Religion*—John Calvin, Translated by John Allen, 7th American Edition, Philadelphia, 1936—Chapter 20, Sec. 1, 23, 25.
95. Quoted in Troeltsch Op. Cit; note 282. P. 871
96. *The Social Sources of Denominationalism.* H. Richard Niebuhr, Meridian Books, 1962, P. 84.
97. Ibid P. 104-105
98. *Religion from Tolstoy to Camus*—Selected and Introduced by Walter Kaufman: Harper Torchbooks New York, 1964. P. 27.
99. Malcolm Hay—Chapter I of "Europe and the Jews", Kaufman, Op. Cit. P. 350.
100. Ibid P. 351
101. Ibid P. 354

THE PRACTICE OF FREEDOM:
A Prerequisite for the Catholic-Marxist Rapprochement

by
GEORGE H. HAMPSCH

"Freedom is so much the essence of man that even its opponents realize it. . . . No man fights freedom; he fights at most the freedom of others. Every kind of freedom has therefore always existed, only at one time as a special privilege, another time as a universal right."
Karl Marx, *Debatten über die Pressfreiheit.*

"For freedom Christ has set us free; stand fast therefore, and do not submit again to the yoke of slavery. . . . For you were called to freedom, brethren; . . . through love be servants of one another. For the whole law is fulfilled in one word, 'You shall love your neighbor as yourself.' But if you bite and devour one another take heed that you are not consumed by one another." St. Paul, *Letter to the Galatians.*

Very serious difficulties block the way to a meaningful rapprochement between the Catholic Church and Marxist thought—especially as that thought is represented by what has been called the "socialist world." On this all are agreed. Yet it is imperative that men of good will in both "camps" work away at this seemingly hopeless split so as to reduce the gap to some degree from both sides.[1] Neither Communism nor Christianity seems destined for an early demise. The viability and longevity of both indicate that both are meaningful to modern man.[2]

The task of closing the gap can proceed at a quicker pace than is now commonly predicted, if properly approached. The accomplishment of this work can be viewed as a three-pronged but simultaneous process. The initial area of labor involves the clearing away of ignorance and obvious misunderstandings of each other's position, as well as the lingering suspicion on the part of each that the motives of the other are less pure than its own. The second area consists in the recognition of common errors and common distortions and misapplication of principles in practice. The final phase involves the recognition of mutually acceptable positions or tenets.

We cannot hope to treat of all possible subject matter where the opportunity of applying these three steps exists. We will restrict ourselves to one area which is both immediate to experience and is the key to a fruitful dialogue on the more basic and complex problems of monism, the existence of God, faith and the religious reflex, and the sociological problems of the human significance of labor, violence, revolution, socialism, and so on. This is the problem of human freedom.

An objective look at this problem leads us to the following conclusion: both Christianity and Marxism by reason of their principles should be totally committed to freedom of the highest order, yet both the Catholic Church and the World Communist Movement have acted historically in such fashion that each can with a good deal of justice accuse the other of being the enemy of freedom. The rest of the world generally concurs with both.

The misunderstandings of both the Christian and the Marxist in regard to the other's notion of human freedom arise primarily from the abuse by the other of his own principles. The misunderstandings are, of course, greatly intensified when these abuses stem from the activities of certain of the structured institutions which have been established within both positions—such as the Roman Catholic Church and the several Communist Parties. The Catholic Church and most of the Communist Parties that have gained political control have been accused of being totalitarian in nature and of restricting basic freedoms. There is much justification in these charges, as outstanding figures of each position readily admit.[3]

The history of unfreedom within the Church is well known. She had indeed a lengthy history of autocracy, persecution, censorship, coercive sanction—moral and otherwise—as well as the lesser infractions of paternalism, nepotism and self-perpetuating cliques. Hardly had she recovered from her own period of persecution when she begain to imitate her persecutors.[4] The Arians, Donatists and Manichees suffered greatly at the hands of the Church during the early period. The Catharists, Albigenses, Waldenses and Templars in the Middle Ages suffered persecution and death, with even the theological support of the otherwise-great theologians, Leo I and Thomas Aquinas. In the modern period Christians have actively persecuted Jews, Muslims and fellow Christians.

The Inquisition, above all else, has made the Church appear as

123

the purveyor of evil and enemy of freedom. Terrible trials, imprisonments, tortures and death have indelibly impressed on the consciousness of the world the unholiness and inhumanity that exists within the Church. The cruelness of the Inquisition was lessened during the period of the Enlightenment, but, sad to say, some of the spirit of the Inquisition and its attitude towards freedom linger on in the Church of the twentieth century.

Unfreedom in the Church is exercised not only against her enemies but against her faithful members as well. As the contemporary Catholic theologian, Hans Küng, points out, someone examining the Church critically from the outside would see her walls to be more like the walls of a prison than those of a sanctuary. Within those walls, the lack of freedom is found in every nook and corner:

> . . . servility pretending to be obedience and cowardice pretending to be prudence; power politics masking itself as spiritual service, and dishonesty as defense of truth. Above all, . . . [there is] at every level, low and high, a constantly recurring, appalling, cowardly, worldly fear: fear by which all Christian responsibility, courage, boldness, initiative, all Christian freedom, is in so many people struck dead and buried.[5]

This disregard for, and abuse of freedom finds its roots, first of all, in the crude interpretation, or rather the mis-interpretation of Christian tenets. Then there is too, the ever-present temptation of man to abuse the exercise of power, and his tendency to unduly centralize the authority that comes from power.

The mis-interpretation of Christianity is exemplified in the first place by the attitude of "triumphalism" which has plagued the Church from her early ages; secondly, by a certain crude interpretation of the doctrine of infallibility which would turn the believer into more of an intellectual robot than a human person, if taken literally—and which has, in effect, made this tenet something of a laughingstock to those outside the Church. A third mis-interpretation of Christian principles is one that gives to the teaching office of the Church the authority to make moral pronouncements binding, irrespective of the believer's conscience.

Triumphalism is best characterized, as Archbishop D'Souza complains, by the attitude: "Although we are sinners, we Catholics possess the whole truth; and this is our great superiority. We possess the truth; the others say the same things as we do or they are in error; therefore, we need not listen to them except to refute them."⁶ This attitude is still common despite the fact that the Church has never been free from a generous number of theological errors, cherished not only by her rank and file members, but by her clerics and bishops as well. Such self-congratulation and lack of intellectual humility have undoubtedly turned untold numbers of the human race away from any serious consideration of the claims of the Church, or from any attempt to examine the gospel of Christ with an open mind.⁷

The doctrine of infallibility, too, has been a scandal to many within and without the Church. Much of the abhorrence of this doctrine stems from a lamentable ignorance of its content and limitations, to be sure. Yet it cannot be denied that a crude but common interpretation of the teaching authority of the Church by clergy and laymen alike, has contributed to the almost total rejection of that authority by intellectually-serious men. According to this crude interpretation, the Church autocratically appropriates to herself and seizes possession of God's revelation. The Church, and the Pope in particular, divinizes authority, makes it immediate, original and something transcendent. Instead of the Church's authority consisting of a "humble, obedient, unsubjective service," some prefer to see it operate with "an arrogant tone, a loveless attitude, frequent denunciations, authoritarian interventions without reason given and condemnation without a man's being heard in his own cause, totalitarian repression of free discussion, petty censorship [and] dissemination of an atmosphere of fear and unfreedom."⁸ As such, the Church and its hierarchy, with no great surprise, have been labeled autocratic, totalitarian, and even fascist. Yet as we shall see presently, such use of authority within the Church is quite unevangelical, *i.e.*, contrary to the gospel.

Another sore point and cause of much misunderstanding and ill-will is a position held by many churchmen that the Church is the depository of all learning and the final arbiter of all questions —and especially moral questions. But Christ gave the Church no commission to control the world of learning, as the Galileo case and the question of evolution have so definitively shown. It is primarily in the arena of moral judgments, however, that those critical of the Church see an abuse of human freedom. Many within the

Church still feel that the Church is competent to provide them with detailed instructions on how to solve each and every moral problem. These people wish to act with the firm conviction that their every act is morally justified because the Church has judged it so. Every moral problem should have its "Catholic position" to which the faithful must subscribe if they would be considered loyal and obedient sons and daughters of Holy Mother the Church. But does the Church have such powers? Does the gospel empower the Church to give such direction and so manage the lives of people? "The Church is commissioned to teach the morality of the gospel, which is the moral revolution of Christian love," writes the Catholic biblical scholar, John L. McKenzie.

> The New Testament reduces all morality to the commandment of love. This implies no commission to teach philosophical morality. . . . If authority solves a moral problem by philosophical reasoning rather than by application of the gospel, its position has no more strength than its philosophical reasoning. It will be as strong or as weak as an ecclesiastical commission met to settle the question of whether the sun moves round the earth. . . . The teaching office is not commissioned to tell people what to do, but to make it possible for people to decide what to do. . . . The Church does best what Jesus Christ empowered it to do, and he did not empower the Church to be everyman's schoolmaster and everyman's conscience.[9]

Whenever the Church attempts the impossible it invariably loses prestige. The Church is beginning to recognize that in the area of moral theology she is as vulnerable to another Galileo-type case as in the area of science. Fr. McKenzie, writing on the problem of birth control, informs us:

> A moral proposition, supported a generation ago by several arguments, has suffered the erosion of each of these arguments. The clergy know the difficulty of imposing an obligation on the faithful when the clergy have no clear and obvious explanation of why that which is forbidden is wrong. Now the clergy find themselves saying equivalently: "We used to tell you birth control is against the Bible and against natural law. We can no longer tell you that it is against the Bible. The explanation of how it is against the natural law is too complicated for us to give you. Now we tell you it is wrong because we have been telling you that it is wrong; and if we withdraw from this position, the infallibility of the Church will be compromised." Whatever the ultimate issue of this moral discussion, the position of both the clergy and the laity at the time of this writing is intolerable.[10]

This kind of moral imperialism has seeped into the very marrow of Catholic thought and leadership. As one example, it has led to the questionable conclusion that one must be a professed anti-Communist to be a "good" Catholic.[11] In this or in any other matter, nearly every Catholic at one time or another, has experienced a tension between his conscience and official moral pronouncements —at least in their stricter interpretation. This is due in great part to the remaining vestiges of what has been called the Carolingian outlook of the Church towards the secular world. Thomas Merton has recently summed up this outlook remarkably well in the following passage:

> This [the Carolingian] is a worldview which was rooted in the official acceptance of the Church into the world of imperial Rome, the world of Constantine and of Augustine, of Charlemagne in the west and of Byzantium in the east. In crude, simple strokes this worldview can be sketched as follows: We are living in the last age of salvation history. A world radically evil and doomed to hell has been ransomed from the devil by the Cross of Christ and is now simply marking time until the message of salvation can be preached to everyone. Then will come the judgment. Meanwhile, men being evil and prone to sin at every moment, must be prevented by authority from following their base instincts and getting lost.
>
> They cannot be left to their own freedom or even to God's loving grace. They have to have their freedom taken away from them because it is their greatest peril. They have to be told at every step what to do, and it is better if what they are told to do is displeasing to their corrupt nature, for this will keep them out of further subtle forms of mischief. Meanwhile the Empire has become, provisionally at least, holy. As figure of the eschatological kingdom, worldly power consecrated to Christ becomes Christ's reign on earth. In spite of its human limitations the authority of the Christian prince is a guarantee against complete chaos and disorder and must be submitted to—to resist established authority is equivalent to resisting Christ. War on behalf of the Christian prince and his power becomes a holy war for Christ against the devil. War becomes a sacred duty.[12]

Primarily in the three practices of triumphalism, autocratic dogmatism and moral imperialism has the Church of the twentieth century prolonged this Carolingian outlook. Consequently, she still stands accused of condoning and perpetuating unfreedom. And yet these attributes of the historical Church not only have no solid biblical foundation, they are obviously in conflict with the letter and deepest spirit of the gospel of Christ. In spite of its many shortcomings, the Second Vatican Council has quite successfully made *this* point clear—though not without internal struggle. Yet Dostoevski, in "The Legend of the Grand Inquisitor" in the novel *The Brothers Karamazov* had already made the point, perhaps with greater cogency, years prior.[13]

Christianity is truly a religion of freedom. In spite of its many failings in the course of Church history, Christianity and its notion of freedom has had a noticeable and favorable influence on the spread of at least the *concept* of liberty in the Western world, as most objective scholars, Marxist[14] and non-Marxist alike, readily admit. The biblical foundation of the position of man seeking his personal and social fulfillment through a freedom based on love and human creativity cannot be challenged. This freedom consists first and above all in a new relationship of man to God made possible through Christ.[15] Through such a relationship man sees his fellow men as brothers whom he loves and respects because of his love of God. But such love brings a mature freedom with it in accordance with the mandate: *ama et fac quod vis* (love and do what you will). This freedom leads to an interacting relationship between the person, his fellow men and the objective world of nature. "Freedom," writes Cardinal Feltin, "lies at the very heart of Christianity, which seen from without might look like a system, but thought and lived from within is a living bond between persons. . . ."[16] To his fellows the Christian extends love, and helps create love in them as a consequence. The world of nature he humanizes and "re-creates" by actively shaping the social environment.

The acts of loving and creating are those which make man distinctively human, and to the Christian, make man God-like. Being human means to live vicariously and analogously the life of man's Creator, Love Itself. But not that of a God enthroned "out there" beyond the sight of the highest flying cosmonaut. Rather, the life of the Christian is like the life of a God who, as Thomas Merton puts it, is the "absolute future who will manifest himself in and through man, by the transformation of man and the world through science orientated to Christ."[17] Such a life is necessarily free, though it will never include activities that violate the relationship of friendship or love through the *compulsiveness* of spite, hate or selfishness. Nor will it bow passively to a mechanistic and seemingly over-powering environment. Love and creativity demand freedom, but freedom must necessarily tend towards the life of love and creativity, or the freedom is illusory.

This life of freedom is not ready-made. Man is not born free, says Christianity, he is born *to be* free. The life of freedom demands a struggle—a struggle against one's own compulsive instincts, a struggle against the evil perpetrated by other men, and a struggle against the dehumanizing aspects of the mechanical organization of the world. Man in and of himself is helpless in this struggle, though only he can wage it. "I do not understand my own actions," complains St. Paul.

> For I do not do what I want, but I do the very things I hate. . . . I can will what is right but I cannot do it. For I do not do the good I want, but the evil I do not want is what I do. . . . For I delight in the law of God, in my inmost self, but I see in my members another law at war with the law of my mind and making me captive to the law of sin which dwells in my members.[18]

These contradictions in man are overcome not necessarily only by means of class struggles and historical changes in the modes of production, but principally by God's free help through grace. "Who will deliver me from this body of death? Thanks be to God through Jesus Christ our Lord!"[19] The struggle is difficult and unending. It stretches throughout the history of man. Its goals are both social and personal. Success is indeed registered but it only serves to more clearly delineate the work still left undone.

From what has been said it becomes clear that Christianity demands a dynamic view of man and society. It requires liberty and openness and the consequent willingness to take certain risks. The world is not something to be shunned by the Christian, or to be held in suspicion and ridicule. It is rather, as Merton writes, ". . . a living and self-creating mystery of which I am myself a part, to which I am myself my own unique door."[20] A door through which I am to understand and re-create the world for man—a world in which I can come to know my brothers and myself. Any individual, any organization or any society that restricts man in his struggle for increased human love and creativity, is by the very principles of Christianity, interfering with that process of salvation wrought by Christ. Whatever other attributes may be ascribed to that person, organization or society, surely "Christian" can not be one of them.

The Catholic Church has been accused, with much justification, of unnecessarily restricting man's freedom both internally, by certain ecclesiastical attitudes and restrictions in the area of theology, morality, canon law and liturgy, and externally, by acting as an ally or servitor of political and economic forces that exploited men.[21] This happened in spite of a founder, a doctrine and theological principles that clearly sought to liberate man; principles whose very acceptance and workability demanded freedom! But have not the almost identical charges been leveled against the World Communist Movement in general, and against the Communist Parties and political regimes (be they Soviet, Maoist, Titoist, Castroist) in those countries where Marxism is established, in particular? And can it be denied that notwithstanding the ignorance and malicious distortions of fact on the part of some anticommunist forces abroad in the world, more than a kernel of truth is to be found in these accusations?

Is there not more than a passing similarity in the abuses of freedom perpetrated by the Church and by World Communism? Is there not the same tragic irony and paradox when the professed humanistic aims of both are contrasted with their mechanistic, dehumanizing bureaucratic centralism and totalitarian leanings in practice?

The Church stands indicted for a certain "triumphalism" based on pseudo-rationalization and intellectual duplicities leading to placidity and ineffectualness, but nevertheless based on an avowedly mysterious transcendent faith. But what can be said for the dogmatism of certain Communist leaders and theoreticians, their blind faith, their uncritical "authority-quoting" attitude towards their own principles, their condescending and over-critical attitude towards other philosophical positions, when Marxism is avowedly based on an unmysterious, empirical, dynamic, dialectically open-ended attitude towards reality and truth?[22] Certain European Marxists[23] to be sure, have recognized this "triumphal" attitude for what it is worth, but by and large, it still prevails among Communist leaders and theoreticians.

A crude interpretation of her teaching authority has caused the Church at times to appropriate to herself certain powers and totalitarian attitudes. Certainly the same can be said to have happened in the socialist world through an equally crude and vulgar interpretation of the Leninist principle of *"partiinost"*—that tenet whereby the Communist Party, the avant-garde of the proletarian class and its most progressive segment, interprets the real, objective interests of the proletariat, properly applies the Marxist classics to the practical aspects of everyday life and guides the evolutionary development of Marxist-Leninist ideology.[24] Under a simplistic but prevalent interpretation of this complex epistemological principle, how many loyal citizens, dedicated party members, philosophers, artists, scientists — and even logicians! — have been humiliated and perhaps suffered violence at the hands of a party politico? Have not the C.P.S.U., the C.P.C. and other Parties frequently assumed (to re-use Hans Küng's description of certain Catholic Church activities) ". . . an arrogant tone, a loveless attitude [with] frequent denunciations, authoritarian interventions without reason given and condemnation without a man's being heard in his own cause, totalitarian repression of free discussion, petty censorship, [and] dissemination of an atmosphere of fear and unfreedom."?[25]

Abram Tertz, who himself has recently suffered the consequences of the current interpretation of *partiinost* in the Soviet Union, beautifully satirizes this interpretation, precisely by expressing it in theological language:

> It is with . . . joyous facility that this artist accepts the directives of the Party and the government from the Central Committee and its First Secretary. For who, if not the Party and its leader knows best what kind of art we need? It is, after all, the Party that leads us to the Purpose in accordance with the rules of Marxism-Leninism, the Party that lives and works in constant contact with God. And so we have in it and in its leader the wisest and most experienced guide who is competent in all questions of industry, linguistics, music, philosophy, painting, biology, etc. He is our Commander, our Ruler, our High Priest. To doubt his word is as sinful as to doubt the will of God.[26]

Within the tight party discipline, secret police activities, strike prohibitions, bureaucratism, excessive directives, censorship, over-centralization of power, there breeds a totalitarian climate that cannot help but lessen freedom. Such practices weaken all arguments—however sincere—that Communists might present concerning the freedom of the worker under socialism. By a strange irony, Marxist humanism as practiced, appears to many as *in*human; not a few have difficulty distinguishing Communism from its ideological contrary, Fascism. Lenin's principle of democratic centralism seems to appear as centralized autocracy. Socialism in practice is often difficult to distinguish from state capitalism. The bureaucracy appears as a new Establishment; its members, a new, privileged aristocracy. Why must this be?

If the Catholic Church stands accused of moral imperialism, what is to be said of the moral self-righteousness and ideological "chauvinism" of the Communist world? How often do Communist writers portray the moral struggle between the Marxist and non-Marxist worlds in purely black and white terms? Do not their arguments often reduce merely to crude diatribes and condescending sermons on the moral ignorance or malice of others?[27] Is not many a Communist Party as guilty as is the Catholic Church of a certain superciliousness in its moral pronouncements? Do they not both attempt to bind their members, and perhaps even non-members, to an obedience and conformity that appears to override the individual's conscience?

If the Catholic Church is plagued by its Carolingian outlook towards the non-religious world, the Communist World Movement has an analogous problem. While the struggle for the future society of freedom and human maturity goes on, man is still imperfect and prone to evil and misjudgment. The words of Marx and Lenin have often as not been interpreted to mean that men must be prevented by authority from making these errors. Their freedom must be taken from them, for freedom at present is their greatest peril to future freedom. For the time being they must be told what to do. The already established socialist states stand as the bulwark against the powers of exploitation, and as figures of the eschatological society which will embrace all mankind. In spite of their human failings, these socialist states, under the guidance of their Communist Parties, are the only guarantee against the forces of evil, and must be submitted to—to resist established authority is to resist mankind, progress and history itself. If violence be necessary in behalf of this cause, it becomes a crusade, a holy war against slavery and exploitation. To fight becomes a sacred duty.[28] There is no justifiable reason for dissent. To speak out against authority makes one a traitor to the cause. A party member who opposes the position of the Party becomes thereby a heretic and must be purged. He is to be allowed back to the communion of believers only on condition he repents and does suitable penance.

One might ask: What have such practices to do with Marxist

132

humanism? Could not a Soviet or Chinese author of the genius of Dostoevski write a new *The Grand Inquisitor* substituting Marx for Christ? Marx looked to socialism as a mode of production under which man could for the first time in his history live within a free society—a society which makes possible the existence of the free human personality and stimulates its growth. To reach a free society demands a struggle, to be sure, but *"the struggle for a free society is not a struggle for a free society unless through it an even greater degree of personal freedom is created,"* writes the Marxist philosopher Gajo Petrovic.[29]

But this humanistic aspect of Marx is often distorted and abused. According to the "collectivist" interpretation, "the personality is asked to 'merge' completely with his class, to subordinate all his personal thoughts, wishes, hopes, apprehensions and passions to the requirements of the class struggle."[30] But such an interpretation is no more Marxist than an *auto-da-fé* is Christian. Just as a society is not free if somebody else decides its fate, neither is a personality free if somebody else decides its fate.

> Those who . . . demand the subordination of the personality to "class" do not realize that *there is no revolutionary class struggle without free personalities* capable of raising themselves above the factual level of their class and of realizing its revolutionary, universally human potentialities. . . . Great personalities are indeed necessary to class, nation and mankind, but no less necessary are those seemingly "lesser" personalities, which regardless of their own modest working and intellectual "capabilities" evince high qualities of humanity.[31]

Of course the Marxist is careful not to reduce human freedom to a pure individualism, or a Sartrean notion of complete autonomy with its infinite choice of goals. For not only is there personal freedom but there is social freedom and class freedom as well, having equal need to be cultivated according to the historical process in its present moment. But the possibility of these various aspects of freedom is not to be taken as meaning that each is peculiar to itself and mutually disassociated. "All forms of freedom are mutually conditioned, and each of them is one form of freedom." As Marx himself puts it:

> As in the solar system each individual planet revolves around the sun only while turning around itself, so in the system of freedom each

133

of its worlds circles around the central sun of freedom by circling around itself.[32]

Whenever a particular form or aspect of freedom is violated or denied, the excuse almost invariably given is that the unfreedom is *necessary,* demanded by the requirements of a more important form of freedom. But to the Marxist such an approach either misunderstands the very nature of freedom, or it is meant to serve as an apologia for the assertion of the freedom of an individual or group at the expense of someone else's freedom. "No man fights freedom itself," wrote Marx, "he fights at most the freedom of others."[33]

Freedom must be unqualified—not in the sense of an unlimited scope of activity—but as the necessary foundation of all meaningful activity. The freedom of each man is the condition for the freedom of all.[34] Likewise, the freedom of all is a necessary condition for the meaningful freedom of each. One cannot be said to be acting freely or seeking freedom if he lessens someone else's freedom in the process. Once again, Karl Marx:

> Each form of freedom is the condition for the rest of them as one member of the body is for the others. Whenever a specific freedom is brought into question then freedom itself is brought into question. Whenever one form of freedom is rejected, it is freedom which is rejected, and it can continue to carry on only a fictitious life because henceforward it is pure chance at which point unfreedom will manifest itself as the predominating force.[35]

There is no true personal freedom unless there is political freedom; no meaningful political freedom unless there is freedom from poverty and economic exploitation; no real freedom from exploitation unless there is freedom of conscience; no meaningful moral freedom unless there is freedom from alienation, and so on.

Authority is meaningless unless it operates with some degree of free consent of those responding. The use of power, be it domestic, social, political, economic, moral or religious, becomes inhuman to that degree to which the freedom of those upon whom the power is exercised is lessened.

Man remains alienated as long as he remains "outer-directed." Yet only by becoming a "species-being" through human socialization can he become, in the full sense, a person—for the free person seeks the freedom of others as his own. The "outer-directed" man

134

is unfree because his activities are subordinated to the freedom of others; the "socialized" man is free because he finds his freedom in the freedom of all. In true community man lives according to his free nature and, consequently, freedom is universal. In alienated society man is degraded, either because his freedom is denied him by others, or because he lives alone and apart from his fellow men—his "freedom" being at best a series of egoistic acts in which other men become means or objects to manipulate.[36]

Freedom demands non-alienation, and non-alienation demands love of one's fellow man. On this both Marxism and Christianity agree in theory, in spite of the almost unbelievable aberrations of this theory in the historical practice of both.

Much of this disparity between idealized theory and practice is explained by the fact that human freedom is a historical process, ever-growing but never complete. Man has only gradually come to understand what is implied in the notion that freedom is of the very essence of man. Even less speedily has he applied this knowledge to practice.

As the Marxists have so pungently but correctly observed, the tragic weakness of Christianity is that it finds itself seemingly powerless to reduce its message of freedom and brotherly love from abstractions to the world of reality, *i.e,* to social practice. Perhaps realizing this weakness, at least implicitly, religion almost invariably has sought the support of the secular powers that be— either by outright control or through the securing of privilege. There is no need to spell out this long history of church-state relations and their consequences, beginning with Constantine and extending down to the anti-missionary atrocities in contemporary Africa. What is more than a little disturbing to many is that there is no great assurance that the Church has learned from her own history all that she should. Practical efforts to bring her message of freedom and love to mankind still, at this late date, often as not reduce that message to one of authoritarian, moralistic legalism.

The Marxist will argue that this could have been foreseen, and that the phenomenon is explained adequately from the standpoint of historical materialism. Christianity has existed as part of the superstructure of several successive modes of production that made the practice of universal freedom and human comradeship, out of the question. Influenced in itself by these modes of production, religion, often as not, served in a reactionary role, actually assist-

135

ing a mode of production and prolonging its existence. It has found itself consequently in the awkward position of being the official prophet of equality, justice, freedom and brotherly love, while engaged in the practical order as the defender of authority and order in an economic and political system that has made the real, concrete exercise of these humanistic values on a social scale literally impossible. If Christianity is ever to see its message of social justice successfully implemented, this must come about within the socialist mode of production. If the Church is really more interested in the spread of the gospel message of social freedom and brotherhood than in the continuation of her privileges, her property, her authority and her power, then she can do no better than to seek the advancement of the world socialist cause.

But the Marxist is embarrassed to find that the existence of a socialist mode of production does not assure that humanistic values prevail. Efforts to reduce the socialistic message of a free community of men to practice have almost without exception resulted in an authoritarian, moralistic legalism, with a political bureaucracy to boot. Attempts to explain away the inconsistencies have not been wholly successful.

Be that as it may. The purpose of this extended comparison of Marxism, the Catholic Church and their respective positions regarding freedom, is to point up the possibilities of a rapprochement and its direction. Both Communism and Catholicism have been guilty of roughly the same "sins" against freedom. Yet both possess in their tenets not only a profound respect for freedom, but a positive injunction to make man free. Each has alienated the other as well as large numbers of mankind by its failures in practice of freedom, yet as Roger Garaudy has pointedly observed: "the future of mankind cannot be built in opposition to those with a religious faith, nor even without them; the future of mankind cannot be built in opposition to the communists, nor even without them."[37] If this be true, then not only the possibility of dialogue on the level of theory, but the very future of freedom among men depends on both Christians and Marxists committing themselves to the struggle for freedom—not only against *others* who seek to destroy it, but, perhaps at this stage, more importantly against the unfreedom found *internally* within both. What Gajo Petrovic writes concerning freedom within socialism can be applied equally (*mutatis mutandis*) to freedom within the Catholic Church.

136

The problem of freedom in capitalism is still theoretically interesting; but the problem of freedom in socialism is nevertheless newer and more interesting. And regardless of what is more interesting the problem of freedom in socialism is certainly incomparably more important, not only from the standpoint of the internal development of socialism but also from that of the contemporary world as a whole. *The development of socialism as a free community of free personalities is the most effective criticism of capitalism.*[38]

When Christianity in general and the Catholic Church in particular show to the socialist world a sincere and total commitment to freedom in practice, and when the socialist world in its turn does the same, then and only then can any meaningful rapprochement come to be. Until this happens, there may be the possibility of a superficial dialogue on the level of ideas alone, but each will turn a jaundiced eye on the other when there is a question of cooperation on the level of action.[39] Yet a dialogue of ideas which does not lead to action and cooperation, regardless of how intellectually refreshing it may be, is contrary to the best thought of both traditions.[40]

Of course, for each to live up to its teachings on freedom is at best only a prerequisite for the rapprochement and not the solution of the theoretical and practical difficulties involved. And the depth and complexity of these difficulties cannot be overemphasized—whether they be the first order questions centering on the problem of God, the matter-spirit dichotomy and the anthropological critique of religion, or the related second-order, sociological questions bearing on the human significance of labor, the condemnation of capitalism, the suppression of established classes and the building of socialism.[41]

But freedom is necessary for a dialogue on these questions to be fruitful. For such a dialogue demands not only an openness, but a liberty to travel a course somewhat tangent to the official party or hierarchial "line," if need be. At the same time, the dialogue must be instituted without precondition. Neither side may require of the other to stop being what it is, but on the contrary, ask only that it live up to its ideals more fully. Dialogue does not imply concession of any basic principles on the part of either. It does imply the presence of that freedom which is required if one is to *grow* in human understanding.

As Garaudy remarks, the Christian must be free to refuse theological intervention in the field of science. He must be free to see in technical and scientific progress, not a danger to salvation, but a legitimate affirmation of the power and grandeur of man. He must have the liberty to break from any social philosophy that makes sacral class divisions and social inequality, looking upon them as conditions required by God in expiation for sin. He must be free to reject if need be, the popular assumption that private ownership of the means of production is a necessary guarantee or requirement for the liberty of the human person. He must have the freedom to recognize in socialism and communism a form of organization of social relations that is possibly superior to capitalism. He must have the liberty to love life and to view knowledge and earthly happiness as legitimate goals for man.[42] He must be free to recognize the natural law to be not a body of ready-made moral absolutes given from somewhere on high, but a law to be discovered in the concrete events of an evolving history. He must be able to recognize the immense contributions of communists and others who have focussed the attention of the world on the work of the world, teaching Christians the true meaning of "ransoming the time."[43]

In his turn, the Marxist too must have his freedom. He must be free to break from any dogmatic approach that reduces the analysis of religion merely to the summary formula: "Religion is the opium of the people." He must be able to recognize along with Marx, that Christianity too is a "protest against real suffering."[44] He must be free to recognize that there need be no struggle between science and religion. For while it is true that science destroys superstition, magic and myth, science, as Garaudy correctly points out, cannot touch upon what is fundamental in religion. Neither the existence of God, nor questions of a moral nature are open to strictly scientific investigations or conclusions. And it is on these questions that the crucial debate between Marxists and Christians must take place.[45] While his belief in his task does not presuppose a necessity for, or any appeal to a God, the Marxist, nevertheless, must have the freedom to recognize that he is not required by his tenets to rob men of any dimensions of reality historically arrived at from a starting-point of a faith in a transcendent deity. He must be at liberty to perceive that belief in this transcendent deity need never limit nor retard the progress of humanity, but may in fact, enhance man's creative energies in the struggle for the realization of the completely fulfilled man.[46]

138

The Marxist must have the freedom to reject any attempt at social betterment that reduces itself to a kind of patronizing surveillance and domination of the earth. He must be free to reject any programmatic future that limits man's destiny to the blurred vision of still-alienated social planners.[47] In political discussions, he must have the freedom to support Christian and other non-Marxist reformers who are engaged in significant social reforms—shunning a doctrinaire approach which would condemn any such social phenomena that fail to fall within the rigid classical categories of the class struggle.[48]

With mutual freedom will come mutual enrichment. From dialogue between a small number of isolated pioneers who are often suspect among their own, will come in time a true dialogue between whole Marxist and Christian communities who have opted for the future. Then can Marxists and Christians begin to *work* together for that future—free men seeking greater freedom in order to better love one another while respecting the different outlooks. In the touching words of Roger Garaudy:

> As far as faith is concerned, whether it is a question of faith in God or of faith in our task, whatever may be the divergence or what its source is, though it be for one party a bowing to the will of God and to the other a purely human creation, it imposes upon us the duty of making every man a man, that is to say a living focus of initiative, a poet in the profoundest sense of the word—that which makes every day of his overreaching himself creative of what the Christians call his transcendence and we, his true humanity.
>
> This ideal is high enough and difficult enough of realization to demand the combined efforts of all, even if we must, in the fire of that dialogue which will enable us to meet each other in the very center of ourselves, on the threshold of the fundamental, see consumed all that is in us which prevents us from becoming what we are, in the wonderful sense given by Nazim Hikmet to this flame of purification and sacrifice:
>
> > How will the darkness
> > If I do not burn,
> > If you do not burn,
> > If we do not burn,
> > Become light?[49]
>
> Let us all begin to burn!

NOTES

1. Cf. *Pastoral Constitution on the Church in the Modern World*, 21, in *The Documents of Vatican II*, ed. by Walter M. Abbott, S.J., New York, Guild Press, 1966, pp. 218-219; Pope John XXIII, *Pacem in Terris*, 159, 160, NCWC transl., Boston, St. Paul Editions, n.d., pp. 53-54; William Wainwright, "Catholics and Communists," *Marxism Today*, 7 (September, 1963), pp. 267-270; Leslie Dewart, "Christians and Marxists in Dialogue," *Continuum*, 1 (Summer, 1963), 139-153; Louis Dupré, "The Challenge of Marxism," *Cross Currents*, 12 (Summer, 1962), 327-335; Oskar Schatz and Ernst Florian Winter, "Alienation, Marxism and Humanism: A Christian Viewpoint," *Socialist Humanism*, ed. by Erich Fromm, Garden City, Doubleday, 1965, pp. 288-304; *Catholics and Communists*, New York, Political Affairs Press, 1964. See also the "Marxism and Religion" Issue of *Political Affairs*, (July, 1966).
2. Cf. Roger Garaudy, "The Marxist-Christian Dialogue: Possibilities, Problems, Necessity," *Continuum*, 3 (Winter, 1966), 403. This article is also in *The Marxist Quarterly*, No. 17 (Spring, 1966).
3. See, for example, Adam Schaff, "Marxism and the Philosophy of Man," in *Socialist Humanism*, p. 137; Hans Küng, *Freedom Today*, New York, Sheed and Ward, 1966, pp. 34 ff, also in *Commonweal*, Vol. 78 (June 21, 1963), 343-353.
4. Cf. Küng, *Freedom Today*, pp. 38-39.
5. *Ibid.*, p. 44. See also, John L. McKenzie, S.J. *Authority in the Church*, New York, Sheed and Ward, 1966, especially pp. 137-150; Eugene D'Souza, Archbishop of Bhopal, India in *Council Speeches of Vatican II*, ed. by Hans Küng, Yves Congar, O.P. and Daniel O'Hanlon, S.J., Glen Rock, N.J., Paulist Press, 1964, p. 132.
6. *Council Speeches of Vatican II*, p. 213; cf. Leon Arthur Elchinger, Coadjutor Archbishop of Strasbourg, France, *ibid.*, pp. 215-221; McKenzie, *Authority in the Church*, p. 129.
7. Cf. *The Church in the Modern World*, 19, *Documents of Vatican II*, p. 217.
8. Hans Küng, *The Council in Action*, New York, Sheed and Ward, 1963, p. 199. Cf. Joseph Descuffi, Archbishop of Smyrna, Turkey in *Council Speeches of Vatican II*, pp. 68-71; Ernest Primeau, Bishop of Manchester, U.S.A., *ibid.*, pp. 83-86; McKenzie, *Authority in the Church*, pp. 123 ff; Daniel Callahan, "Freedom and the Layman," in *Freedom and Man*, ed. by John Courtney Murray, S.J., New York, P.J. Kenedy, 1965, pp. 152-167.
9. *Authority in the Church*, pp. 134-135. Cf. Bernard Häring, C.S.S.R., *The Liberty of the Children of God*, Staten Island, N.Y., Alba House, 1966, pp. 35-54, 118-120.
10. *Authority in the Church*, p. 133.
11. On this point, see Dewart, "Christians and Marxists in Dialogue."
12. "Is the World a Problem?," *Commonweal*, Vol 84 (June 3, 1966), 306.
13. At least in Aloysha's interpretation of the legend. Cf. Ellis Sandoz, "Philosophical Anthropology and Dostoevsky's 'Legend of the Grand Inquisitor,'" *Review of Politics*, 26 (July, 1964), 374.
14. See, for example, M. A. Kamyshan, "Concerning an Objective Criterion of Moral Progress," *Filosofskie nauki*, 1962, No. 5, translated in *Soviet Studies in Philosophy*, Vol. 1, No. 4 (Spring, 1963), pp. 58-63. Mark Twain however is not quite so ready to admit this: "The church here rests under the usual charge—an obstructor and fighter of progress; until progress arrives, then she takes the credit. The church . . . always condemned progress as heresy."

Quoted by Philip Foner, *Mark Twain: Social Critic*, New York, International Publishers, 1958, p. 148.

15. Galatians 5:13; 1st Corinthians 7:21-24; John 8:31f; Romans 8:14-22, etc.
16. Quoted by Norman St. John-Stevas in "Catholicism and Religious Toleration," *The Wiseman Review*, No. 488 (Summer, 1961), p. 105. Cf. *Declaration on Religious Freedom*, 10, *The Documents of Vatican II*, p. 689.
17. "Is the World a Problem?," p. 308.
18. Romans 7:15-23.
19. Romans 7:24-25. On the nature of Christian freedom see the excellent essays by William F. Lynch, S.J., "The Freedom to be Human," in *Freedom and Man*, pp. 70-86, and Jean-Yves Calvez, S.J., "Freedom in Tomorrow's Society," *ibid.*, pp. 168-182.
20. "Is the World a Problem?," p. 308.
21. Cf. I. Chiari, *Religion and Modern Society*, London, Herbert Jenkins, 1964, p. 180; Garaudy, "The Marxist-Christian Dialogue . . .," pp. 413-414.
22. Cf. Dewart, "Christians and Marxists in Dialogue," pp. 150-151, note 2.
23. In the writings for example of Roger Garaudy, Maximilien Rubel, Adam Schaff, Georg Lukacs, Karel Kosik, Gajo Petrović to mention only a few, certain blind spots in Marxist philosophy caused by dogmatism are recognized with candor. Cf. Howard L. Parsons, *Humanistic Philosophy in Contemporary Poland and Yugoslavia*, New York, The American Institute for Marxist Studies, 1966.
24. Cf. V. I. Lenin, *Urgent Tasks of Our Movement*, *Selected Works*, New York, International Publishers, 1943, Vol. II, p. 11; Joseph Stalin, *Problems of Leninism*, Moscow, Foreign Languages Publishing House, 1953, pp. 164-188; N. S. Khrushchev, Speech at Kiev, April 26, 1958, in *Soviet World Outlook*, 3rd. ed., Washington, U.S. Dept. of State, 1959, p. 35; Mao Tse-tung, *Problems of Art and Literature*, New York, International Publishers, 1950, pp. 33-34; "Edinstov teorii i praktiki," *Voprosy filosofii*, 1954, No. 2, p. 5.
25. *The Council in Action*, p. 199.
26. *On Socialist Realism*, New York, Pantheon Books, 1960, p. 42.
27. As one among numerous examples, see S. Kerbyatyev, "Lecture Was Not Given," *Izvestia*, Nov. 27, 1965, as translated in *The Current Digest of the Soviet Press*, Vol. 17, No. 48 (Dec. 22, 1965) where there is presented a very crude (and much too typical) anti-religious position.
28. Compare this with Merton's description of the Carolingian concept of the Church, "Is the World a Problem?," p. 306. On the point of loyalty, see G. Anaskin and N. Babin, *Freedom of the Individual in the U.S.S.R.*, Moscow, Foreign Languages Publishing House, n.d.
29. "What is Freedom," *Praxis* (International Edition), 1965, No. 4, 430.
30. *Ibid.*, Cf. Raya Dunayevskaya, *Marxism and Freedom*, 2d ed., New York, Twayne Publishers, 1964, pp. 62-66. Marx refers to this as "crude communism" and rejects it. *Economic and Philosophical Manuscripts of 1844* in *Karl Marx: Early Writings*, ed. and trans. by T. B. Bottomore, New York, McGraw-Hill, 1964, pp. 153-154.
31. Petrović, "What is Freedom," p. 430. See also his "Man and Freedom," in *Socialist Humanism*, pp. 250-255, and Adam Schaff, "Marxism and the Philosophy of Man," *ibid.*, pp. 129-137 Cf. Marx, *Critique of the Gotha Programme*, *Selected Works*, Moscow, Progress Publishers, 1962, Vol. II, p. 24.
32. *Debatten über die Pressfreiheit*, *Werke*, Berlin, Verlag Dietz, 1957, Band I, pp. 69-70, as translated by Petrović,"What is Freedom," 431. Cf. Y. Frantsev, *Communism and Freedom of the Individual*, Moscow, Foreign Languages Publishing House, n.d., pp. 21 ff.

141

33. *Debatten über die Pressfreiheit,* p. 51.
34. Cf. Marx and Engels, *Manifesto of the Communist Party, Selected Works,* Vol. I, p. 54.
35. *Debatten über die Pressfreiheit,* pp. 76-77, as translated in Petrović, "What is Freedom," 431.
36. Cf. Marx, *On the Jewish Question,* in *Karl Marx: Early Writings,* pp. 13, 26-27; *Economic and Philosophical Manuscripts of 1844, ibid.,* pp. 126-128, 208, and *passim.*
37. "The Marxist-Christian Dialogue . . .," 403.
38. "What is Freedom," 432. Cf. Adam Schaff, *The Philosophy of Man,* New York, Monthly Review Press, 1963, pp. 121 ff.
39. Cf. "Marxism as Propaedeutic,"—An Editorial, *Continuum,* 3 (Autumn, 1965), 338-339. This article is also found in *Political Affairs,* 45, No. 7 (July, 1966).
40. See James 1:22-25; Marx, *Theses on Feuerbach,* XI.
41. Cf. Jose Gonzalez, Ruiz, S.J. *Juventud Obrera* (February, 1965), as cited in Garaudy, "The Marxist-Christian Dialogue . . .," 404-405.
42. "The Marxist-Christian Dialogue . . .," 416.
43. "Marxism as Propaedeutic," 341, 342.
44. *Contribution to the Critique of Hegel's Philosophy of Right,* in *Karl Marx: Early Writings,* pp. 43-44. Cf. Garaudy, "The Marxist-Christian Dialogue . . .," 414.
45. "The Marxist-Christian Dialogue . . .," 414.
46. *Ibid.,* 414-415.
47. "Marxism as Propaedeutic," 340.
48. On this point, see Thomas P. Anderson, "Needed: A Communist Reappraisal," *Continuum,* 3 (Winter, 1966), 506-509.
49. "The Marxist-Christian Dialogue . . .," 416-417.

THE PROPHETIC MISSION OF KARL MARX *

by Howard L. Parsons

According to Marx, what holds man in the grip of the deep divisions within his life are not only the institutions of private property (class behavior) but also the ideas which are the reflexes of actual life. These ideas pertain to the family, the community, law, morality, economics, the state, religion, and the other institutions of the society. Two such ideas are particularly persistent and harmful, for they prevent social change. They are the illusions concerning commodities and the gods. They grow out of the same error of endowing the products of human activity with an independent reality standing over against man and exercising an alien power over him. Commodities are produced by collective production and exchange. They are the crystallizations of social labor, having value only as they originate in human activity and terminate in some use for that activity. The world of religion is "the reflex of the real world,"[1] of man's inner dissociation and loss of power. While it may, like a pearl, appear pure and beautiful, it is in fact the precipitate of man's material irritation and suffering. But like the fetishism of commodities it holds man in thrall. And as capitalists feed on living laborers, so the gods, born of a dichotomized human world, feed on the energies of man. God is made in the image of an economic despot—an all powerful, arbitrary dispenser of good and evil.

The mouthpiece of the gods is the priest. He intervenes between man and his free self-activity in the realm of thought just as the capitalist intervenes between man and his free labor. He extorts surplus value in the form of ideas. Initially, man's alienation brings into being a priestly class with its paraphernalia of fantasy, and this then reacts back on man so that he must sell his soul (his free consciousness) in order to win a certain amount of security in the spiritual realm. The ascription of reality and value to religious

* Reprinted, in part, from THE JOURNAL OF RELIGION, January, 1964, XLIV, No. 1 (with permission).

ideas is a species of idolatry. But idolatry occurs on a collective scale wherever men believe that any form of their alienated social life—the family, the state, the law—is final or conclusively determinative of their existence. Man's idolatry is his enchantment with some illusion, his captivation by some form of his life, which when thus dominant over man thwarts his unfoldment and prevents him from becoming truly human. The fetishism of objects is only one form of this, and it is peculiar to bourgeois political economy, which holds that "the social and economic character of things . . . is a natural character."[2]

The chief form of man's idolatry for Marx is his attachment to the particular economic forms of his society. This attachment occurs through the fact that "the ruling ideas of each age have ever been the ideas of its ruling class."[3] For Marx, idolatry consists in man's production of a good on which he depends, which commands his devotion without his entirely knowing that it does, which man accepts with a certain degree of consciousness (and hence choice) as the center of his life, and which progressively destroys man because it stands in the way of man's free, unalienated labor, his fulfilment, and the creative transformation of the economic and social order. This idolized "good" determining man's destiny rises up in demonic power to cast a spell over him. At the present stage of history this consists in the property relations of man's present society. These relations weave a network of invisible threads about man until he is caught fast by the "sorcerer"[4] he has called into being.

Man's enslavement to machines and the property relations they create is reinforced by his enslavement to the ideas which are thrown up as their camouflage and justification. With all of his energies invested in his place in the social system and the modes of production and exchange underlying it, man then defends his position and system by defending the official ideology of the system. He refuses to see anything inconsistent or wrong in it. His conservatism and the momentum of the system lead him to suppress from consciousness all awareness of those ideas that conflict with the system. Even more, he tends to universalize and absolutize his ideas of good. He equates his own self-interest and class interest with the interest of the community: "What's good for GM is good for the country"—and for the world. Every idea, every social product, becomes subject to the distortion of idolatry. Every relative thing may be held up as absolute, every particular universalized, every created thing turned into a god. The mechanism of this idolatry is the "objectification"[5] of the process of human labor, a dividing off of man and a consequent direction of human energy toward a fragment, the material product itself—the hollow, lifeless image of a god.

Here, probing like a prophet into man's predicament, Marx restates an old truth. But he does it in a new way, showing on a vast historical scale how men and societies, under the lash of economic necessity, fail to see beyond the forms of their own social organization. Marx's formulation of man's flaw can be thought of now as a special version or application of a Darwinian law—that man's brain, mind, meanings, and values are inevitably turned into instruments of survival. Driven by the impulse to live, men stretch, compress, and twist their worlds (perceptions and meanings and values) so that the worlds will seem to sanction, support, and preserve those driving organic interests. Thus economic advantage displaces truth, might becomes right, expediency become principle, and the interests of a class are identified with the interests of mankind. Thus, in short, idols come to be worshiped as gods.

❋   ❋   ❋

Let us now turn to the question of whether Marx was a prophet.

1. *A prophet is a radical realist.*—A prophet is ordinarily dismissed as idealistic. But idealism, in the sense of fantasy, is furthest from his mind. He takes the most direct route to reality he can find. He will not rest with half-truths and half-way houses. He yearns for raw reality, unencumbered by custom, cliché, theory, or artifice. Only simplicity will please him: an ideal that may call for a return to the days when life was purer, more direct, more honest. Fed on the pap of popular superstition and myth, the mass of men prefer mush to the rocky hardtack thrown back at them by the prophet. They fear reality with its rough edges, its disruptions, its anguish-producing ambiguities. So, to salve their own inversion of things, they call the prophet visionary. They stone him with temple stones. But he does not mind. His house belongs to another kingdom and stands on another ground, prepared for men from the foundations of the world.

A prophet can bind himself to his reality because he has been liberated from what immures most men. This is their blind devotion to the existing order and their protective identification with it. The prophet's disenchantment with the establishment makes possible his preternatural perception and criticism. He shows appearance for what it is because he takes the standpoint of reality. To see one's own society for what it is, one must live on a mountain of solitude, eat the locusts of ostracism, and sharpen one's eagle eye. A prophet nurses no illusions about his people. He has suffered himself to be stripped of the last vestige of sentiment toward the status quo. His alienation is total, for he sees the alienation of his society as total. His exile is self-imposed. Yet he still feels identified with the deeper and meliorative dimension of his people. He shares the burden of their failure and their need for redemption.

A major aim of Marx's mission is the exposure of the bourgeois Western world for what it is: an exploitive system of human relations sanctioned by a tissue of religious, philosophical, political, and other illusions. What are these illusions? Capitalism is the paragon of economic systems; freedom and individuality are the sublime virtues of the Western world; law and order represent its advance over barbarism; education is the key to progress; war puts the stamp of nobility upon people; democracy is the best system of government devised; morality is comprised in the Ten Commandments and the Sermon on the Mount; and religion is the expression of man's highest values. The truth? Marx tells it: capitalism is a system for maintaining the profits and power of the few at the expense of the many; "freedom" for this power élite means the freedom to make money, for the masses means the ideas of a kept press, and for the intellectuals means reprisals for non-conformity; the laws and courts are fashioned to favor the privileged and wealthy; education is the captive of minds who themselves are captives of the powers and values that reign; the glory of war is a disguise for "the gospel of greed"; "representative democracy" represents the ruling interests, arrogantly ignoring the needs of the people; the prevailing morality is trafficking in human beings, self-aggrandizement, graft, fraud, bribery, the ruthless exercise of power over persons, acquisitiveness, waste, indifference to the disadvantaged, the young, the old, and the docile; and religion, oblivious to established injustices, is the bourgeois betrayal of man in the name of God.[6] In short, the reality of man's life is a hell on earth, at the foundation, and a fantastic heaven in its ideology. Man is swathed like a living mummy in two layers of unreality

146

masquerading as real—capitalism and the system of ideas hiding its enormities. But the real, still breathing man underneath is yet to be freed and realized: productive, cooperative, realistic, free, responsible.

In this war of the few against the many, Marx allies himself with the many dispossessed of their birthright. His intellectual passion for truth finds its counterpart in the search of the masses of men for their own reality, and merges with that. Truth is one. Intellectual truth must finally find confirmation in and grow out of the trueness of man's being, the authenticity of his productive life. So, consciously alienated from the unrealities of his social and ideological system, Marx identifies himself with the destiny of the masses. He helps to articulate for them their true destiny. He throws a burning light on the decay and restoration, the corruption and promise, of the human situation.

2. *A prophet perceives an ultimate order of goodness.*—This order transcends the existing social order, which has grown alienated from its source in the ultimate order. Whereas the ultimate order is invariant, universal, integral, and health-giving, the social order is seen to be variable, provincial, disintegrating, and sick. The prophet "sees" and grasps this unseen order—and is grasped by it. He is a "seer" of the divine order. (I use the term "divine" here in its original sense of day, shining, high, lifted up, excellent.) He has a special sensitivity to it.[7] He is gripped by its power and feels commanded to speak for it. Personally he may be reluctant or averse toward the task of prophetic testimony (as Moses, Isaiah, Jeremiah). But, like them, he shoulders the responsibility.

A prophet is a radical with a regard to the problem of man's ultimate significance. He is driven by a concern to know this, to communicate it to others, and to commit himself in action to it. He speaks in the optative and imperative moods. But his voice is not mere personal caprice. He speaks for something greater, for what is and ought to be. He proclaims the rightness in reality. Yet it is not he who speaks so much as the rightness which speaks through him: "Thus saith the Lord."[8] While what he speaks for and points to may not be heard or seen by the prophet's generation of men, it will in time, he believes, reveal itself. The prophet's declaration will then be vindicated in the eyes of men: he will be a "true prophet." In advance of his own generation, the prophet has eyes which other men do not. In this sense he foresees the truth

147

and foretells it. He foretells the joy or doom to descend upon men as they respond or do not respond to this reality.

The supreme message of Marx is that there is a ruling power of right in human history which man must comprehend and commit himself to. This is the power of the dialectical process expressing itself progressively in the free, creative, social labor of men. In the struggle to live and the class struggle, men still strive to act in integral, productive ways. Lacerated and fragmented by the division of labor and the exploitation of man by man, the creative ordering power within man and between man and man still stirs and starts forth anew. Torn by destructive competition, man yet in his deepest disposition desires to be constructive and co-operative. The reason is that the order of health lies under all suffering and will in time prevail—in and through man. A study of the primitive communism of prehistory intimates what this ideal and fulfilled life might be. And we now have glimpses of this life in Marx's description of French socialist workers: "Smoking, eating and drinking are no longer simply means of bringing people together. Society, association, entertainment which also has society as its aim, is sufficient for them; the brotherhood of man is no empty phrase but a reality, and the nobility of man shines forth upon us from their toilworn bodies."[9]

In creative social labor, man with increasing effectiveness, confronts, explores, understands, controls, and directs the conditions of his common life, both in history and nature. Here man's freedom is the singular and decisive feature of his situation. Man *does* make himself and his own history—by creative choice, in knowledge and in action—or by default. Marx sides with those "Possibilists" of the eighteenth century, and indeed with all the Utopians of his time dating from Saint-Simon and Fourier, in asserting the improvability of man. Marx's "materialism," far from ruling out man's freedom, makes it meaningful. His materialistic view of history is intended to show precisely that man's past, present, and future display an order and direction that can be understood and acted upon. Because of this, man can discover significant knowledge about himself and take significant action for himself. Marx's announcement that history is orderly and essentially teleonomic was as shocking as it was revelatory. Shocking because many Westerners had lost faith in the Judaic-Christian belief that history has a definite plan. Revelatory because it repudiated both the idealistic notion of disembodied freedom and the mechanistic notion of necessity. Marx puts freedom in the context of necessity, the individual in the context of society, and man in the context of history. (The detailed metaphysics of this dialectical position are not worked out.) Marx's materialism is a way of showing that man's history is an objective process; that the vast mode of his productive apparatus determines man's character and institutions; and that by understanding the movement of contradictions within this apparatus man can freely guide the necessary order of his life to a liberating issue.

3. *A prophet criticizes and judges the existing social order.*— Such judgment is entailed as the brute facts, the vices and follies of his society, are exhibited before the bar of the ultimate order of values. Consequently this judgment is apt to be total and devastating. For the values of every social system tend to insulate themselves against criticism and to pyramid themselves into monuments of self-love and the pretense of eternity. Because, as Emerson said, "the virtues of society are the vices of the saint,"[10] the prophet's mission is "To root up and to pull down, to wreck and to ruin, to build and to plant."[11] When man lies a large lie, the the prophet must speak the even larger truth. And this will surely seem a lie to men committed to the lie by which they live. If men live by exploitation, then the prophet who declares that men are and ought to be co-operative will be "esteemed stricken" by the exploiters. But the exploited may welcome him.

Governed by the rule of right in reality, the prophet must pronounce "Woe to those who call evil good, and good evil."[12] He must dethrone the false gods, destroy the destroyers, negate the negators, and expropriate the expropriators. He lifts up the standard of what is supremely significant for the human situation. He brings down that standard upon concrete situations (where it is all the time), rightly dividing the word of truth, laying the ax to the root of the tree of human iniquity and human presumption. Like a Dante or a Daumier, he paints life as it is: you can recognize the human characters. But he sees below the surface to the corruption in the vitals of man, and below the corruption he sees yet the goodness. He judges man as he appears by what man really is and might be.

The prophet hungers and thirsts after righteousness. He desires to have that righteousness become truth, both in word and deed.

149

He speaks from the perspective of a standard which is independent of any given situation but concretely participates in every situation: he is "one who is inspired by God."[13] And in his effort to save men from destruction and for construction, he would, if he could, incarnate the character of the divine. The prophet hurts to have the hurt of humanity removed. The hurt is there, but it is hidden by the averted eye, the deceitful heart, the weak, compliant will, the sacred myths gargoyling and buttressing the system, the ignorant mind, the drudgery of labor, the inertia of custom, the timidity of the masses, the insolence of rulers. Hence the prophet is the eternal dissenter, preaching up a storm, rousing the outcast, stirring up the dust of discontent toward received opinions, established morals, august dogmas, and institutionalized cruelties. He is the critic of "common-sense" beliefs, the enemy of the truistic and mediocre, the idol-smasher. He is the gadfly in Athens, the scourge of those who are at ease in Zion.

Marx's critique and judgment of his society concentrates upon those points where the human norm of free, creative, social activity is most deformed. But those points define the whole circle of human activity, namely, man's way of life, his economy, his ecology. Man's way of living is his way of making his living, that is, his way of producing his life in his relations to material things and to other persons. Thus Marx's criticism is total, because man's economy embraces the totality of his life. All man's institutions are weighed in the balance and found wanting.

In his specific and often heart-rending accounts of factory life and in his excoriation of the factory system dominated by the "were-wolf hunger for surplus labor,"[14] Marx echoes the cry of Isaiah: "I am a man of unclean lips, and I dwell among a people of unclean lips."[15] Like the Biblical prophets, he dreams of a time when nations shall learn war no more. He joins Amos, Isaiah, and Jeremiah in declaiming against the extortion of surplus value: "Woe to him . . . that makes his neighbor serve him without pay and gives him not his wages."[16] Marx documents the prophets' indictments against man's inhumanity to man in the forms of capitalist accumulation—wage-labor, rent, and interest. In his passion to right wrongs, he speaks like Amos: "Let justice roll down like waters, and righteousness like a perennial stream."[17] When Marx cries out against the "capitalised blood of children,"[18] he amplifies the righteous indignation of the prophets against neglect and oppression of children and orphans, an indignation that rises to a climax in Jesus: "Whoever hinders one of these children who believe in me might better have a great millstone hung around his neck and be sunk in the open sea."[19]

Marx's judgment is the prophetic judgment that man's life is rotten at the foundations. There is no way for man to save himself but to build the house of his culture on new and incorruptible foundations. But an inveterate blindness prevents man from facing the rottenness of his situation. That is ideology—in particular, religious ideology. Thus, like the prophets before him, Marx reserves his heaviest blows for the idols of religion. The reason is that religion has always been the archenemy of the divine in human life because in it men have focused all their evil impulses under the facade and symbolism of some final good. Marx sees in religion the crowning perfidy of the ruling classes, the omnipotent illusion, the deflection of man's energies from his appointed task of destroying property relations and building the brotherhood of man. We are reminded of Jesus' bitter denunciations of the guile and hypocrisy of the Pharisees, who "lock the doors of the Kingdom of Heaven in men's faces."[20]

4. *A prophet is committed to action and demands that others commit themselves to action.*—Concerned with knowing and feeling reality, a prophet is also turned toward *realization*. He not only wants to see and hear the reality of the right. He longs to speak and reveal it, to open the way for it, to relate himself to it, to share it with others, to have it, to be had by it—to become identified with it. A prophet passes from perception and vision to action. He is Zarathustra, carrying his ashes to the mountain of his immolation, receiving his message there, and returning to impart that to men. Popularly he is pictured as an agitator, busy in the dissemination of ideas that move and upend people, disturbing the peace of the social order. He is considered (and is) dangerous, because he works in the underground of that dim, crepuscular, unpoliced region of the human mind, the unconscious. His ideas agitate and excite. They get under the skin and work on people. But the prophet does not cherish ideas and social change for their own sakes. His goal is a great revelation of reality. He must tear away illusions and blast away blockages to the full manifestation of the real. But if the real is real, why not let it be and realize itself? The prophet believes it is not enough to leave

151

the world alone. Things are not what they might be—really. Something has gone wrong—calamitously wrong. Action is called for. Rooted in reality and accountable to that portion of it over which he has responsibility, the prophet feels called to affirm its demands in his own life. He "will not rest from mental fight" or from his revolutionary practice until reality in the fulness of its nature has come to fruition. Therefore his commitment to this is serious, passionate, categorical, continuous, and total.

These marks of prophecy stand out boldly in Marx's career. His early sense of engagement in a universal human cause as shown in his letters to his father; his lifelong identification of his personal destiny with the destiny of the workers of the world; his adoption in his Ph.D. thesis of the creed and image of Prometheus, undergoing punishment for the sake of the liberation of mankind; his running quarrel with the authorities and defenders of the status quo—his criticism of Prussian censorship, the suppression of his *Rheinische Zeitung*, his expulsion from France and Brussels for radical activity, his trial for treason in Prussia (he opposed the king's dissolution of the National Assembly, advocating non-payment of taxes and armed resistance), his expatriation from Prussia; Marx's singleminded devotion to his cause, so that he took upon himself and his family dismal surroundings, poverty, disease, degradation, and death (for three of his children) in a London slum; his unbroken absorption in his work, forsaking food, sleep, and the supernumerary pleasures of the flesh; his sacrifice of money, comfort, position, fame—in a word, personal aggrandizement—for the sake of the lives of millions he would never see; his unwavering faith in the cause of the underdog, a cause at once weak, uninformed, vacillating, and factional; his endurance in writing *Capital* "amidst carbuncles and the daily calls of creditors"; [21] his love of his wife, children, working men, and the children with whom he often talked and played on the heath at Hampstead or in Maitland Park; his uncompromising hatred of injustice, of the brutal use of power by one man over another, of deception and dishonesty, of human loneliness, weakness, and fantasy; the time-consuming years spent on the International Workingmen's Association—all these define Marx's character as prophetic.

It is the quality of his *outward* passion, objectively practiced, that separates a prophet from ordinary men. What makes Marx unique is the zeal of his attack on the alienations and idolatries of men; his undaunted persistence in his belief that the good life is possible; the urgency of his call for social reconstruction; his profound sense of man's indebtedness and responsibility to history, lying behind, below, and in front of man; his apocalyptic sense of destiny; and his expectation of the imminent transformation of history. Marx moves in the tradition of Biblical prophets who mightily strove to purge from the comings and goings of men all that hinders their honest-to-goodness human existence.

5. *A prophet warns men of destruction and promises fulfilment.* —He carries two instruments, a sword that delivers the coup de grâce to men in an already dying civilization, and a scalpel for cutting away the rotting flesh of men who may be healed. Prophetic criticism points downward to damn. It also points upward to the standard in virtue of which all judgments are made; it lures and promises. So the prophet curses and blesses. Discerning what abides, as well as the signs of the times, he anticipates the consequent suffering of the evil doings of men. He foretells the undoing of men. He predicts dire consequences: blood on the moon, brother turned against brother, wars and rumors of wars. But as the decay deepens and the darkness gathers around men, the prophet glimpses the light of the transcendent power, both an ever present power and an ideal. He tells of it and foretells its reappearance to the yet blind, despondent, or fickle eyes of men. He is the voice crying in the wilderness, the lone optimist in the ruins, calling on men to rebuild their world on truer foundations. (Or, as he has found those who have ears to hear, his band may have gathered about him.) He lifts the standard for the future—and for all time. The foundations and the broad plan for man in history are always there. They are implicit in man's nature and situation. What remains is for man to grasp them as the prophet does and respond to their demands. The prophet calls men back to their true selves, disowns their false selves, warns them of the harvest of unhappiness in living by the false self, and promises them the rewards of living by the true self. The prophet urges—he almost physically coerces—men to revere, understand, and obey the source of their lives, their true divinity.

Doom is a main theme in Marx. Capitalistic society is headed downhill in a wild ride that can end only in the breakup of the system. Marx describes with lightning brilliance and thundering power the brutal dehumanizing of workers, "the idiocy of rural life," civilized "barbarism," "the universal war of devastation," "class struggles," the "slaves" of "the industrial army," deepening "pauperism," bourgeois idleness, proletarian misery, the prostitution of women, the exploitation of children.[22] But more: crises worsen and conflicts increase; the proletariat, aroused to full consciousness of its power, will awaken from its slumber, throw off its fetters, and spring into the air "the whole superincumbent strata of official society."[23] Thus downfall is the augury of upheaval. Characteristically prophetic, Marx holds that things must get worse before they get better. But ahead there is for certain, he believes, the good society. Marx is inspired by the prophetic dream —at once a remembrance, a hope, and a spur—a dream of man's honest labor, both physical and mental. This draws man into relations of trusting, just, and fruitful exchange with his fellow man and binds him into productive relations with the things of nature, where he both creates and is created.

The principal tocsin of Marx is tolled out against the economic alienation of man. Religion is accused too, as an ideological ally of exploitation. Like some instrument of slow torture, both squeeze out the essence of man. Religious thinkers (Christians)[24] and philosophers (Feuerbach),[25] alienated themselves, turn some abstract, ideal feature of man into concrete man. Their error is to see man as only a shadow—yet that is what he is in capitalism—and to claim then his shadow self is his real self. His real self is man in "the ensemble of his [social] relations."[26] So Marx warns that to be independent and human, man cannot live by the favor of others.[27] He must reject the attitude of "natural religion," which makes of nature a "completely alien, all-powerful and unassailable force."[28] He must realize that "man makes religion, religion does not make man."[29] At the same time man must reject the economic form of his servility. The growing remnant of the oppressed must free themselves from bondage. Only in this way can they genuinely be promised fulfilment.

All the while, however, individual man remains indefeasibly dependent on his active relations to other men for his fulfilment. Concrete man is social, and social life is practical.[30] True, "the critique of religion ends with the idea that man is a supreme being for man."[31] True, men are "the authors and actors of their history,"[32] Still, the collectively created history of men, and their modes of production and exchange, make individual men. The

154

great moving matrix of man's natural, historical, productive life, preceding (in part) and sustaining all individuals and cultures, makes the human species, cultures, and individuals. Consciousness does not primarily determine this,[33] though it can and will increasingly. So while history is *our* history and we make it, we interpret it, we change it—still it makes us, it changes us. The promise of our fulfilment is tempered by the knowledge of our individual relatedness to other individuals, past history, and nature.

Bent on combating man's crippling subservience to other men and a despotic social system, Marx stresses man's self-mastery. But his awareness of the undergirding power of the cultural process—in both its beneficent and malignant aspects—is no less real and important. It is Marx's perception of this iron law of history, moving on dialectically to its end, that qualifies him as a prophet. On the basis of its objective existence Marx warns of the dissolution of the current social order and promises the progressive ascendancy of man. Continue in your oppression and your flight from reality, declares Marx, and you shall suffer mounting miseries; but move with the directive in history and you shall be saved. Bearded and recusant like that outlaw John the Baptist, the black-maned, leonine Marx cries out to men: "Repent, for the kingdom of man is at hand. You generation of vipers, fly now from the wrath to come. Every tree that brings forth evil fruit will be hewn down and cast into the fires of history. Repent, and do only those deeds meet for repentance. And you who are appointed to be the saving remnant of mankind, unite, rise up, and take possession of the kingdom destined for you from the creation of the world."

* * *

We come now to an estimate of Marx as a prophet. Immediately some will say that Marx was not even religious.

There is first the atheism of matter. Can a man be a materialist and be religious? In one sense of the word "materialism," a man cannot be materialistic and be anything else but matter, and dead matter at that. Marx's materialism means that man makes his own history. It means that the process of producing his living (food, shelter, clothing) precedes, accompanies, and determines all else that he does. Man must live before and as he lives well. But the process of producing is a *human* process. It is free, linguistic, social, intelligent, purposive, creative. From the moment of the most primitive human act of tool-using, human productivity is unique. In it the self, others, and nature in its import for man are created and transformed. Such an act carries pregnant in it all the distinguishing features of humankind—ranging from food-producing to art and mathematics. "Surviving" is the first and continuing stage in the expression of such productivity. This is an enterprise carried on in, and understandable in the framework of, a spatiotemporal nature. There is nothing strange or contradictory about the "early" and "later" Marx or about Marx's "materialism" and "humanism." Marx's humanism is a creative or dialectical materialism (or "organic mechanism," in Whitehead's language), and the economics of the later Marx simply analyzes the economic conditions obstructing man's humanistic development.

Classical materialism and traditional religion have been mortal enemies. Establishing religion on the basis of materialism, says Engels, is like regarding modern chemistry as true alchemy.[34] But Marx's neomaterialism or naturalism places it in a different case. With classical materialism, one had either to deny religion altogether or to establish its source beyond the natural world. But with naturalism a third alternative arises: a naturalistic religion, an effort by man to realize significance within the immanent bounds of nature and history. Marx's prophetic mission lies here.[35]

There is second the matter of atheism. (Why must people repeatedly confuse the discussion of religion with this question?) While Marx rejects religion as the illusory hope of the hopeless masses, he also refuses, like Camus, to take atheism seriously. It misses the point. What is needed is a positive and constructive view of man growing out of a "positive human self-consciousness" which as practiced begins to reconstruct the conditions of man's social life. Marx demands "the *positive* supersession of all alienation, and the return of man from religion, the family, the state, etc. to his *human*, i.e., *social* life."[36] Prima facie Marx cannot be written off as an atheist any more justifiably than can a prophet who calls down damnation on the God of the temple. We must find out first what gods he opposes. We must find out second what Marx regards as truly worthy of man's commitment in order to measure him against alternative positions.

Marx opposes all religions, all gods. Why? They are illusory and antihuman. He fights that religion which alienates and divides man, making him to suffer once more for his distress. But here he

makes common cause with a long line of "religious" figures themselves: certain Biblical master spirits, Taoists, Buddhists, Zen
masters, Stoics, Jesus, the communal heretics of Christian history,
the great mystics like Eckhart, the Renaissance humanists, the
religious men of the Enlightenment, progressive Protestants,
Catholics, Jews, Muslims. Can this criticism of religion, then, be
called "religion" or "religious"? For Marx, no. Indeed, in the ideal
Marxian society, all forms of alienation—ideology, religion, the
family, the state—must be and will be superseded.[37] They will be
replaced by the descriptions of the special sciences and "the
science of thought and its laws—formal logic and dialectics."[38] By
"ideology" Marx and Engels mean an idealistic reflex of a materialistic and alienated base—unconscious, "independent" ideas reflecting society's antagonisms and using imagination to fill in the unknown.[39] As men and societies become healthy, their ideas will
reflect that health, and, sloughing off ideologies, they will express
truth.

But such an interpretation assumes a perfect state of non-
alienation in which man infallibly possesses the truth and requires
no criticism. It assumes the removal of changes, relativities, antagonisms — inescapable in dialectical materialism. It assumes the
formulation of an all-sufficient set of principles for interpreting the
world, performing the functions of understanding and controlling
the facts of experience, functions traditionally served by ideologies.
To say that only one set of organizing principles, dialectics—even
if "non-ideological"—will survive in the ideal society is not a descriptive truth but a prediction and prescription. But we cannot
know which organizing principles will prevail among sound men
until sound men in a sound society prevail. The materialistic
principle that practice precedes ideas requires that this be so.
Moreover, the principle of relativity entails that every idea is
limited and thus subject to criticism. Hence the critical or prophetic function—wherein men appraise values and claims to ultimate values—appears inescapable. Whether this is called "religious" is a terminological question. But hitherto prophets (at
the safe distance of the centuries, to be sure) have been called
"religious."

Marx asks, "What transformation will the state undergo in
communist society? In other words, what social functions will
remain in existence that are analogous to present functions of the

state?"[40] Similarly, it could be asked, "What transformation will religion undergo in the good society? What social functions will remain in existence that are analogous to present functions of religion? What are the progressive, lastingly human, and ultimately important values of religion? What will man—ought man—trust as the source of his significance?" These are questions that the prophets asked—and tried to answer. And in this they themselves transformed the character of religion, from a priestly to a critical and progressive function. If the forms with which "religion" is identified are so changed that they are not recognizable—just as the wars and infanticides of the Old Testament are hardly recognizable as religion—men committed to such change cannot be disturbed about the loss of identifiable form. What matters is not the idolatrous preservation of past form but creative transformation.

What *is* of final significance for man?

For Marx, the answer is clear: man must and will trust a creative process operating in and between men and between men and the rest of nature. This directive power is an object of discernment and devotion in religious traditions, particularly the Judaic-Christian: man must see a great light, he must be born again, he must be transformed, he cannot yet know what he shall be.[41] The renewal of man through his effective identification with the divine movement in human history means that he is empowered to be more fully human: more sensitive, expressive, responsive, empathic, co-operative; more integral, self-aware, self-reliant, self-directing, resourceful, effective; more realistic, imaginative, appreciative; more trustful, transcendently absorbed, concerned, caring, courageous, committed. Marx is ambiguous as to just how this transformation of man occurs. At times (when Marx has in mind the idealists) it seems to be solely a deliberate, conscious achievement of man. At other times(when Marx has in mind the movement of history) it is a change which, together with man's developing insights, is worked in man and culture through the directive events of the historical process.

Like his favorite Greek writer, Aeschylus, Marx takes as his purpose the purging of the prevailing thought forms of fantasy and fatuous beliefs. Aeschylus adumbrates a God above gods, a "Father of ancient days" who stands behind the many subjective gods of men's minds. In the magnificent defiance of Prometheus, Aeschylus protests against the capricious injustice of Zeus and affirms the freedom and dignity of man. He asserts that children do not suffer for their fathers' sins; that the chain of sin may be broken by confession and repentance; and that suffering is not an arbitrary decree of the gods but is the natural price of deepened wisdom. Here is a prophetic cleansing of the temple of superstition in the great tradition. Marx is the modern Aeschylus—a prophet of wrath, driving the predatory gods and money-changers from the temple. To drive out is to let in—or to protect what is there and has been usurped and corrupted by alien elements. What was Marx protecting in the human situation? The developing brotherhood of man.[42] The creative power in and through and beneath the conscious, social labors of men; the rights of man to share freely, equally, and fraternally in that creativity; the responsibility of man to that power.

What was Marx driving out? The unrighteous ruling few, who wronged the many by robbing them of the products of their collective labor, and by harnessing them like slaves in Egypt to alien gods: property relations, modes of distribution and exchange, social relations and institutions. Marx's mission was to free the human species—and hence each and every man—of the burden of his own self-deception and self-slavery, evident in both man's way of life (capitalism) and his way of thought (religion). For class structure is the alienation and incapacitation of each individual man writ large, and the "ruling few" represent outwardly the inward rule of each man by an alien master.

The question of whether Marx is a true prophet is a question of whether Marx had a true theology, that is, a true view of the divine. Like the biblical prophets, Marx carried on a war to the death with established religion. Marx's critique of religious and other forms of alienation is not primarily impelled by metaphysical or even scientific purposes. It is humanistic and prophetic—in the sense of exposing the depths of good and evil in those day-by-day issues where men struggle, suffer, despair, hope, live, and die. The whole point of Marx's extracting the "rational kernel" from the "mystical shell" of Hegel's thought[43] is not intellectual. It is to find a key for unlocking doors into man's liberation.

Critics who quote Marx to prove his atheism and hence his opposition to all that is human, holding that Marx "despises all the gods," forget to quote the full statement, which gives the *reason:*

159

"In one word, all gods are my enemies. They had good from me. They return me evil."[44] Prophets have ever been the adversaries of evil gods. "The progress of religion is defined by the denunciation of gods."[45] The only gods the prophets consent to respect must be congruous with man's highest good. Thus, prophet-wise, the proper study of the gods must begin and end with man. In Marx's motto, *nihil humani a me alienum puto*.[46] The question is not whether man will have unquestioning faith in whatever gods there be—God knows modern man has filled the world with as many gods as did ancient man! The question is whether man will have the courage and faith to resist the gods that wrong his better self, clinging to what he knows in his heart to be right. In doing so, man, following his prophetic intuition, may discover a value beyond all gods.

The course of prophecy in history itself signifies the divine in human life. As the gods are cursed and the judgments of time topple and erode the idols, the true good and right of man stands more clearly revealed, like the statue dimly emerging from the stone. Prophecy is cumulative; it grows. Man's insight into the nature of the real and the right, his power to deal with reality and respond to it, his capacity for knowing and achieving value are all progressively sensitized and widened. Marx moves in this direction; this progression in the human spirit is what moves him, this yearning for the things of greatest import for man. Marx finally revered the concrete historical process that lifts man to the heights of his thrust toward realized significance. His whole life was dedicated to a prophetic mission: first, to the task of tearing down the false gods, the idols he considered to constrain man's progress; second, to the burden of building the conditions of man's fulfilment.

NOTES

C, I—CAPITAL (Vol. I), etc.; EPM-*Economic and Philosophical Manuscripts*, in E. Fromm, MARX'S CONCEPT OF MAN (Ungar, 1961); GI-GERMAN IDEOLOGY (1935); CM-COMMUNIST MANIFESTO (1948 edit.); LF-Engels, LUDWIG FEUERBACH AND THE END OF CLASSICAL GERMAN PHILOSOPHY (1950 edit.); TF-Marx, THESES ON FEUERBACH

1. *C, I,* 79.
2. *C,* III, 257.
3. *CM,* p. 29; *GI,* p. 39.

4. *CM,* p. 14.
5. *EPM,* pp. 95 ff.
6. For example, see Conference on Economic Progress, *Poverty and Deprivation in the United States. The Plight of Two-fifths of a Nation* (Washington, D.C., 1962); Fred J. Cook, "The Corrupt Society. A Journalist's Guide to the Profit Ethic," *The Nation,* CXCVI, No. 22 (June 1-8, 1963), 454-97; and Gibson Winter, *The Suburban Captivity of the Churches* (New York: Macmillan Co., 1962).
7. J. M. Powis Smith, *The Prophets and Their Times* (Chicago: University of Chicago Press, 1925), p. 4.
8. Cf. "It is no longer I that live, but Christ that liveth in me" (Gal. 2:20). All citations from the Bible are in An American Translation.
9. *EPM,* p. 150.
10. "The Oversoul."
11. Jer. 1:10.
12. Isa. 5:20.
13. "Prophet," in Madeleine S. Miller and J. Lane Miller, *Harper's Bible Dictionary* (New York: Harper & Bros., 1961), p. 582.
14. *C.* I, 265.
15. Isa. 6:50.
16. Jer. 22:13.
17. Amos 5:24.
18. *C,* I, 756.
19. Matt. 18:6.
20. Matt. 23:14.
21. Marx-Engels, *Selected Correspondence* (Moscow, n.d.), p. 232.
22. *CM, passim.*
23. *Ibid.,* p. 20.
24. *C,* I, 79.
25. *TF,* VI.
26. *EPM,* p. 138.
27. *GI* pp. 19-20.
28. *Towards the Critique of Hegel's Philosophy of Right,* in L. Feuer, ed., *Marx-Engels: Basic Writings on Politics and Philosophy* (Garden City, 1959), p. 262.
29. *TF,* VI, VII.
30. Marx's "Introduction to the Critique of Hegel's Philosophy of Law. Critique of Religion," in Fromm,*op. cit.,* p. 13.
31. Quoted in Fromm, *op. cit.,* p. 13.
32. Karl Marx, *A Contribution to the Critique of Political Economy,* translated from the second German edition by N. I. Stone (Chicago: Charles H. Kerr & Co., 1904), pp. 11-12; Hereafter *CCPE.*
33. *LF,* p. 49.
34. *EPM,* p. 140.
35. *Ibid.,* p. 128.
36. *Ibid.; GI,* p. 14; *CCPE,* p. 12; *LF,* pp. 81 ff.
37. Friedrich Engels. *Socialism: Utopian and Scientific* (New York; International Publishers Co. 1935), p. 51.
38. *LF,* p. 83.
39. *Ibid.,* p. 69.
40. Karl Marx, *Critique of the Gotha Programme* (Moscow: Foreign Languages Publishing House, 1954), p. 41.
41. Isa. 9:2; John 3:7; Rom. 12:2; I John 3:2.

42. *EPM*, p. 150.
43. *C*, I. 20.
44. Aeschylus, *Prometheus Bound*, trans. Edith Hamilton in *Three Greek Plays* (New York: W. W. Norton & Co., 1937). David Grene renders the lines (975-77) in this way: "In a single word, I am the enemy of all the Gods that gave me ill for good" (see *The Complete Greek Tragedies*, Vol. I: *Aeschylus*, ed. by David Grene and Richmond Lattimore (Chicago: University of Chicago Press, 1959).
45. A. N. Whitehead, *Adventures of Ideas* (New York: Macmillan Co., 1933), p. 12.
46. "Confession," in Fromm, *op. cit.*, p. 257.

THE POLITICS OF HOPE

by Martin J. Corbin

"For the lover of truth discussion is always possible"
—Pope Paul VI

A Communist writer whom I respect, Roger Garaudy, has accurately defined the essentially novel character of the positions taken by the late Pope John XXIII, in his magnificent encyclical, *Pacem in Terris* (1963), especially in so far as they have a bearing on the kind of dialogue being conducted in these pages. In his analysis of the encyclical, published shortly after its appearance,[1] Garaudy called attention to three major advances in papal thinking:

(1) The spirit of hope that pervades *Pacem in Terris* and Pope John's manifest confidence in the powers of human beings will do much to foster increased collaboration between believers and non-believers, on the basis of the "natural morality" they have in common.

(2) Pope John refused to rest content with simple moral exhortations against war. By addressing himself to the concrete problems that the abolition of war will entail, he prepared the way for common action directed to specific goals.

(3) In the Church's dealings with the Communist world, the spirit of dialogue is beginning to replace the spirit of anathema. Catholics must be prepared to engage in practical collaboration with Communists on specific issues, without presupposing any ideological compromise on either side.

Pope John's central preoccupation was with the avoidance of war; inevitably so, since his all too brief pontificate was passed in an era in which the great powers continue to indulge in the crudest kind of power politics, only now equipped with arsenals of scores of thousands of hydrogen bombs, a single one of which possesses more explosive force than the sum-total of all the explosions produced in history. It is hardly an accident that the most

163

exhaustive papal treatment of the problem of modern warfare contains no reference to the traditional distinctions between just and unjust war, so painstakingly elucidated over the centuries by Catholic moralists. Pope John was clearly convinced that in the Age of Overkill these elaborate constructs have little or no relevance, hence his insistence that it is "hardly possible to imagine that in the atomic era war could be used as an instrument of justice".[2] The other great spiritual leader of the past decade, Dr. Martin Luther King, Jr. was echoing the thought of Pope John when he warned us recently that the choice confronting mankind is no longer that between violence and non-violence, it is between non-violence and non-existence. Marxists might likewise ponder the implications of Khrushchev's wry observation that the Bomb is the only reality in contemporary society that does not possess a class character.

In his perceptive commentary on *Pacem in Terris*,[3] an informed American theologian, Father Peter J. Riga, has remarked the significance of the choice of the plural form of the noun *terra* in its title. This was the first encyclical in history to be issued, not as a directive to the body of the faithful, but as an open letter to the whole world. If there is one theme plainly reiterated it is Pope John's serene conviction that what men have in common is infinitely more important than what divides them. He proposed a dialectic of human rights and reciprocal duties, which can be translated into concrete political and social changes, by men living under diverse political regimes. The unprecedently warm response evoked in all quarters, East and West, by the promulgation of Pope John's letter is proof that the world is ready to listen to a Church that will use unambiguous language in speaking of the desperate problems that afflict humanity: the stockpiling of weapons that imperil man's continued existence as a species, the hunger and squalor that are the daily lot of two-thirds of the world's inhabitants, the brutal neo-colonialism that is eroding the painfully won independence of the young nations of Africa and Asia. Pope John's approach to these international evils was anything but parochial.

In a recent magazine piece on the opposition of American intellectuals to the Vietnam war, Professor Eric Bentley observed: "Whether or not one can envisage the world acting on the lines laid down in *Pacem in Terris*, one can surely believe that the spirit the encyclical embodies might influence the world. If one cannot believe this, one's view of politics is wholly cynical. Not to give up politics in that way is to bear witness to a degree of faith in human possibility."[4] It may be added that Pope John's faith in human possibility was grounded in an optimistic and humane theology, sensitive to the implications of the primary Christian doctrine of the Incarnation and fully conscious of man's role as co-creator in a redeemed universe. By unmistakably affirming the legitimate autonomy of the temporal order, Pope John made certain that the Christian can no longer evade the trials and perplexities of social commitment by withdrawing to the security of a real or metaphorical "cell". The artificial separation of the spiritual and temporal spheres, which has bedeviled Catholic thought and practice for centuries, is beginning to crumble. It might be more accurate to say that Catholics are increasingly coming to understand that such matters as the nature of the social systems that men construct, the ordering of their economic affairs, and the kind of property relations that exist between them, *are* matters of vital spiritual concern. As Berdyaev has reminded us, while bread for myself may be a "material" question, bread for my neighbor is a spiritual question.

Throughout the entire encyclical, a framework of peaceful co-existence is assumed. In past history, wars have never settled the right or wrong of anything; today, anyone who imagines that he can impose his ideology on the world through force is conniving at global suicide. Moreover, the readiness to renounce violent forms of struggle is necessary, but it is not enough. If Christians and Marxists are to compete, even on the ideological plane, they must eschew the kind of psychological annihilation that would implicitly deny the effective humanity of hundreds of millions of people on one side or the other. If there is to be an ultimate triumph, it will go to the side that exhibits the deeper understanding of the nature and real drives of man; whatever competition is engaged in must take the form of ministering to man's authentic needs.

Christians have particular reason, anyway, to be wary of ideological crusades; not only did the historical opposition between Catholics and Protestants, for example, result in an incalculable number of senseless deaths; it also drastically retarded that process of mutual enrichment of thought which is only now beginning to take place. That is why Pope John's "opening to the Left" is so important and so welcome to those of us within the Catholic Church who have long been convinced of the necessity for responsible communication between Catholics and Marxists. In a celebrated passage of *Pacem in Terris*[5] Pope John gave his full approbation to this view. First, he said, we must always distinguish between error and the person who errs. But to have stopped at that point would have been to remain at the level of truism. He went on to remind us that day-to-day contacts between believers and those without the faith can be fruitful occasions for the discovery of truth. The words that immediately follow represent a remarkable innovation in papal theory:

> It must be borne in mind, furthermore, that neither can false philosophical teachings regarding the nature, origin, and destiny of the universe and of man be identified with historical movements that have economic, social, cultural, or political ends, not even when these movements have originated from those teachings and have drawn and still draw inspiration therefrom. For these teachings, once they are drawn up and defined, remain always the same, while the movements, working on historical situations in constant evolution, cannot but be influenced by these latter and cannot avoid, therefore, being subject to changes, even of a profound nature. Besides, who can deny that those movements, insofar as they conform to the dictates of right reason and are interpreters of the lawful aspirations of the human person, contain elements that are positive and deserving of approval?[6]

His conclusion is that forms of joint action for practical goals that were formerly deemed "inopportune or unproductive" may now or in the future be opportune or useful. Three conditions are laid down to guide the Catholic in his prudential judgment as to when to undertake such common activity: it must be in accord with the principles of the natural law, with the social teaching of the Church, and with the directives of ecclesiastical authority. Although this passage contains no explicit reference to Marxism, there is little doubt in the minds of commentators as to which contemporary ideology Pope John had chiefly in mind. (I am aware that its adherents would not describe Marxism as an ideology, since the term has a rather specialized and pejorative connotation in the writings of Marx and Engels. Throughout this article I use the word in its commoner and more generalized sense, to designate movements of thought that have, for good or ill, significantly shaped the course of history.)

166

When it comes to undertaking this kind of dialogue, nothing would be more out of place than a proselytizing approach to one's interlocutor. The orthodox Christian should bear in mind Cardinal Newman's warning that no one has ever been argued into the faith and refrain from acting as if he had a mandate to convert his opponent to Christianity, or even to some form of theism. The Marxist could profitably study the instructive posthumously published "testament" of Palmiro Togliatti, secretary-general of the Italian Communist Party, in which he frankly acknowledged that traditional Left-wing anti-religious propaganda has in practice proved worthless and even pernicious, for it has only succeeded in causing the workers to suspect hypocrisy behind the apparent openness of the "outstretched hand" policy. (There is perhaps a similar lesson for Catholics in the fact that the Communist vote in Italy, a largely Catholic country, has gradually increased since the promulgation of the Holy Office interdict on collaboration with Communists in 1949). The only indispensable preconditions for authentic dialogue are a degree of respect for the sincerity and integrity of the other party and a readiness to grant at least the possibility that in his search for truth he may have hit upon valid insights that could quicken our own understanding.

I hope I may be pardoned at this point for referring the reader to a recent issue of the *Catholic Worker*,[7] which included an exchange of ideas that suggests the possibilities of this kind of discourse. In this case the exchange consisted of articles on the subject of atheism by two young Czechoslovakian intellectuals, one a Marxist, the other a Catholic, along with a commentary by James Douglass, a brilliant American lay theologian. The dialogue should be read as a whole for its intrinsic interest; what is noteworthy in the present context is that, in the course of debate, as Mr. Douglass points out, each writer arrived "at an increasing respect for the other's hierarchy of values and a consequent effort in the fulness of truth to reach out and appropriate elements of it to enrich his own commitment."

What strikes the reader of both communications is the passionate concern for social justice manifested by each writer and the candor and intelligence with which they treat of the subject that represents the most potentially divisive issue between Marxists and Christians. The Marxist contributor, for example, has this to say about official attempts to interfere with religious belief: "When

167

there should have been serious efforts made to understand the religious believer as a human being, in his inner struggles, the unforgivable mistake was made of applying gross administrative interference." And the Catholic writer in turn acknowledges: "Christians have betrayed their mission to the world. They have allowed their faith to be used to support the powerful against the weak, to become a weapon against the small, contributing to their bondage. We cannot erase these facts from the history of Christianity. We can only learn from them . . . in a spirit of deep humility before our Father and his Son, Jesus Christ."

If the exigencies of peaceful co-existence render meaningful dialogue a moral imperative at this juncture in history, we are entitled to expect that even more positive benefits will accrue from such colloquies, in the way of purification of concepts and liberation from outmoded and rigidified categories of thought. Catholic thinkers in the past have notably added to the corpus of their knowledge by assimilating the achievements of a host of original thinkers, from Aristotle to Freud, who arrived at their insights within a non-Christian framework. Why then should we have any hesitation in exploring the great nineteenth-century revolutionary tradition, of which Marx and Engels were among the most influential exponents? Unless, of course, we have made the fatal error of identifying Christianity with the bourgeois spirit and with the capitalist method of amassing and distributing wealth. One need not subscribe to the dogmas of historical materialism in order to appreciate the incisive quality of Marx's critique of capitalism and his masterful demonstration of the way in which economic realities so often underlie political and social transformations, his description and analysis of the way economic systems actually operate. I do not think it fanciful to suggest that many Marxian insights will one day be incorporated, with whatever necessary modifications and adaptations, into that presently amorphous congeries of propositions known as the "social teaching of the Church."

Could a closer knowledge of the Christian's traditions and some acquaintance with his sources of inspiration provide the Marxist with any valuable increments of knowledge? In the nature of the case, this is perhaps not for me to say; I would prefer to cite the testimony of Garaudy, whom I mentioned at the beginning of this article. He is a trained philospher and a high official of the French

168

Communist Party. In a sensitive commemorative tribute to the Jesuit paleontologist and mystic, Teilhard de Chardin, published on the tenth anniversary of his death,[8] M. Garaudy wrote, in part:

> Thanks to Father Teilhard, who speaks the language of our times, a Marxist can more easily appreciate the Christian heritage: the opening to the infinite in thought and action that characterized the birth of Christianity after the sealed-off humanism of the Greeks and Romans; the Christian idea of love, according to which each human person only comes to know himself and fulfill himself by and through others, and which provides such a lofty image of man and of the meaning of life that Marxism would be impoverished if Saint Augustine, Saint John of the Cross or Father Teilhard were to become strangers to it.
>
> The Marxist conception of religion cannot be reduced to the bare formula: "Religion is the opium of the people", as if religion, everywhere and at all times, acted as a brake to labor, to research and to struggle. Undoubtedly this formula has a very wide field of historical application, especially from the eighteenth century up to our own days, when religion has usually been identified with scientific obscurantism and social reaction. But to take only examples near at hand, religion has sometimes not been an opium but a ferment in movements for national liberation of oppressed peoples who have often waged their struggles in the name of God before waging it in the name of the fatherland. One of the achievements of Father Teilhard, and not his least, was to have demonstrated that it was possible for Christianity once again to play a progressive role.

That the attitude of mind displayed in this passage does not reflect a personal whim or aberration is proved by the fact that one of Father Teilhard's books, with a preface by M. Garaudy, has recently been translated into Russian and published in the Soviet Union. This is undoubtedly the first work by a Catholic theologian to be published in the U.S.S.R. since the Revolution.

The Catholic seeking points of concordance with Marxism will sooner or later encounter two apparently formidable obstacles, in that: (1) the Catholic Church has invariably affirmed the right of private property and (2) Popes have been unanimous in their condemnation of socialism.

Let us take the question of private property first. Even the most traditional Catholic teaching on the matter is a little more nuanced than the customary popular presentation of it would suggest. Saint Thomas, for example, from whom the papal teaching largely derives, held that while private *ownership* of wealth is legitimate, its *use* must be subordinated to the common good of society. In the article of the *Summa* in which he treats of private property,[9] he admits that it is a human institution, determined by human convention, and that it is an acquired, rather than a natural right. "Ownership of goods," he says, "is not contrary to the natural law, but is superadded to the natural law by the determination of human reason." It is interesting to observe that it is by a similar appeal to the *"jus gentium"* rather than to the natural law that Saint Thomas managed to justify the institution of human slavery. It is not surprising, then, that there are contemporary Catholic churchmen who are convinced that the traditional teaching of private property could bear re-examination and who tend to agree with the socialist contention that the right to individual appropriation should be restricted to articles of personal consumption and those that constitute an extension of personality, and need not apply to those instruments of production that make possible the exploitation of labor.

We can be certain that private ownership of property is not commanded by the natural law, since a rather strict communism, at least in regard to the distribution of goods, was practiced by the very earliest Christian communities. (Cf. the Acts of the Apostles.) Catholic defenders of the *status quo* will reply that such a communism is fitting for monastic orders but that it is impracticable and undesirable for the laity. They should be made aware that their contention was formally condemned as long ago as 1417, at the Council of Constance. Those who readily invoke Saint Thomas' defense of property usually manage to overlook his animus against the taking of interest and his reprobation of the uninhibited pursuit of wealth, which was severe enough to compel the late R. H. Tawney to his conclusion that: "The true descendant of the doctrine of Aquinas is the labor theory of value. The last of the Schoolmen was Karl Marx."[10]

The central concern of the Popes has not been to sanctify the institution of private property as such but to safeguard the human person from being swallowed up in the collective. John XXIII, in *Mater et Magistra,* made a point of reiterating the teaching of Pius XI that the State or other public agencies can legitimately appropriate public goods that "carry with them an opportunity too great to be left to private individuals without injury to the community at large".[11] Many industries that are either monopolistic

170

by nature or have become so with the development of capitalism could be included in that category. The important point is that the Popes have recognized the legitimacy of both public and private property; consequently, questions as to the desirable extent of each and the proper balance between them become empirical ones, subject to the prudential judgment of men. The governing criterion for such decisions will be the principle of subsidiarity, according to which properly individual initiative should not be subsumed unnecessarily by large social organisms. The Popes are sensitive (and in my opinion, correctly so) to the dangers inherent in Statism and excessive centralization. A social order approximating the Christian ideal would be markedly pluralistic and federalistic. Such a society might well be based largely on genuine workers' cooperatives, in which the workers themselves would own the means of production and participate directly in the decision-making process at every level. This could be combined with a certain amount of public control (not necessarily in the form of nationalization) of unwieldy industries and a measure of private property (small business and individual artisans). Whether such a society could properly be called socialistic can, of course, be debated. To my mind, the essence of authentic socialism is embodied in the goals outlined by the Catholic thinker Emmanuel Mounier, who founded the Personalist movement in France:

> The abolition of the proletarian condition; the supersession of the anarchic economy of profit by an economy directed to the fulfillment of the totality of personal needs; the socialization, without state monopoly, of those sectors of industry which otherwise foster economic alienation; the development of co-operative life; the rehabilitation of labor; the promotion, in rejection of all paternalist compromises, of the worker to full personality; the priority of labor over capital; the abolition of classes founded upon the division of labor and wealth; the priority of personal responsibility over the anonymous organization.[12]

Furthermore, the Popes have been unanimous in advocating the widest possible distribution of property rights, and such a demand constitutes a radical criticism of the present system. As J. M. Cameron and others have pointed out, capitalism is unjust in its essence, not only because it has brought about vast disparities of ownership and income, but because it has effectually abolished property rights for the mass of individuals. Most Catholic thinkers are aware of this contradiction; unfortunately, they have tended to argue that the remedy lies in distributing property more widely within the present system. Such an amelioration is theoretically possible, but if it were really carried out, it would put an end to capitalism. For, as Marx pointed out, if the capitalist economy is to operate, the worker must be free in a double sense; he must be able, unlike the slave, to sell his own labor power on the market, and he must have nothing to sell *except* his labor power. If the worker acquired enough property to free him from this necessity, he could become a capitalist himself. Marx demonstrated that such a relationship is not somehow in the nature of things but a result of prior historical development.

It may be objected that the papal social encyclicals have not questioned the legitimacy of the wage contract and have concentrated on showing how the system can be rendered "just". But this is to misinterpret the primary function of the encyclicals, which is to pronounce on the moral issues involved in the existing social system. In past ages, the Church did not formally condemn human slavery or feudalism as institutions. But the eventual recognition that the continued existence of these institutions was grossly at variance with the implications of the Christian concept of the dignity of the person hastened their dissolution. Should men freely decide that an alternative economic arrangement is to be preferred to the wage system, the Church will then have to examine the new problems that arise. To argue otherwise is to assume that the Church's existence is bound up with a particular economic or social regime, which is an untenable position for a Catholic. By the same token, the Catholic who is committed to radical social change cannot maintain that the type of society he advocates is the *only* one compatible with Christianity.

What meaningful conclusions can we draw, then, from the papal condemnations of socialism? In the first place, we must carefully discriminate between statements that express "transcendental" assertions and those that are merely "historico-prudential" assertions. This is what Father Hervé Chaigne, the Franciscan writer, has done in his illuminating survey of the key papal statements on the subject of socialism.[13] Father Chaigne's examination of these texts leads him to three major conclusions: 1) There has been a considerable shift, amounting to an almost complete reversal of attitudes, in a little over a hundred years. In

172

1849, Pius IX reacted to the burgeoning socialist movement with total and uncomprehending hostility; the encyclicals of John XXIII, with their guarded approval of "socialization," tacitly vindicate many of the socialist claims. 2) The socialist movement has not been purely and simply condemned; rather, it is on trial and must be continually interrogated in the light of Christian moral principles. In so far as socialism means total materialism, systematic violence and the reduction of man to *homo oeconomicus,* it must be rejected; to the extent that it represents an attempt to liberate man from the alienations and built-in injustices of capitalistic society and to construct a truly human commonwealth, it is positive, but not without its peculiar dangers. 3) What we know as the "social teaching of the Church" has been hammered out in response to the socialist challenge. Unfortunately, the counter-proposals have usually been retarded and inadequate. The Church was at first anxious to reform capitalism from within; when this reformism proved a failure, Pius XI tentatively proposed to replace it with a kind of corporatism that had dangerous affinities with fascism. With Pope John, the emphasis is on increased participation by the workers in all phases of social and economic life and greater popular control of socio-economic structures.

Nor is this trend likely to be curtailed or reversed during the pontificate of Pope Paul VI, who is determined to achieve a "vital synthesis of the faith and the technological outlook" and who has deplored the "rupture of the symbiotic union" between what he describes as the two supreme expressions of human activity: the faith and labor. A sampling of his recent allocutions provides evidence that Pope Paul has made a greater effort than any of his predecessors to come to grips with the specifically Marxian criticisms of religion and the social order. Speaking to a group of Italian workers, for example, he asked the following questions:

> Is it possible, really possible, for labor in its modern form to discover in the Christian view of life new and authentic inspiration that can illuminate its human and social depths? Is it possible for human labor —which tends to dominate natural objects and energies in order to make them yield immense, marvelous and extraordinary services—to evoke just as fully and marvelously the laws and conceptions that the divine labor has infused them with? Is it possible for the agent of this human labor—whether he be laborer, technician, or business leader— to thus engage in a wonderful dialogue with God the creator from

which will issue, not that alienation of the worker which religion is accused of promoting, but his exaltation and redemption, his supreme dignity, his superior worth, his profound consolation and infallible hope? Is it possible to give back to the worker the possibility of devoutly loving what he is doing and what he is? Is it possible to render him capable once more of the Christian sentiments of peace, good will, and love?[14]

It appears that the Pope is attempting an almost point-by-point refutation of Marx's celebrated characterization: "Religion is the general theory of that (reversed) world, its logic in a popular form, its spiritualistic *point d'honneur*, its enthusiasm, its moral sanction, its solemn completion, its universal ground for consolation and justification."[15]

Even though Marx regarded religious alienation as a secondary and derivative phenomenon, he insisted that "the criticism of religion is the condition of all criticism." This criticism is necessary, partly for pedagogical reasons, since religious alienation is the type of all alienation, but also because in practice religion preaches resignation to the exploited and provides justifications for the exploiter. In the religious sphere, the internal division of man, reflecting the split between his individual and social nature, is reconciled in an abstract and illusory way; actually, it will only be healed with the abolition of private property and the introduction of communism. The root problem, then, is economic alienation.

In the course of another allocution, delivered to a general, audience on May Day, 1965, the Pope asked: "Did no one foresee that the new mode of labor would arouse in the worker the consciousness of his alienation, that is, the awareness that he is no longer working for himself, but for others, with instruments that no longer belong to him but to others, no longer alone but in conjunction with others?" The question is posed, of course, in a rhetorical form, but it is well known that the existence of this phenomenon is one of the central aspects of Marxian thought, and that Marx formulated the concept as early as 1844: "The *alienation* of the worker in his product means not only that his labor becomes an object, assumes an *external* existence, but that it exists independently, *outside himself*, and alien to him, and that it stands opposed to him as an autonomous power. The life which he has given to the object sets itself against him as an alien and hostile force."[16] What is striking is that this is the first time a Pope has ever explicitly alluded to the theory of economic alienation without immediately dismissing it or attempting to refute it.

On June 8, 1964, Pope Paul delivered an address to the Christian Union of Italian Employers and Managers, which the Vatican itself described as "explosive". Although he lauded his listeners for their praiseworthy attempts on the personal level to apply the moral norms of the "social teaching of the Church" to business dealings, most of his talk was devoted to the fundamental discord inherent in the system itself, which renders it impervious to the most high-minded efforts at reform:

> Are your businesses, the wonderful fruit of your efforts, not causes of disappointments and disputes? The mechanical and administrative structures work perfectly but the human structures do not as yet. Firms, which of their very nature should be centers of collaboration, agreement, harmony, are still today places where minds and interests clash. Often, their very existence is considered as an indictment of those who have founded, directed, and administered them. Is it not said that you are the capitalists and the only guilty ones? Are you not often the target of social argument? There must be something profoundly wrong, radically inadequate in the system itself, if it creates such social reactions . . . What is required therefore, is to overcome that selfish interest and mentality which today opposes capital to labor, private profit to public goods, the concept of class to the organic concept of society, private economy to public economy, private enterprise to one that is rationally planned, national autarky to an international market—in one word, personal advantage to the advantage of the human brotherhood. We must needs have a new, wide and universal view of the world, to which the very course of history invites us and to which Christianity has always spurred us.

Elsewhere in the same address, Pope Paul specifies what is "radically wrong" in the system itself: unilateral ownership of the means of production, the primacy of profit over human values, and the fallacious trust in the economy as a self-regulating mechanism. The class struggle, he reminds us, is not a perverse invention of dialectical materialism but the necessary concomitant of a system in which wealth is produced by modern cooperative methods and appropriated by a single class. When he calls upon his hearers to collaborate in the construction of a new social order incarnating properly Christian values, he is careful to add that "this religious cooperation should not be used as a mere paternalistic and utili-

175

tarian corrective to calm the angry and even subversive feelings of the working class toward their employers."

Pope Paul shows himself aware that pious rationalizations of avarice and "pie-in-the-sky" promises to the oppressed have done much to lend plausibility to Marxian polemics against religion. But if the Church's response to the thrust of revolution has been invariably retarded and often wrong-headed, it is at least arguable that Marxism in turn has been unable to rid itself of excrescences due to the philosophical climate existing when its postulates were first formulated. May not atheism be one of these? At any rate, I would endorse the observation made by Catholic students of Marxism, like Father Marcel Reding, that a refusal to reconsider the question of atheism, whose assumed validity may rest only on a simplistic understanding of the relation between economic "base" and ideological "superstructure" betrays an uncharacteristic dogmatism, altogether alien to the dynamic spirit of Marxism.

* * * * *

It would be disingenuous of me to pretend that I could not have written at equal length on what I consider unacceptable in Marxism, both as to its theory and its revolutionary *praxis*. But what ought to alarm Christians most about Marxism is not its unabashed atheism or even the fact that Marxist regimes have actively persecuted religious believers and other dissidents, but the extent to which it has managed to identify itself, in the minds of millions, with the cause of the poor. What a commentary on the languid and superficial character of our commitment to Christianity! For Christianity, after all, has a *praxis* of its own, which is to be found in the Twenty-fifth chapter of St. Matthew:

> Then the true men will answer him: 'Lord, when did we see *you* hungry and give you food? When did we see *you* thirsty and give you something to drink? When did we see *you* lonely and make you welcome, or see *you* naked and clothe you, or see *you* ill in prison and go to see *you*?
>
> And the King will reply, 'I assure you that whatever you did for the humblest of my brothers you did for me.'

If there is any conclusion to be drawn from this essay as a whole, it is that the revolutionary's thirst for justice will have to be combined with an adherence to those values that transcend time. How or when such a rapprochement will come about remains to be seen. In the meantime, I can only endorse the judgment of a distinguished German Catholic writer, Walter Dirks:[17]

We have reason to be grateful to Marxism for having provided us with the insight into the historical power of riches, of 'interest', of the power-giving quality of riches and of those planned deceptions and self-deceptions whereby men have transfigured and glossed over their will to power through riches and their will to riches through power (and to lust through riches and power). Whoever wishes to orient himself on this aspect of history can do so in the pages of Marx, but he can do it equally well in the writings of the monastic leaders. They proceed from the same facts, except that Marx is stronger as a positive analyst, and the founders of the orders are stronger as healers. If they should once begin to think and talk together, the possibility of an approach to a good theory and practice of history would exist.

NOTES

1. *Cahiers du Communisme,* July-August 1963
2. *Pacem in Terris,* No. 127
3. Peter Riga, *Peace on Earth,* Herder & Herder, 1964.
4. Eric Bentley, "Treason of the Experts," *The Nation,* December 13, 1965.
5. Nos. 158-160
6. Ibid, No. 149
7. "Christian-Marxist Dialogue," *Catholic Worker,* January, 1965
8. "Un pionnier du dialogue," *Le Monde,* April 15-21, 1965 (My translation.)
9. St. Thomas Aquinas, *Summa Theologiae,* II-II, 66, 2.
10. R. H. Tawney, *Religion and the Rise of Capitalism* (Mentor-New American Library), p. 39.
11. *Mater et Magistra,* Polyglot Press, p. 26.
12. Emmanuel Mounier, *Personalism,* Grove Press, 1952. (I have re-translated a couple of words in the text to bring them closer to the original French.)
13. Hervé Chaigne, "The Catholic Church and Socialism," *Cross Currents,* Spring 1965.
14. Paul VI, allocution to personnel of the Gio, Buton and Rosso Antico Society of Bologna, May 15, 1965.
15. Karl Marx, *Contribution to the Critique of Hegel's Philosophy of Right,* in *Marx and Engels on Religion,* Schocken, 1964, p. 41.
16. *Marx's Concept of Man,* Ungar, 1961, p. 96.
17. Walter Dirks, *The Monk and the World,* David McKay, 1954.

MOUNIER'S INTEGRAL REALISM
by Patrick J. Hill

INTRODUCTION

To the casual observer, the contemporary dialogue between Marxism and Christianity is one of the most surprising occurrences of our time. While practical exigencies, especially in Europe, go a long way toward explaining its occurrence, the doctrinal positions of these two great traditions seem so far apart, on several key points, that the somewhat shocked and scandalized reactions of some American Christians (who generally do not share the sense of exigency of their European brothers) are at least understandable. For one thing the significance and the efficacy which Marxism assigns to the collective for achieving the liberation of man, with the consequent depreciation of individual effort, seem sharply and fundamentally at odds with the Christian emphasis on the possibility and worth of the interior transfiguration of individual souls through grace-aided, individual effort. For another, the explicit and systematic exclusion of the supernatural by naturalistic Marxism seems reason enough to suppose that nothing fruitful can be gained in dialogue; and further, especially in the absence of mutual respect, that the continuance of the dialogue in the face of these difficulties evidences either a manipulative hypocrisy or a puzzling subordination of doctrinal considerations to practical ones.

While almost endless responses to the casual observer's reaction are both necessary and readily available, there is something significant and unavoidably true in it. When and where the sense of shared exigencies exists, the question of the existence and significance of the supernatural can perhaps, by mutual agreement, be soft-pedalled until another day. Far less manageable, however, because less postponable, is the question of the individual: his significance, his freedom, his relation to the collective. Although Marxism is by the admission of some of its adherents in need of a philosophy of the individual, the earlier dialogue between Marx-

178

ism and Existentialism ought to have illustrated that its need is not so dire as to induce it to effect a hasty and uncritical merger of its doctrinal corpus with a conception of the individual which might well emasculate its socio-political thrust. Traditional Christianity's primary concern to transfigure the individual in Christ, i.e., to effect through the action of the supernatural within the individual a saving, interior liberation from bondage to this world, from enslavement to its goods,—this concern has in fact, *in the particular way in which it has been implemented,* operated to remove the Christian from the struggles of the earth. The prospect of the enormous benefits to be gained by the cooperative action of Marxists and Christians ought not make us ignore the fact (which more conservative members of both traditions will continue to underline) that fundamental philosophical and theological differences seem to preclude the possibility, or at least question the wisdom, of what is actually taking place.

In short, there are major theoretical lags on both sides of the dialogue, lags that will be judged more or less serious in proportion to how one views the relation of theory and practice. If one's practice is guided solely by expediency, then the doctrinal disharmonies will not be taken seriously since cooperative action in the present emergencies is all that is really valued. But if one conceives the relation of theory and practice more integrally, then the present dialogical experience constitutes a formidable challenge. If, from one standpoint, the contemporary cooperation and the present activity of Christians is somehow judged to be more truly Christian than what has dominated religious concerns in recent centuries, or, from the other point of view, if Marxists find that this activity evidences a hitherto unperceived compatibility of individual and organizational demands, then for both Christian and Marxist, the present theoretical lag will be regarded rather seriously.

Viewing this theoretical lag from a comparatively neutral standpoint, one can easily perceive the general nature of the theological and philosophical reconstructions that would be consistent with contemporary practice. What is needed by both Marxists and Christians is a new conception of the relation of the natural and the supernatural and of the relation of the personal and the communal. What is needed most is a conception of personal life and of the interaction of the supernatural with it such that the pursuit of the highly valued interior transfiguration is not carried on *at*

179

the expense of participation in the great historical struggles of the world community.

To my mind, such a vitally relevant reconstruction of these fundamental notions already exists in the sadly neglected work of Emmanuel Mounier, the founder and long-time editor of the influential French journal *Esprit*. The philosophy of this seminal thinker was in fact cast in the fires of a basically similar attempt of diversely positioned groups to formulate cooperatively the principles of a new civilization. It is my judgment that his thought is capable of becoming a focal point of far-reaching and significant dialogue not only between Marxists and Christians, but also, in a manner challenging to both, between Christianity and the whole of the naturalistic tradition.[1]

Space limitations prevent the presentation here of anything more than an outline of Mounier's thought. As what is really required to reveal his relevance is an exposition of how several key notions hang together, my strategy will be geared, in all but the last section, toward presenting the scope and flavor of his thought more than its depth at any particular point. The central ideas of this study are all Mounier's; my own remarks have been confined to clarifying and structuring those ideas relative to each other and to the contemporary Marxist-Christian dialogue.

The first two sections, as will be seen, provide a necessary interpretive background without which the philosophy of man which follows might well seem an inaccessible re-hashing of old formulas. In the first section, entitled "Historic Supernaturalism," the crucial notions of nature and supernature are re-interpreted in the context of an analysis of the nature of the influence which the Christian hopes to exert upon the course of history. The middle section, entitled "Christian Humanism," although the barest part of the outline, sketches two important features of Mounier's interpretation of Christianity: a philosophy of Christian history called "tragic optimism" and a theology of evil built upon the principle of Christian humanism. The great extent to which the dictates of Marxist and Christian doctrines create practical overlaps, apparent throughout the study, is most pronounced at this point.[2]

The concluding section, "Integral Realism," is the core of the study. Within the framework of the preceding sections, a philosophy of personal life is presented wherein the religious imperatives of interior transfiguration are harmonized with an active concern for cosmic and collective liberation. The exposition is sub-divided in such a way as to illuminate, first, the basis for the present concurrence of Marxist and Christian practice, and secondly, the possibility of maintaining all the while a rigorous and challenging conception of personal life.

HISTORIC SUPERNATURALISM

The interpretation of Christianity given by Mounier, what he calls "total Christianity," is an attempt to grasp the eidectic pattern of Christian presence in the world, i.e., to understand the essential nature of the influence which Christians of any epoch are called upon to exert upon the course of history.

A. Goals of Total Christianity

The Christianity of recent centuries has focused its attention almost exclusively upon the salvation of the individual soul. The first task of total Christianity is to restore the collective and cosmic dimensions of the Christian message, the dimensions which in fact constitute the goal of Christian presence.

(1)   In the perspective of total Christianity, the Gospels are an open message addressed to Humanity taken as a single whole, to a Humanity which has been split asunder in the Fall. The Gospels, according to Mounier,

> . . . announce a *kingdom,* that is to say, a collective liberation and not a consultation for the cure of souls. . . . Christ, is not first of all the friend of the cloistered soul. He is first of all the Gatherer of this dispersed Humanity.[4]

The goal of the redemptive process is thus the healing of this ruptured unity, the effecting of a universal reconciliation. And the central-theological category of sin is to be reinterpreted in this view, as a breaching of the unity; in the depreciatory sense of the word, as an *individualization.*

(2)   Joined to this collective dimension is the cosmic aspect of the Christian message, an aspect which the work of Teilhard de Chardin has returned to the fore of Christian consciousness after a long century of panicky over-reactions to what seemed to Chris-

tians the stark falsities of evolutionary naturalism. The earth itself shares in the fate of fallen Man and in the promise of redemption. From the start, the progress of the earth is linked to the Christian message and endowed with a sacred history in solidarity with the human activity which will, in fulfilling the charge of Genesis, replenish and subdue it. The earth, far from being destined for the destruction of the neo-Platonic apocalypse, will be preserved and transfigured, as will all the human labor that has been expended in its organization, in the new order which the Incarnation of Christ makes possible.

B. Superior Indifference to Means

Of greater importance for the understanding of the nature of Christian presence is the means with which the Christian implements these goals. The goals themselves, loosely, the universal reconciliation of men and the organization of the earth, are not significantly different from those which most of Western humanism might articulate as the ends of its activity. But the means demand close attention, both because they are peculiar to the Christian and because an exact understanding of them is necessary for determining the extent to which Christians either contribute to or impede the progress of the earth.

Mounier's analysis can be considered with specific reference to the New Testament dictum that the Kingdom of Christ is *in* this world but not *of* it. The material on which the Christian works, Mounier would say, and the ends toward which it is shaped, are definitely in this world, but the specifically Christian manner of shaping that material toward those ends is something quite distinct from (though not necessarily more important than) the contributions made by the non-Christian.

(1) By way of explication, Mounier distinguishes two streams that feed the progress of history: for want of better words, the secular and the Christian streams, or what in older but even more misleading language was called the temporal and spiritual orders. The secular stream is the whole series of contributions—the inventions, the ideas, the new sentiments, political developments, etc., whose cumulative effect we generally have in mind when employing the word "progress." What the Christian stream adds to the secular stream is a personalizing quality, a contribution whose

efficacy would assure that the progress of the secular stream is of a hominizing rather than a reifying sort. The way in which the Christian community exerts this influence, unlike the course of the secular stream, is solely through a contagion of interior transfiguration, i.e., only through personal examples which testify to the individual's commitment to the actualizing of the Kingdom. Christian presence in the world is therefore essentially incompatible with the creation of specifically Christian institutions, for its mission in history is to influence through personal example *already existing* secular institutions.

(2) Mounier's thesis is that the influence of the Christian on the progress of history, as compared with the non-Christian's, is always lateral or *indirect*. To say that it is lateral is to say that the Christian, *qua* Christian, is not directly concerned with progress in the same way as a scientist or a social organizer might be; but it is not to say, as Christians have too often led Marxists to believe, that his lack of direct concern is equivalent to *un*concern with the earth's progress. Far from that, for the commitment of the true Christian to the redemptive goal makes it impossible for him to be unconcerned about this. What he is unconcerned about is the *means* which secular civilization employs in the implementation of that goal. The Christian, as a result of his interior liberation, as a result of possessing the pearl of great worth which the Gospels promise, is or ought to be so enthralled and animated with the thirst for actualizing the Kingdom that is to come that he will work energetically and cheerfully *with whatever means* are created and employed by the secular stream in his time, e.g., in the framework of *any* institution, *any* ideology or culture.[5] So free from bondage to the goods of this world and from internal fears and anxieties ought his spiritual treasures have made him, that he will operate with a "superior indifference to means" while passionately and committedly effecting the unification of Man and his earth.

The dynamics of Christian presence might perhaps be clearly illustrated by the mode of its influence on ancient Roman civilization. The Church made no effort to construct a specifically Christian culture. Indeed, the philosophies of Greece and Rome became the vehicles of the Christian message, the pagan basilicas became the first places of Christian worship, and the statue of Bacchus was used as the first representation of Christ. As for the institution of slavery which was thoroughly at odds with the value system of the Gospels, the commitment to work *within* the cultural framework necessitated that Christian presence make itself felt not by interfering with slavery *as an institution,* but rather by the personal example of Christians. The Christian's contribution to the advancement of the collective liberation of Man came in his response to the exhortations of his Church to free his slaves; for in so doing Christians testified to the greater value of the Kingdom within each person, the discovery of which had enabled them to free themselves from bondage to the possessions of this world.

Here, as throughout history, the Christian contributes the personalizing influence. The point is not that political or institutional reform by conventional means is not worth while. Indeed, the Christian might well engage in those activities himself. Rather the point is that the specifically Christian mode of influence is the contagious testimony to the extraordinary worth of personal life. Wherever progress is made, whatever the predominating framework of action, the Christian will be on the scene, participating actively to assure that the quality of the progressive moment will be leavened with values respectful of the dignity of personal life.

C. The Incarnational Economy

Given the nature of the goal, then, and the nature of the specific contributions of each of the two streams which Mounier has distinguished, it is apparent that the two streams require each other in order to effect progress in history. While much can be said about the current separation of streams, the important point for present purposes is the recognition that the secular stream, so long depreciated and ignored by the Christianity of recent centuries, makes what is literally as necessary a contribution to the realization of the Kingdom as does the Christian order. What this recognition amounts to is a telescoping of the distinction between the natural and the supernatural, between the temporal and spiritual. Mounier goes so far as to suggest that the historical and natural be so elevated as to be considered as another source of divine revelation, as *gesta Dei,* alongside the traditionally recognized *verbum Dei* in the sacred texts of the Judaeo-Christian tradition.[6]

By its own admission, recent Christianity has not been animated with such an understanding of the relation of the spiritual and the temporal. In the perspective of total Christianity, Mounier

184

perceives the nature of the abstraction which underlies much of the current irrelevance of Christianity:

> Instead of maintaining at all cost the central point of view of the religion which has the Incarnation as its axis, we have little by little allowed our concept of the spiritual to be contaminated by the eclectic and rootless idea of an idealism in which the spiritual and moral signify the soul without the body, the breath of life without life, good will without the will, culture without the earth.[7]

Mounier's analysis provides the groundwork for what he terms the demystification of the spiritual, for a significant relocating of the current, etherealized notions of the spiritual squarely back in the natural world. In doing so, the concept of the natural is itself rescued from the depreciation that necessarily accompanied the excesses of spiritualistic Christianity:

> For the Christian, the spiritual is, in the strict meaning of the word, the presence in our life of the eternal life, in opposition to our natural activities. But this eternal life is itself bred in the flesh and ordinarily presents itself to us only through the agency of natural activities. . . . We do not have to carry the spiritual to the temporal. It is there already. Our task is to discover it there and to give it life, indeed to sacramentalize it. The temporal in its entirety is the sacrament of the Kingdom of God.[8]

The centrality of the Incarnation in Mounier's analysis is here apparent. The supernatural, he says, has through the Incarnation, been "organically grafted" to the natural in such wise as to make the former unavailable except through the natural. That is the economy of the Christian order. The Christian pursuit of the spiritual, far from being isolatable from the temporal, cannot even be conceived apart from it, as the more socially conscious segment of the Christian tradition has recognized. "The gravity of the Christian world," writes Mounier, is "simultaneously within life and beyond life," for the Christian's life of grace is an *essentially mediated* one.

In the final analysis, then, the two streams of which Mounier has written, while distinguishable, must not be regarded as separate. The organic grafting of these two orders effected by the Incarnation amounts to saying that

. . . there are not two histories alien to one another, sacred history and profane history. There is but one history, that of Humanity on the march toward the Kingdom of God. . . . It is then entirely impossible for the Christian to speak as if he were separating his occupations: to the Church or to the life of faith, the supernatural domain, on the one hand; to this ism or that action, the organization of the earth, on the other. The earth cannot be organized outside the faith nor can the faith develop without the forces of the earth.[9]

CHRISTIAN HUMANISM

The exposition to this point, principally directed toward revealing Mounier's re-rooting of the supernatural in the historic, has perhaps indicated as well the very great extent to which Marxists and Christians might work together in responding to the practical exigencies of their different doctrinal commitments.

Nevertheless, even though we have not yet reached the point in this study where the crucial differences between Marxism and Christianity are to be raised, it is necessary, if the fullness of Christian presence in the world is to be understood and if the mistakes of recent Christianity are not to be repeated, to add an extended modulation of the analysis so far presented. For while the economy of Incarnational theology demands that the supernatural be discovered and nourished only in the natural, it by no means suggests that the natural or the temporal could ever *exhaust* the supernatural. The supernatural, present in the lives of Christians, animates the natural, attempting to effect its organization in the direction of the Kingdom. But until the Kingdom is actualized, the demands of the supernatural necessitate that any and every form of Christian presence be abandoned when the next opportunity appears for widening the basis of human unity. It is this demand that insures that Christian presence will remain uninstitutionalized, dynamic, and forever free from *permanent* commitment to any of the particular manifestations of the supernatural in history:

The law of the pendulum which Bergson formulated from human experience is the irresistible rhythm of an incarnation in which the supernatural cannot fail to incorporate itself and cannot incorporate itself without being both diminished and bemired. And so the life of the Church will swing continually between two movements: a movement of *insertion* within the temporal in which . . . she will ask of the temporal orders the maximum for subsistence within them, and a movement of *recoil* from the temporal in which she will ask of them the minimum of subsistence outside them. . . . We leave one phase to enter another. It is a passion stirring history we are living, different from a crisis of decadence or facility.[10]

A. Tragic Optimism

The difficulties of successfully performing this mission are enormous. A fuller analysis would reveal the extent to which much of the difficulty is inherent in the structure of a religion constructed upon the staggering notion of a God become man, and upon the very audacity of the consequent Christian concerns. In Mounier's judgment, the difficulties are so great as to preclude any facile optimism or self-righteous assurance about the will of God in history. The thirst for universal reconciliation is frustrated again and again by the unyielding resistance of the natural and made anxious by the lack of easily applicable guidelines for action. The situation is such as to introduce the Christian to a tragic dimension in history that is so pervasive as to make him the spiritual brother of the atheist:

> The course of Christian history is like that of those peaceful waters where we know indeed that they flow and whither, but where we cannot see, through gazing at one point, the direction, in which, at this point, they are flowing. The landscapes are confused and values shrouded. Shadow alternates ironically with light, and immediate significance evades apprehension. The man of faith will never experience the total dereliction known to the philosopher of the absurd. But being so made as to create obscurity by the very audacity of his enquiry, he can escape neither creative anguish nor the combat in the night. Thus he becomes brother to all who, like him, are passionately involved in the search for the secret of man's being.[11]

But there is an optimistic dimension to this "Christian agnosticism" as well, severely tempered, to be sure, by the tragic, but which we cannot afford to lose sight of now:

> Yesterday, optimism was the philosophy of the satisfied. Then Christianity needed its Kierkegaards, its Pascals, and its Bloys. But our countries, devastated by weariness, now need the builders of hopes and duties.[12]

A good part of Mounier's studies of Christian history is devoted to the relationship of the Christian's faith and the progress of history. While the details cannot be discussed here, it is Mounier's judgment that the Christian ought to be among the most optimistic of his contemporaries. His optimism, like that of the Marxist, is a function of his cosmic-scale mission which communicates meaningfulness to every event and thereby precludes as we have just seen, some of the absurdities which other men must consider as real possibilities. More importantly, it is the result of the faith that a favorable outcome of man's struggles is guaranteed by the love and generosity of God. While that guarantee is shrouded in mystery and is seemingly not such as to eliminate some of the more fearsome of the possibilities that threaten us, still those who have faith in God's promises cannot doubt but that man will prevail in the future.

B. The Problem of Evil

The pessimism that has prevailed in Christian circles, as Mounier acknowledged, was justified in its situation. But like all such emphases, when the purposes for which they are made are lost sight of, this pessimistic turn in Christianity reverberated throughout its doctrinal corpus in somewhat uncontrolled fashion and resulted in what Mounier considered fundamental doctrinal distortions and vitiations of Christian presence, distortions so serious as to compromise even the possibility of Christianity's returning to its historical mission.

What is at issue is the understanding of the Fall and its repercussions in history. In Mounier's analysis, the Fall resulted in an impairment of the potency of human activity, but did not inflict a fatal or essential wound in its capacity to effect the building of the Kingdom. The body has suffered disorientation, but only the same disorientation suffered by the spirit; and neither is under an irremediable curse. The course of Christian redemption, in this perspective, is the cumulative *eradication* of the maledictions of the Fall by means of man's activity. A Christian theology of evil can speak of more than just the possibility of transcending existing evils through interior acts of transfiguration. In what he calls the principle of Christian humanism, Mounier underscores the basis for unqualified Christian participation in the struggles of the earth:

There is no essential disqualification, no absolute evil in the world, nature, flesh, matter, nor in consequence in the opus humanum, which

188

would make history fundamentally ignoble and predestine it to the lot of irremediable decadence.[13]

The Christian's practical activity, then, in that it is a necessary condition for creating the glory of God's Kingdom, is of enormous value. The body and the machine, the tools of that creation, share in that value. And while the Christian's concerns go beyond those of the Marxist, the organic grafting of the supernatural and the natural in the wide historical perspective of tragic optimism make it possible to see that the concerns which do separate the Christian from the Marxist are not the sort which could presently excuse the withdrawal of the Christian from the struggles of our technological era:

> It is precisely because its task is quite different that Christians should wish to be delivered by automatisms, from the primary and excessive anxieties which paralyze them, so that they and all men should be free for the essential. . . . We need ask nothing more of the Christian who hopes to become an angel by fleeing man and cursing him: let him [like Christ] be made man, fully man: let him be filled with longing for the time when we can say of every man without exception that he had the possibility of making himself man, fully man.[14]

INTEGRAL REALISM

The conceptual problem most crucial to Marxism and Christianity and to their dialogue with each other can now be raised. As promising as is Mounier's vision of Christianity and its role in history, the whole of its thrust, just as that of Marxism, will be vitiated if the conception of personal life and its interior transfiguration is not somehow integrated with the collective and cosmic dimensions. On the other hand, a conception of the interior life which manages at once to transcend *and* transform the natural will stand as a challenge to both spiritualistic Christianity and to materialistic Communism. This is precisely the challenge of Mounier's integral realism.

A. Anti-Spiritualistic Realism

The distinctive feature of Mounier's philosophy of personal life, vis-à-vis all those which he is rejecting, is the defining centrality assigned to the dynamics of personal growth. Metaphysical explanations of a monistic sort are eschewed in favor of a descrip-

189

tion of a three fold movement of exteriority, interiority and transcendence. What is properly personal does not begin until the occurrence of the second movement, which is a temporary separation from the environment. But as the person, like the species man, emerges slowly from nature, there is a great deal prior to that separation which is relevant to personal growth. Mounier's agreements with Marxism, it will be seen, stem largely from the recognition of the profound relevance of the non-personal to the personal. When the person emerges from the non-personal, at that point Mounier and Marx part company

(1) The first step, then, is to locate the person in nature, and that means breaking with the idealistic tradition. Western man, says Mounier, has been "wandering uprooted and unoccupied in a theater of Narcissus" since the 15th century. It is this permanently self-reflexive stance, under the guise of interior aspirations and spiritual isolations, which is at the heart of much modern Christian spirituality. The nobility of the aspirations have obscured the sclerosis and emasculation that the inward turn can produce:

> Excessive rumination dissipates us, too much interiorization leads to over subtlety, and too much self-solicitude, however spiritual, can engender egocentricity that grows like a psychic cancer. The cultivation of a certain image of the self in order to preserve and protect it, may then come to fill the entire horizon of life.[15]

What's worse, this gaze inward may even be self-defeating, for even if the self could be discovered and cultivated in this manner, the ambivalencies which surround this and every movement of personal growth render it more than possible that this ennobled search for self-knowledge may be nought but a camouflage for a surrender to a sub-human, vegetative passivity uninvolved with the transformation of the environment. To this debased and etheralized man, to this misguided and deracinated man, searching for something he is unequipped to find, Mounier issues an urgent and unmodulated plea:

> It is high time . . . to remind the subject that he will never rediscover and strengthen himself without the mediation of the objective: *he must come out of his inwardness if he is to keep his soul alive.*[16]

(2) What Mounier's analysis of idealistic philosophy amounts to is what has been previously termed a demystification of the

190

spiritual. As this demystification occurs in a universe wherein the material has already been re-valuated, i.e., rescued from the depreciation it has suffered in the hands of idealisms and religious evasionism, Mounier is now able to announce the dissolution of the "idealistic alienation" in a conception that integrates the two dimensions of man's life. There is body and there is soul, but "there is not . . . for man a life of the soul sundered from the life of the body." The gates of modernity open to Christianity with the frank and undepreciating recognition that

> Man is a natural being; by his body he is a part of nature and his body is everywhere with him. . . . It is the basis of all consciousness and of all the spiritual life, the omnipresent mediator of the spiritual life.[17]

More strongly and more graphically put:

> Man is a body in the same degree that he is a spirit, wholly body and wholly spirit. His most fundamental instincts, eating and reproduction, he has elaborated into the subtle arts of gastronomy and courtship. Yet the great philosopher is attacked by headaches and St. John of the Cross used to vomit during his ecstasies.[18]

As in Marx, existence itself demands the objectivity of the body. So far has Mounier come from the Cartesian tradition in French thought that even the experience of the self is a bodily experience:

> *I exist subjectively, I exist bodily,* are one and the same experience. I cannot think without being and I cannot be without my body, which is my *exposition* to myself, to the world, to everyone else: by its means alone can I escape from the solitude of a thinking that would be only thought about thought.[19]

(3) The path of these two lines of thought, the demystification of the spiritual and the re-valuation of the material, leads Mounier's integral realism into the camp of the "third way" of contemporary French thought where the concept of an "incarnate cogito" plays a fundamental role in steering between the excesses of Marxism and Sartrian Existentialism. The *cogito,* the bastion of etherealized metaphysical systems, is dislodged from its egocentric retreat and projected into the world of material things. We cannot follow here even the major philosophical repercussions of this school of thought. What is important for present purposes is the essential

need of personal existence for objective mediation. Far from their being a problem, then, of relating the inner life which Christianity wishes to transfigure to the material world, it is unavoidable that they be related:

> People always speak of "engagement" as if it depended upon our-selves: *we are engaged,* embarked, already involved. Abstention is only an illusion.[20]

It is impossible, then, that the goal of interior transfiguration be achieved in isolated withdrawal from the world. "Inwardness," says Mounier, "is achieved only through action." He speaks of an "instinct of exteriorization" and in the light of this and what has preceded defines the person dialectically as

> ... an inside in need of an outside, and the very word "exist" indicates by its prefix that "to be" is to go out, to express oneself.[21]

We are here entering upon that theoretical analysis of personal life wherein lies the basis for the practical agreements and dis-agreements with the Marxists. The realistic dimension of Mounier's integral realism does not end with the recognition of the indispensable function of the body for personal growth. It extends further to an appreciation of the positive function which other material objects can perform. Being and having, to use the familiar terms of Marcel, "are not mutually exclusive alternatives between which our embodied existence is held in tension." Possessed objects stabilize the self and at the same time prevent it from being ab-sorbed into a world of wholly depersonalized objects. The first act of self-affirmation is an act of self-expansion into a world of pos-sessed objects. "Property like intimacy," says Mounier, "is a con-crete requirement of personality." An objective being has essential, objective needs:

> To have at its own disposal a certain range of objects with which it can form relations of intimacy somewhat like those that it seeks with other persons, relations of frequency and of long duration—that is for the person an elementary need. To possess is to make contact, to give up one's isolation, to "bear with something."[22]

Therein lies much of the basis for the present concurrence of Marxist and Christian social goals. The Christian, however pas-

192

sionate his longing for the Kingdom, must recognize that the actualization of the Kingdom, the ability to respond to the higher values of personal life and most of all, to the Personhood of Christ, presupposes not only a liberation from basic anxieties about the vital minimum necessary to sustain life, but also a range of possessed objects which anchors this existent being in his objectivity and his uniqueness. These are the "terrestrial conditions" upon which actualization of the Kingdom waits.

B. Anti-Materialistic Realism

A careful and extended analysis of the variety of ways in which material objects can function begins the discussion of the second and third movements of personal life. Insights born of Christianity's spirituality of dispossession and of the excesses of bourgeois culture, pinpoint a second danger to man, containing as great a possibility for alienation as does the idealistic etherealization of man:

> Narcissus is devoured from within by the malady of the too beautiful soul. He disintegrates before his own eyes. But Hercules is devoured from without by his latest conquest, burned to the quick by the product of his worldly victory.[23]

Personal existence, though in essential need of a movement of exteriorization, can become encysted by that movement in the same fashion as interiorization can. Legitimate, self-anchoring possession, for example, turns, like the reflexive gaze of consciousness, into a dislocated end-in-itself, that is to say, abstracted and isolated from the function it performs for the whole person. A self-confining, stifling ownership replaces the liberating relationship of the person with the world of objects around him. The possessed object, therefore, cannot be thought of as *intrinsically* liberating, nor can its dialectical relation to an inner life be ignored without disastrous consequences:

> The personalist dialectic of having is not so confident, for it sees beyond to the entropic and involutionary function of having. Expansion of personality implies, as an interior condition, a renunciation of the self and of its goods which depolarizes egocentricity; for only in losing oneself can the person find himself.[24]

Mounier, in short, agrees with those Existentialists who have sounded a trumpet call to awaken modern man from the torpor of objectivity, from the immersion in the group, from the functionalization of his being, from an imprisonment, as Valery put it, "that shuts us up outside ourselves." "Personal life," Mounier writes,

> begins with the ability to break contact with the environment, to recollect oneself, to reflect, in order to re-constitute and reunite oneself in one's own center.[25]

(1) To speak of breaking from the environment, of course touches upon the question of freedom. Attention will be turned to this issue, crucial to the dialogue, immediately after completing the description of the movements of personal growth, i.e., after gaining some understanding of what it is that Mounier claims the person is free to do.

The movement of interiority, the dangers of which the Marxist critique of idealism has laid bare, is a *temporary* withdrawal, a stepping back intended to suspend the lived unity of subject and object in order to reflect upon it, and to search for what can only be described as "an active presence," the central secret which is one's personhood. The third movement, the movement of transcendence, is a forward movement, made in the light of the reflection, in which the person struggles against what is given in order to effect his own liberation. Mounier's claim is strong:

> Character is not a fact, but an act. The synthetic unity of character is not a product, it is a living effort and this effort may be effective far beyond what the majority of men consider possible.[26]

Perhaps the briefest and most helpful way to provide some understanding of what the second and third movements of personal growth hope to attain is with Mounier's distinction between the individual and the person, a distinction based on the total orientations of each. The individual, by definition, is correlated with the movement of exteriorization. His life is one dominated by acquisition and by *ownership*. The inner orientation of the individual is marked by dispersion and avarice. Whatever expansion occurs in that life must be sought in the same mode of being, i.e., in ownership, through a self-extension in and through possessions: *my* house, *my* book, *my* wife, *my* position, etc. Acquisitions, achievements, past triumphs thus become constitutive *determin-*

194

ations of the individual. As an entity *wholly given* in what he owns, a constant threat to singularity and well-being is present in the possibility that his possessions be lost, destroyed, discredited. All sorts of defense mechanisms spring up to avoid such occurrences, the most serious of which more or less completely compromise the *availability* of the individual. Locked up outside of himself, his responses are limited and determined.

The life of the person, is dominated by generosity. In sharp contrast to the dispersion of the individual amidst possessed objects, the inner orientation of the person is characterized by self-possession and self-determination. It too grows or extends itself in its own mode of being, i.e., by *dispossession* and renunciation. The person is, consequently, essentially a *prospective* (as opposed to a retrospective) entity, one whose being is not given in the present, but turned toward the future. It, like man himself, can be defined only as a continual self-surpassing. The very nature of the person demands that the only manner by which it can maintain itself in existence is by constantly denying itself the objectifications acquired for its life:

> The realization of the person . . . is, by reason of the transcendence of the person, a constant effort at advancement; therefore, at renunciation, dispossession, and spiritualization. Therein lies the process of spiritualization that is characteristic of a personalist metaphysics. It is at once a process of dispossession and a process of personalization.[27]

Such is the movement of transcendence, breaking down the provisional boundaries of the biological, social and psychological subjects seeking always the "inaccessible center" that supplies the force, and the "intuition which animates those essential objectifications."

This mature person, having emerged from nature and gained inwardness through objectification, is essentially *available* to others. Loosed from the bondage which possessed objects may effect (though not from need for objective mediation), loosed from individuating factors, the personal mode of being is essentially communal:

> Human communion is implanted in the very heart of the person as an integrating factor of its existence. . . . The person, by the very movement which is its being *exposes* itself. It is thus communicable by

195

nature and is lonely from the need to communicate. We must start from that primordial fact. . . . One might almost say that I have no existence save in so far as I exist for others.[28]

In thus finding the "we" anterior to the "I," the primary action of the person is established as the sustenance of a society of persons. Like the tri-une God in whose image he is made, man's being is "of its very essence the negation of solitude." Personhood can be achieved and maintained only in intimate dialogue between persons.

(2) Though the exposition here has been necessarily brief, the hope is that this much was accomplished: a conception of personal life has been presented wherein neither engagement, nor community is sacrificed in the concern for the development of a challenging and rigorous inner life. The major works of Mounier have to be studied in all their details before a final assessment should be made. But the main lines of the vision are here, a challenge to those who have isolated either the cosmic or the personal.

The burning question, of course, the crucial question is man's freedom. Can the person do what Mounier's philosophy claims is possible? Everything depends on that:

Freedom is the life and source of personal being. . . . Action is less than human unless it transfigures the most obstinate data by the magic of its spontaneity.[29]

The first thing to be said about Mounier's notion of freedom is that it is not, despite the heroic sound of the above statement, the absolute freedom of Sartre. In Mounier's view, "a minimum of physical development, health, security and material ease is essential" for the great number of men to be enabled to respond to the higher appeals of humanity.[30] More strongly, no matter at what level of development or what level of material ease one finds himself, freedom is still not absolute. To be is to be located, engaged, both essentially and uniquely situated; the conception of freedom must recognize that as fundamental:

To be free is, in the first place, to accept this position, to accept this position and base oneself upon it. Not everything is possible, or not everything at every moment.[31]

Both the lack of realism in the Christian approach and the paternalism of Marxist practice are being questioned here: freedom must be treated contextually and developmentally, as a "freedom under conditions." It is the transformation of *whichever* obstacles to a fuller life are present *in this or that situation* which constitutes freedom; not the ability to achieve some end or solve some problem or respond to some lofty appeal which someone else considers the fullest life. Freedom is distorted if it is discussed only vis-à-vis certain abstract goods that we wish to see realized in people's lives or in society. Freedom exercises itself on *whatever* expansive possibilities are present in a concrete situation for a particular person.

But *is* man free? Does he have the capacity to transform his environs? If the question is so framed, i.e., as a question about empirical fact, then Mounier will answer "no." As indicated previously, Mounier agrees with a good deal of Existentialism's analysis of the soporific effects of contemporary Western society.

But the freedom of which Mounier speaks is not discoverable by objective, dispassionate observation. In a paragraph that well illustrates why he described his characterology as a science *fighting* for man, Mounier offers not a proof but an exhortation:

> It is the person that *makes himself free,* having first chosen to do so; but nowhere does it find freedom given or instituted: nor does anything in the world assure it of freedom unless it enters courageously into free experience.[32]

Each person himself and he alone can discern and exploit the opportunities that are present in his life. Failure to do so results in an increasingly enslaving torpor. To begin the struggle is to begin the long ascent to the heights of personal life, to independence, self-control, unification, self-determination and the capacity of love. The only weapon the person possesses is what the Christian tradition called fortitude, a force "which is at once internal and efficacious, spiritual and manifest."

(3) We are now in a position to examine Mounier's critique of the Marxist philosophy of man. "The essential error of Marxism," he wrote, "is its misconception of the interior reality of man, that of his personal life." Marx's version of the realistic tradition needs to be complemented so that it contains principles both of externalization, and internalization. Marxists have violated what Mounier calls "the first great postulate of human statics and dynamics," *viz.*:

> . . . the inward man exists only in virtue of the outward man; the outward man exists only through the strength of the inward man.[33]

In the absence of such a dialectical understanding of interiority, no acceptable conception of the person was available to the Marxists. Though the exclusion of a concept of the person did not of itself necessarily make the system anti-personalistic, the exclusion manifested itself in just such a fashion throughout the system:

> Marx's whole doctrine of alienation presupposes that the individual is incapable of transforming himself and of escaping from the befuddling mystifications of bourgeois liberalism.[34]

Mounier, it must be emphasized, is not going back on his recognition of the enormous influence exerted by non-personal factors upon the individual. Economic disorders still require economic solutions. He is merely underscoring the nature of the judgment that underlies Marx's analysis:

> Left to himself the individual stumbles about in vain efforts and succeeds only in alienating himself more. The collective mass, on the contrary, is strong, balanced and creative. It keeps the individuals on the ground and transforms them by directing them, so to say, into its own currents.[35]

The individual, treated only as a politico-economic animal, is subsumed under the class to which all transforming power is transferred. Despite the fact that the analysis may have been and may still be politically true, the abstraction is calamitously dangerous for the whole man:

> To ignore the actual presence in our unhappy history of the living principle of liberation, not only in its historical and social form (the succession of "progressive classes"), but also in its trans-historic form; to misunderstand the power of the person both for breaking down and building up, on the pretext that the person is still a slave; to do this is to risk atrophying the only force that is capable of making the leap from necessity to liberty.[36]

What class movements can transform is limited to material conditions, and hence Marxism becomes a humanism of material comfort only. The collective, moreover, becomes the source of value, replacing the individual again, and the individual's role is reduced to that of conforming to these values. As the individual has been stripped of creative responsibility, this conformity can only be brought about by the agency of the collective, by training and not through the education and experience of the individual.

A "radical pessimism," says Mounier, indeed a "deep contempt" for the capacities of the person is at the heart of the Marxists' doctrine. The individualized benefits of science will be of little use to class members rendered spiritually bankrupt by the class methods.

Marxism ends by turning into its opposite. From the point of view of Mounier's understanding of the person, Marxism is a dictatorial rationalism that depreciates the role of experience, a radical pessimism, and, in denying the conditions for a true community of persons, "a more malignant kind of individualism."

CONCLUSION

The work of Mounier is relevant to contemporary problems for many reasons and in many areas. He has gained heightened relevance, however, with the emergence of the Marxist-Christian dialogue; for in his work, the fundamental notions central to the past and present relationships of these two great traditions have been re-worked. For those engaged in the dialogue, for those concerned to harmonize lagging theory with the contemporary cooperative experience, more detailed study of Mounier might well provide the conceptual clarifications necessary for mutual understanding and for self-criticism. At the very least, his work would serve as an excellent focal point for the structuring of the dialogue in the future.

NOTES

1. Mounier died in 1950, while still young and at the peak of his productivity. As he was a thinker pre-eminently involved with the problems of his time, much of what he wrote has already become dated. But the core of his thought remains relevant.
2. In a longer study of Mounier's work, which I have already completed and will appear in *Cross Currents* (Winter, 1968), these first two sections are considerably expanded with special reference to the relevant portions of the Christian doctrinal tradition and to Mounier's analysis of contemporary Christianity.
4. Emmanuel Mounier, *Studies in Personalist Sociology* (*La Petite Peur Du XXe Siecle*) published as a single volume with *What is Personalism* (*Qu'est ce que le Personalisme?*) under the title *Be Not Afraid*, trans. Cynthia Rowland (New York: Sheed and Ward, n.d.), pp. 76-77. These two works will be abbreviated throughout as *SPS* and *WP* respectively.

   The greater part of Mounier's work has been collected in four large volumes, *Oeuvres de Mounier* (Paris: Editions du Seuil, 1962). As the most significant portions have already been translated, I will refer to the available English books throughout this study, although I have frequently made slight modifications of the translations. Unless otherwise noted, the emphasis in quoted passages has been added.
5. Mounier makes the qualification, unimportant in this general analysis, that the means be not such as intrinsically do violence to the justice of God.

6. The basic term for Mounier is "history" rather than "nature," in that he does not recognize any absolute nature apart from man's interaction with it. It is in this perspective that he coins the phrase "historic supernaturalism."
7. "Christian Faith and Civilization" (*Feu la Chrétienté*), *Cross Currents*, Vol. I, no. 1 (Winter, 1950), p. 3. Hereafter abbreviated as *CC*. This article and the short book *Spoil of the Violent* (*L'Affrontement Chrétien*), trans. Katherine Watson (West Nyack, New York: Cross Currents Corporation, n.d.), provide a fine introduction to Mounier's understanding of Christianity.
8. *Ibid.*, p. 9.
9. *Ibid.*, pp. 16-17.
10. *Ibid.*, p. 20.
11. *SPS*, p. 84.
12. *Ibid.*, p. 104. The optimistic dimension in Mounier's work no doubt suggested the phrase *Be Not Afraid* as a title for studies to which reference has just been made.
13. *Ibid.*, p. 90. Mounier is not forgetting that there are rigorous conditions to be met to redeem the world. The point is rather that the evil can be eliminated.
14. *SPS*, p. 106.
15. *Personalism* (*Le Personalisme*), trans. Philip Mairet (London: Routledge and Kegan Paul Ltd., 1952), p. 43. Hereafter referred to as *Pers.* See also *The Character of Man* (abridged from *Traité du Caractere*) trans. Cynthia Rowland (New York: Harper and Bros., 1956), pp. 215-16. Hereafter as *CM*.
16. *Ibid.*, pp. 4, 12.
17. *Ibid.*, p. 3.
18. *Ibid.*, p. 11. Mounier's emphasis.
19. *Ibid.*, p. 92. Mounier's emphasis.
20. *Ibid.*, p. 44. This movement outwards is the movement of exteriority which was mentioned above.
21. *Ibid.*, p. 39. See also *CM*, pp. 196-200.
22. *WP*, p. 155.
23. *Pers.*, p. 40.
24. *Ibid.*, p. 34.
25. *CM*, p. 17.
26. Exactness in defining the person cannot be obtained precisely because this is an undetermined entity. To define or to enumerate its characteristics would be to dissolve it. For the problem of self-identity, see *CM*, pp. 220-21.
27. A *Personalist Manifesto* (*Manifesto au Service du Personalisme*) trans. by monks of St. John's Abbey (New York: Longmans, Green and Co., 1938), p. 88. Hereafter as *PM*.
28. *Pers.*, p. 59.
29. *CC.*, p. 22.
30. *Pers.*, p. 59. For the relation of this conception of freedom to that of Jaspers and Sartre, see Mounier's *Existentialist Philosophies* (*Introduction aux Existentialismes*), trans. Eric Blow, (New York: The Macmillan Co., 1949), pp. 65-66, 102-103.
31. *Ibid.*, p. 56.
32. *WP*, p. 163.
33. *PM*, p. 64.
34. *Ibid.*
35. "The Present Tasks of Personalism" ("*Taches Actuelles d'une Pensée d'Inspiration Personaliste*"), trans. by the Personalist Group of London: Personalist Pamphlets, No. 4, n.d.), p. 13.

ARCHBISHOP TEMPLE ON
DIALECTICAL MATERIALISM

by RICHARD GREENLEAF

1.

The middle decades of the Twentieth Century have seen, throughout those parts of the world where Christianity is the dominant religion, three great phenomena of upheaval and reform. Within the Roman Catholic Church there has been a vast revision of liturgy and polity, with an accompanying—though not so prominent—change in many ideological concepts. Within the Protestant churches, there has been a widespread and profound re-examination of man's image of God and of God's role in history. Within all the churches there has been an attempt, on the part both of laity and clergy, to come to grips with the ideas of history and morality advanced by Marx, Engels and Lenin.

Plainly, these are but three aspects of a single social and intellectual movement. A Marxist would say that in the final stages of capitalism there was bound to be strain and wrenching within this portion of the ideological superstructure of capitalist society. And, to be sure, there is no more complete way than that to account for what is going on. But how does it all look from the point of view of religion and the religionist? Unless the student of political-economy makes an effort to see these changes as the religious person sees them, he cannot play a significant role in bringing about that rapprochement between Christian groups and radical political groups which is so vital if war and domestic violence are to be kept at a minimum during the transition from capitalism to socialism.

This paper will in no way attempt to trace the origins and consequences of the Second Vatican Council, nor will it assay the current Death-of-God movement within Protestant theology. Both of these devolpments are certainly worthy of consideration from the Marxist viewpoint, and it is to be hoped that such studies will

201

be forthcoming. But they are beyond the scope of the present essay.

Our province here is the work of a writer whose major works lie now some three decades in the past. They dealt, in substantial part, with the parallels between authentic Christian doctrine and Marxist doctrine. They suggest, as we read them today, a manner of looking at the relations between these two great bodies of ideas such that the situation of Christianity appears, not as a belated and embarrassed effort to "get with it," but as an unfolding and revealing of an ancient philosophy whose existence was precedent to and causative of Marxism.

2.

William Temple (not to be confused with the Seventeenth-Century diplomat and man-of-letters of the same name) was born at Exeter in 1881, the son of Frederick Temple, who became Archbishop of Canterbury in 1896. William attended Rugby, where he became a lifelong friend of R. H. Tawney, the socialist historian and author of *Religion and the Rise of Capitalism*. Following graduation from Balliol in 1900, Temple became a Fellow of Queens, and studied at Jena in 1906. From 1908 until 1924 he served as president of the Workers' Educational Association, a Church body. In 1918 he joined the Labour Party, a membership which he retained throughout the remainder of his life, thus becoming the first Archbishop of Canterbury to be so enrolled.

After holding a number of clerical posts he became Canon of Westminster in 1919, and was elected Bishop of Manchester in 1921. In 1924 he played a central role in the inception and conduct of a world-wide Christian Conference on Politics, Economics and Citizenship. In 1928 he was elected Archbishop of York, and in 1942 Archbishop of Canterbury and Primate of All England. He died in 1944. His writings are numerous and extensive. The principal books are *The Faith and Modern Thought* (1910), *Nature, Man and God* (1934), and *Christianity and Social Order* (1942).[1]

3.

In *The Economic Review* for April, 1908 (the year in which he was ordained deacon), Temple published an essay entitled "The Church and the Labour Party: A Consideration of Their Ideals." It will be well to quote extensively from this at the beginning, not because the ideas there expressed remained unaltered in his mind, but because they show the position from which he started as a young cleric:

> . . . in [the] Epistle to the Ephesians, where St. Paul achieves the completion of his doctrine, he preaches the fullest scheme of evolutionary socialism, so far as all fundamental points are concerned, that has yet been conceived by man. . . .
>
> . . . the philosophy of the Incarnation certainly involves the principle that spirit needs bodily expression if it is to be operative; and the actual conduct of the Incarnate gives no support to [a] concentration upon the purely spiritual side of life.
>
> . . . even the least in the kingdom (or sovereignty) of God is greater [than John the Baptist]—the least citizen, that is, of the regenerated society which Christ was founding, wherein the supremacy of God over all things, material as well as spiritual, should be manifest and His will be done 'as it is in Heaven'. . . .
>
> The Church is bound to recognize the justice, the essential Christianity, of the Labour Movement; the alternative is internal decay and ultimately dissolution. . . . This movement is in a deep and true sense Christian; to stand aside from it would be to incur the guilt of final and complete apostasy, of renunciation of Christ, and of blasphemy against His Holy Spirit.
>
> . . . we also are to take our bodies, give thanks for them, and break them in the service of men, if we would show our remembrance of the Lord.
>
> . . . Socialism (which is the polar opposite of Communism in one direction as it is of Anarchism in another) is the economic realization of the Christian Gospel. . . . The alternative stands before us— Socialism or Heresy; we are involved in one or the other.[2]

Such Fabian ideas, coming from a young Anglican clergyman, were far less shocking in 1908 than they would be today. Both in England and in the United States, such conceptions were in the academic and ecclesiastical air in the decade which preceded the October Revolution. And it will be seen at a glance that, as expressed in this essay of Temple's, they were without any real philosophical underpinning.

Had Temple "outgrown" them, as most men in his walks did, they would be in no way remarkable. Instead, he carefully over the years provided the underpinning which they required from philosophy and theology. It is with this structure that we shall be mainly concerned. But we may turn first to some socio-religious ideas which he expressed at later stages in his life, to assure ourselves that he stayed faithful to the main conformations of his youthful declaration.

"It was not crime or vice," he pointed out with dramatic restraint, "that sent Christ to the Cross; it was respectability and religious stagnation and compromise." [3]

A fascinating evocation of life under socialism as he envisioned it:

"Still city and country life with all their manifold pursuits, but no leading into captivity and no complaining in our streets; still sorrow, but no bitterness; still failure but no oppression; still thoughtless luxury, no grinding destitution; still priest and people, but both alike unitedly presenting before the Eternal Father the one increasing sacrifice of their own lives in body broken and blood outpoured; still Church and world, yet both together celebrating unintermittently the one Divine Service, which is the Service of mankind." [4]

On the so-called Christian doctrine of non-resistance to evil:

"It is the spirit of resentment, not the act of resistance, that our Lord condemns." [5]

On the nationalization of public resources:

"There are four requisites of life which are given by the bounty of God—air, light, land and water. These exist before man's labor is expended upon them, and upon air and light man can do nothing except to spoil them. I suppose if it were possible to have established property rights in air, somebody would have done it before now, and then he would demand of us that we should pay him if we wanted to breathe what he called *his* air. Well, it couldn't be done, so it hasn't been done. But it could be done with land, and it has been done with land: and, as it seems to me, we have been far too tender towards the claims that have been made by the owners of land and of water as compared with the interests of the public."[6]

On the Christian view of history:

"The Christian understanding of history has much closer affinities with the Marxist view than with the interpretations of Christianity in terms of idealistic thought which were lately prevalent." [7]

These are scattered references from writings published over a long period. Temple's *magnum opus,* and that work in which he grappled with dialectical materialism, was *Nature, Man and God,*

*being the Gifford Lectures delivered in the University of Glasgow
in the academical years 1932-1933 and 1933-1934* (London, 1934).
To this we now turn.

4.

"At one time," wrote Temple in his Preface to this work, "I
thought of giving to these Lectures a descriptive sub-title: *A Study
in Dialectical Realism.* But that might suggest an ambition to inaugurate a philosophical tradition suitably so designated. I have
no such desire. But I believe that the Dialectical Materialism of
Marx, Engels and Lenin has so strong an appeal to the minds of
many of our contemporaries, and has so strong a foundation in
contemporary experience, that only a Dialectic more comprehensive in its range of apprehension and more thorough in its appreciation of the inter-play of factors in the real world, can overthrow
it or seriously modify it as a guide to action. I certainly have not
supplied that more comprehensive and more thorough Dialectic;
but I have sought to make a contribution towards it." [8]

Such effort, whether or not it was philosophically successful,
claimed little attention either from Christian philosophers or from
Marxist philosophers. The former (or such of them as studied
Temple) seem to have decided to ignore his remarks on Marx; the
latter seem to have had some difficulty in catching up with the
Archbishop. I instance the confession of Joseph Needham:

"More emphasis ought . . ., in justice to traditional Christianity,
to be laid on the materialist elements in it; for example, the sacra-
mental principle. In the poetic symbolism of the sacrifice of the
lucharist, we take clearly materialistic things, bread and wine,
and with them we offer and make, to a God anciently conceived
as both immanent and transcendent, a holy and efficient sacrifice,
remembering that (in this language) material objects are necessary as carriers of grace. Grace can have no existence in isolation.
If we love not our brother whom we have seen, how can we love
God whom we have not seen? The material bread and wine of this
sacrifice ought to teach us that the most exalted spiritual things are
connected with, and have arisen in evolution out of, the most
primitive processes of living and dead matter. Christians themselves rarely seem to understand this." [9]

And Needham says in a footnote at this point: "But long after
I had written this, I found that Archbishop Wm. Temple does. In

his Gifford lectures . . . he says, 'Christianity is the most avowedly materialist of all the great religions.'. . . And later he approximates his own position to that of dialectical materialism. . . ."

These are the passages from Temple which Needham mentions:

> "It may safely be said the one ground for the hope of Christianity that it may make good its claim to be the true faith lies in the fact that it is the most avowedly materialist of all the great religions. It affords an expectation that it may be able to control the material, precisely because it does not ignore it or deny it, but roundly asserts alike the reality of matter and its subordination. Its most central saying is: 'The Word was made flesh,' where the last term was, no doubt, chosen because of its specially materialistic associations. By the very nature of its central doctrine Christianity is committed to a belief in the ultimate significance of the historical process, and in the reality of matter and its place in the divine scheme."[10]

The second passage:

> "There is reason to think that [the] conception of the intimate unity of spirit and matter affords the chief hope of securing for the spiritual an effective control over matter throughout any period now worth considering. This may surprise those who recognise it as closely akin to the so-called Dialectical Materialism of Marx, Engels and Lenin. But a close examination of this Dialectical Materialism, strongly distinguished as it is by its upholders from Mechanistic Materialism, suggests that its own dialectic will destroy its character as materialist, except in so far as it is opposed to the idealistic view of matter as existing only 'for mind'. Dialectical Materialism so-called, asserts the temporal priority of matter, as we have been led to do; it regards mind as appearing within matter, as we have done; it asserts that mind, so appearing, acts by its own principles, which are not reducible to the categories of physics and chemistry; while mind is regarded as originating in, and out of, what is material, it is not itself regarded as identical with matter. What is postulated by this view is not an identity of mind and matter, but a unity of mind and matter; to present mind and matter as identical is condemned as Mechanistic Materialism."[11]

Only the greatest of Marxist writers have perceived the essential materialism of Christian doctrine. It is not a theme one encounters frequently in recent Marxist commentary upon the religious scene. Indeed, Needham stands out as having explored this realm. It is a realm whose exploration requires the long perspectives of the historian of antiquity. He is talking about *traditional* Christianity, by which he means Christianity in its original elements and intentions, and these are things which it is difficult for the untrained eye to see. It is no accident that Needham, having devoted his life to the study of a civilization and a religion much older than ours—i.e., the Chinese—should be equal to the challenge of this paradox.

But, for the matter of that, only the greatest of Christian writers have perceived the essential materialism of Christian doctrine. Temple's lectures are both daring and neglected. They run hard against the persistent degeneration of Christian doctrine, by which Jesus, a sort of precursor of the flying saucer, descended from the realm of Spirit and scooped up what little he could retrieve of humanity for a rather pagan feast beyond the stars. Temple, with his religion that acknowledges the reality—indeed the primacy— of the material, and seeks to master it by human thought and labor, was bound to be ignored and suppressed by those who use religion as a buttress for the socio-political *status quo*.

These two passages from Temple may seem rather general— though perhaps less so when viewed against the background of the socialist affirmation of his youth. We need to pursue his thought in greater detail to learn whether it does indeed correspond with Marxist thought upon more specific philosophical problems. This I propose to do under several headings.

5.

Freedom and Necessity

The dialectical relationship between necessity and freedom is central to Marxist philosophy "Freedom . . . consists in the control over ourselves and over external nature which is founded on knowledge of natural necessity; it is therefore necessarily a product of historical development." [12] Temple's way of putting this stems from the Old Testament: "We are clay in the hands of the Potter, and our welfare is to know it." [13] But his concept of freedom has the same relation to history as that of Marx and Engels: " . . . human History is nothing other than ourselves; and we make its meaning by living out its process in the power, already available to us, of the Eternal Life which is at once the source of that meaning and its culmination." [14]

How can man have purpose when the universe is ruled by natural law (or by God)? It is the existence of human purpose, according to Marxism, which marks man off qualitatively from all of the stream of prior evolution. Temple parallels this closely: "It is . . . in [the] constant direction of attention, rather than in the moment of action, that freedom is found to be effectively present." [15] And further: "To feel God's hand upon one impelling and directing, and to find oneself actively pursuing some course or serving some cause, are not two experiences but one." [16]

Man's purposiveness is again and again presented by Temple as the very essence of his humanity: "Constancy of purpose is a noble characteristic, but it shows itself, not in unalterable uniformity of conduct, but in perpetual self-adaptation, with an infinite delicacy of graduation, to different circumstances, so that, however these may vary, the one unchanging purpose is always served." [17] And again: "Freedom is not absence of determination; it is spiritual determination, as distinct from mechanical, or even organic, determination. It is determination by what seems good as contrasted with determination by irresistible compulsion." [18]

Man's role, with Temple as with Marx, is to change the world: "The most significant characteristic of Mind, after all, is not such knowledge as is possible to us while we are subject to the conditions of our present life, but purpose—not the apprehension of the world as it now is, but the constant effort to make it something else." [19]

Man as a Social Being

Man, in the Marxist view, has no existence whatever apart from society. With this Temple is in hearty accord: "Membership, such as carries with it a share in a common weal and woe, is an essential element in our nature; and an effort to repudiate it is always found to be a reassertion of it by implication." [20] The essentiality of membership reaches and affects man's highest pursuits: " . . . a man's relation to Truth and Beauty is . . . a social relation . . . [and therefore] the claims of Truth and Beauty constitute an obligation, and not only the offer of an august satisfaction." [21]

Indeterminacy and Idealism

Ignorance and seeming indeterminacy, Marxists hold, are constantly seized upon by reactionary social forces as buttresses for that idealism which stifles progress. Against this Temple repeatedly warns and guards: " . . . a conviction of the independence and the supremacy of mind or spirit . . . [is not] a conviction of the non-existence of matter. On the contrary, it is from an assertion of the reality of matter that we reach our conviction of the supremacy of spirit." [22] He will not accept recruits to his own brand of Theism who come because of indeterminacy: "That anyone should be turned from Atheism to Theism by a belief that electrons act unaccountably seems inconceivable." [23]

Science and Human Values

Positivism and empiricism are characterized by the Marxist as essentially bourgeois philosophies whose purported exclusion of values from the world of science conceals the importation of narrow values. Temple expresses this, not in class terms, but with a clarity which must have a social effect: "When we remember the place which belongs to the mind as a subject of value-judgments in the initiation of scientific enterprise, it becomes absurd to say that value itself has no place in the world which science seeks to comprehend." [24] And Temple, like the Marxists, refuses to see the natural sciences as the foe of human commitment: "We serve truth as a whole most effectively, not when we seek to impose religious ideas upon science, nor when we seek to impose scientific ideas upon religion, but when, studying both religion and the physical world with open and unprejudiced minds, we seek to read their lesson." [25]

Art and Experience

The conception of the artist held by the Marxist is much akin to that advanced by Temple. "The climax of Art," he writes, "is found when the great artist takes the repellent and hostile elements in experience and, welding them into the completeness of his harmony, makes them— while still in their isolation horrifying— constituent and contributory elements of the sublime." [26]

6.

As for the dialectical method itself, there is not a great deal on this in *Nature, Man and God*. But there are revealing passages in

209

less formal writings of Temple's which show that he was not only an admirer of this method, but a satisfied user as well. The following is from a letter he wrote in 1913 to Father Ronald Knox:

> "I try to think neither deductively nor inductively, but (deliberately) in circles—or in pendulum-swings. I approach a group of facts, they suggest a theory; in the light of the theory I get a fuller grasp of the facts; the fuller grasp suggests modifications of the theory—and so on—until we reach a systematic apprehension of the facts, where each fits into its place. As old Caird used to say, 'There is no harm in arguing in a circle if the circle is large enough.' "[27]

A somewhat more formal statement of the dialectical method is given in a book published a quarter of a century later. "Dialectic, at the end of the day," Temple wrote, "only means conversation or discussion. It is the attempt to reach truth by the putting of different points of view over against each other and trying to do justice to them all. It is the method which always refuses to dismiss any alleged fact or widely held belief on the ground that it will not harmonize with theories already adopted." Dialectic he said, is "a process of working round and round the available material until it is found gradually to fit into place and make a coherent scheme. . . . the real test is not usually to be found in the history of the discovery but in its subsequent vindication." [28]

7.

It is not to be assumed from this array of quotations that Temple was never critical of Marxist method or of Communist behavior. There are, I feel, certain inconsistencies to be found within *Nature, Man and God* on this score. We have seen how well Temple followed, and how careful he was to insist upon, the distinction between Mechanistic Materialism on the one hand and Dialectical Materialism on the other. In this regard he faltered somewhat when he said toward the close of his Gifford Lectures: " . . . Marx and Lenin, though insisting on the contrast between Dialectical and Mechanistic Materialism, and on the distinct reality of mind and its own processes, yet limit the activity of mind to reaction, according to those processes, to situations presented by the material order, so that mind is always secondary and dependent." [29]

The word "secondary" is a fair one, but the word "dependent" is certainly inaccurate and unfair. The Marxist would say, rather, that mind, while dependent upon matter for its existence, possesses behavior which is not reducible to the terms of matter.

In the field of social ethics, a reflection of the same confusion can be seen in this passage, taken likewise from the last of the Lectures:

"Communism seeks to create by force a world of mutual cooperation, believing that those who grow up in such a world will be freed from acquisitiveness and self-concern. But the effect will only be to direct these motives upon other subjects than wealth, such as honour and influence. And the initial trust in force, which is always an appeal to self-concern, will stimulate the sentiment which it aims at destroying." [30]

This is an ancient bogey, and it is sorrowing to see the Archbishop stumble into it at the close of so heroic a turn. No Communist "seeks" to establish socialism or communism "by force". Persuasion is better by far, and Marxists have recourse to it at every juncture. But they make— as Temple makes again and again throughout his works—a distinction between unjust wars and just wars. When revolution has recourse to war, if the revolution is genuine the recourse is justified. There is no showing in history that men who have fought for freedom have been more self-concerned than those who have been willing to let it go by the board.

8.

The insistence of this leader of modern Christian thought upon the materialism of his own position, and his equal insistence that materialism comes directly from the founder of this religion, will come as a great surprise to many Marxists of today. And they are not altogether to be blamed for their want of knowledge in this field, for Christian thought has been notoriously fickle among its epistemological and ontological suitors. Its nearest approach to a lasting pledge of the heart has been, of course, to Thomas Aquinas, but before him there was Aristotle, and before him there was Plato. Over the centuries, the official Christian commitment has been more and more strongly to idealism.

But that, it seems clear, has been because the commitment of the churches has been, historically, first to feudalism and then to capitalism. To most of the faithful, the philosophy espoused by

211

their church has seemed a relatively unimportant thing. Religion, the cry of the oppressed, the heart of a heartless world, belongs only peripherally and provisionally to the schoolmen. Their task has been to see that its social fangs are drawn—that good, hard reasons are invented for believing that the world which the meek are to inherit is not this world at all but another in the sky. To the meek, except in time of vast crisis, the point seems hardly worth arguing about, so long as they have the promise of *something*.

But the fangs keep growing back in. Vast crises arrive with increasing frequency. The pie is no longer in the sky but in the next block; Plato and Aristotle and St. Thomas, who would show us that both the pie *and* the hunger are illusory, fall into disregard, and the voices of Democritus and Marx and Lenin are heard around the churches and perhaps within them as well.

When this happens, it behooves the followers of Marx and Lenin to keep on their toes with open ears. Such has not always been their attitude, and such is not always their attitude now.

Thus, the Soviet publication of 1963, *Fundamentals of Marxism-Leninism*, which, under the comprehensive heading "Contemporary Bourgeois Philosophy", discusses existentialism, modern positivism and neo-scholasticism, casts no glance toward such Christian materialism as that of Temple.

There may be sound as well as unsound reasons for such disregard. Perhaps the authors found that Temple has no followers today. Perhaps they felt it would be incorrect to classify his as a bourgeois philosophy. Unfortunately, both of these motives are rendered implausible in the light of such a passage as this:

" . . . many philosophers—and sometimes even scientists—continue to insist that the external world has no objective existence, that the statements of science do not contain objective truth, that man cannot know the real nature of things, so that the wisest course is to place one's trust in the supernatural and accept the teachings of the Church." [31]

Such a categorical dismissal of "the Church" is certainly anachronistic in an edition published since the great 1961 encyclical of Pope John XXIII. The Church, it is true, always has had and still does have teachings as to the reality of the supernatural. But, insofar as it heeds the adjurations of John, it no longer refuses to co-operate with those who deny that reality. Thus he wrote:

" . . . in the exercise of economic and social functions, Catholics

212

often come into contact with men who do not share their view of life. On such occasions, those who profess Catholicism must take special care to be consistent and not compromise in matters wherein the integrity of religion or morals would suffer harm. Likewise, in their conduct they should weigh the opinions of others with fitting courtesy and not measure everything in the light of their own interests. They should be prepared to join sincerely in doing whatever is naturally good or conducive to good." [32]

The contrast here is striking, particularly if it is drawn with the later (1963) encyclical, *Pacem in Terris.* A significant passage is the following:

> "Meetings and agreements in the various sectors of daily life between believers and those who do not believe, or believe insufficiently because they adhere to error, can be occasions for discovering truth and paying homage to it.
>
> "It must be borne in mind, furthermore, that neither can false philosophical teachings regarding the nature, origin and destiny of the universe and of man be identified with historical movements that have economic, social, cultural or political ends, not even when these movements have originated from these teachings and have drawn and still draw inspiration therefrom.
>
> "This is so because the teachings, once they are drawn up and defined, remain always the same, while the movements, working in historical situations in constant evolution, cannot but be influenced by these latter and cannot avoid, therefore, being subject to changes, even of a profound nature. Besides, who can deny that those movements, in so far as they conform to the dictates of right reason and are interpreters of the lawful aspirations of the human person, contain elements that are positive and deserving of approval?
>
> "It can happen, then, that a drawing nearer together or a meeting for the attainment of some practical end, which was formerly deemed inopportune or unproductive, might now or in the future be considered opportune and useful.
>
> "But to decide whether this moment has arrived and also to lay down the ways and degrees in which work in common might be possible for the achievement of economic, social, cultural and political ends which are honorable and useful, are problems which can be solved with the virtue of prudence, which is the guiding light of the virtues that regulate the moral life, both individual and social." [33]

Almost as explosive as the encyclicals of John XXIII was the little book called *Honest to God* by the Anglican Bishop John A. T. Robinson. [34] Like the pronouncements of the Pope, the repercussions of this reformulation of Protestant theology constitute a subject for separate treatment. But some earlier assertions of Bishop Robinson serve as well as the encyclicals to show how wide of the mark is any dismissal of contemporary Christian philosophy in the name of Marxism. Robinson said of a 1953 symposium on Marxism and Christianity:

"Christians no more than Communists are other-worldly, in the sense that their hope is not a hope for history. Their concern for it is just as serious, in fact it must go much deeper, since they see it, not as a fortuitous concourse of atoms, but as God's creation. Their prayer is precisely that His Kingdom shall come on earth as it is in heaven." [35]

And on Marxism:

" . . . the Marxist, with no belief in an after-life, is in a real sense closer to the biblical outlook than the Christian who pins everything upon it. The Communist conception of 'the new world', as something that is coming *despite* the death of the individual, is at this point nearer to the New Testament, though in treating every generation but the last, and consequently every individual within a generation, as a means to an end, Marxism has a radically sub-Christian doctrine of man." [36]

This must be hedged as some of Temple's thoughts on Marxism must be hedged. But the direction is encouraging, and we may well follow Robinson farther:

"What does [St. Paul, I Cor. 7.31] mean by ['the form of the world is passing away'], and what does the New Testament as a whole mean by language like this, of which there is a good deal? Again, perhaps the best analogy for understanding it is provided by Marxism. The Marxist has a strong sense that the system which determines the configuration of the present order is passing away." [37]

And finally:

"There is no more facile analysis than to conclude that, while Communism is 'materialist,' Christianity is 'spiritual,' and that is that. Christianity is not spiritual in the sense that it denies matter, nor, if you really study Marxism, will you find that it denies spirit." [38]

214

Obviously, the spirit of William Temple is not dead, though his lectures may have been shoved to the back of the shelf and may create something of a scandal when they are taken down and opened. In the world revolution which is now proceeding, there is no certainty that the Christian establishment will be on the side of capitalism until the last battle. Indeed, at this moment powerful Christian bodies are opposing the imperialist adventure of the United States in Southeast Asia, and for many years they have played a significant role in the battle against racism.

For, as Temple wrote, "Only if God is revealed in the rising of the sun can He be revealed in the rising of a son of man from the dead; only if He is revealed in the history of Syrians and Philistines can He be revealed in the history of Israel; only if He chooses all men for His own can He choose any at all; only if nothing is profane can anything be sacred."[39]

Father Ronald Knox once twitted Archbishop Temple on being too concerned with the opinions of the modern sceptics—with asking too frequently, "What will Jones swallow?" Bishop Robinson is now under a similar attack. Temple's reply to Knox can serve any conscientious Christian who is accused of relating his faith to his love of his fellows: "I *am* Jones, asking what there is to eat." [40]

NOTES

1. The official biography is Frederic A. Iremonger, *William Temple, Archbishop of Canterbury; His Life and Letters* (Oxford, 1948). A useful biographical sketch is included in Joseph Fletcher, *William Temple, Twentieth Century Christian* (New York, 1963). The latter work affords the best survey of Temple's thought in all fields.
2. *The Economic Review*, Vol. 18, No. 2 (April, 1908), pp. 190-202.
3. *The Kingdom of God* (London, 1912), p. 65.
4. *Repton School Sermons* (London, 1913), pp. 58-60.
5. *Christianity in Thought and Practice* (New York, 1936), p. 83.
6. *The Church Looks Forward* (New York, 1944), p. 116.
7. *What Christians Stand For in the Secular World* (London, 1944), sec. 4.
8. *Nature, Man and God*, pp. ix-x.
9. Joseph Needham, "Thoughts of a Young Scientist on the Testament of an Elder One (John Scott Haldane)". Written in 1936 and reprinted in *Time, the Refreshing River* (London, 1943). The passage quoted is at p. 126. The reference to "a holy and efficient sacrifice" is faulty. The Prayer of Consecration refers to a "full, perfect and sufficient sacrifice"; the Invocation speaks of a "reasonable, holy, and living sacrifice." Needham was obviously quoting from the typically faulty memory of a one-time Anglican.

10. *Nature, Man and God*, p. 478.
11. *Ibid.*, p. 487 ff. The earlier passages in the Lectures, to which this passage makes reference, will be taken up below.
12. Engels, *Anti-Dühring*.
13. *Nature, Man and God*, p. 402. Cf., Isaiah 64:8: "And now, O Lord, thou art our father, and we are clay; and thou art our maker, and we are all the works of thy hands." The Collect for Peace is addressed to a God "whose service is perfect freedom."
14. *Nature, Man and God*, p. 451.
15. *Ibid.*, p. 237.
16. *Ibid.*, p. 381.
17. *Ibid.*, p. 267.
18. *Ibid.*, p. 229.
19. *Ibid.*, p. 207.
20. *Ibid.*, p. 187
21. *Ibid.*, p. 190.
22. *Ibid.*, p. 491.
23. *Ibid.*, p. 228.
24. *Ibid.*, p. 281.
25. *Ibid.*, p. 474.
26. *Ibid.*, p. 358. Cf. *Ernst Fischer, The Necessity of Art: A Marxist Approach* (Dresden, 1959): " . . . the permanent function of art is to re-create *as every individual's experience* the fullness of *all that he is not*, the fullness of humanity at large. And it is the magic of art that by this process of re-creation it shows that reality can be transformed, mastered, turned into play."
27. Cited in Robert Craig, *Social Concern in the Thought of William Temple* (London, 1963), p. 13. Edward Caird was Master of Balliol during Temple's years there.
28. *Christianity in Thought and Practice*, pp. 20-23.
29. *Nature, Man and God*, p. 498.
30. *Ibid.*, p. 513.
31. *Fundamentals of Marxism-Leninism.* English version edited by Clemens Dutt. Moscow: Foreign Languages Publishing House, 1963. p. 47.
32. *Mater et Magistra*, par. 239.
33. *Pacem in Terris*, Part IV.
34. Philadelphia, 1963.
35. John A. T. Robinson, "The Christian Hope", in D. M. Mackinnon, ed., *Christian Faith and Communist Faith* (New York, 1953).
36. John A. T. Robinson, *On Being the Church in the World*. Philadelphia, 1962. pp. 13-14.
37. *Ibid.*, pp. 15-16.
38. *Ibid.*, pp. 34-35.
39. *Nature, Man and God*, p. 306.
40. Related by David L. Edwards, ed., in *The Honest-to-God Debate* (Philadelphia, 1963), p. 72.

RELIGION AND THE SOCIALIST MOVEMENT IN THE UNITED STATES

by CATHERINE R. HARRIS

Today the Left-wing sectors of socialist thought in this country and elsewhere are largely out of touch with the religious traditions and beliefs of the past and from contemporary developments in the field of religious thought and religious studies. Most intellectual socialists are scientific humanists, not interested in religion. The fact that this outlook predominates, reflects chiefly the fact that many religious persons during the past generation have failed to maintain an interest in problems of basic economic and social change.

There was a time, before World War I, when the moral and intellectual climate in this country permitted the emergence of liberal and radical forms of religious socialism. In the future, there is again likely to be a broadening of the radical front. Political and radical religion is a helpful adjunct to a political radical movement.

We may hope that the day is not far off when there will be a revival of religious and Christian socialism in this country on a perceptible scale. The entrenched antagonism and lack of sympathy with the religious outlook which in the past has characterized important Marxist sections of the socialist movement is now in process of being rapidly overcome.

On the basis of my interest in the growth and unification of the socialist movement, I have undertaken the following historical review of the earlier ambivalent and complicated relations that existed between religious and non-religious types of socialism prior to the period of World War II. Most of the survey will be devoted to a description of events that took place before 1917.

The Labor Movement and Social Christianity

The tension that arose in nineteenth century Europe between the proletarian socialist movement and the beliefs and institutions

217

of organized religion was to be found also on this side of the Atlantic.[1] It was to be expected that anti-religious attitudes would be imported into the United States by radical European immigrants, especially by those coming from Germany.

Side by side with this influence, there was also an indigenous anti-clericalism and antagonism to conventional church attitudes in the broader labor movement. This movement included workers of diverse ethnic origin, many of whom were of English-language background and readily assimilated for that reason into the mainstream of American culture. The anti-religious sentiment was not always specifically socialist in character. It was aroused in the course of trade-union struggles of this period. The middle and upper class churches were hostile to the trade-union movement. This fact was bitterly resented by articulate labor leaders who made their reactions public in no uncertain terms.

The labor attack on religion was both pragmatic and moralistic. While the Marxist attitude toward religion was derived partly from the scientific rationalism of the enlightenment, we find in the American labor movement a more purely social emphasis. The working-class leadership rejected Protestant Christianity because of the way it operated in the sphere of human relations. The protest was in itself typically Protestant, attacking the conventional churches on the authority of the Bible, accusing them of falsifying the original democratic gospel of Jesus.

In the urban areas the average middle or upper class church emphasized the administration of a patronizing kind of charity to the poor, which was resented by many of the recipients. Many persons in the Protestant urban working class were alienated from church membership and activity.

A good many years before the Civil War, a moral accusation against organized religion was being voiced by labor representatives who were conscious of their democratic dignity, of their right to speak authoritatively and to call the churches to account for dereliction of duty. A resolution introduced at the Second Industrial Congress of 1847 representing seven states read in part as follows:

> ... we are constrained to declare, more in sorrow than in anger, that the great body of the so-called Christian Church and clergy of the present day are fearfully recreant to the high and responsible duties placed upon them. That they sustain the blood-stained banner of

capital and fraud in their crusade against labor . . . therefore we would warn them that if they would have those principles which they preach, and by which they profess to be governed, influence the people of this country, they must infuse into their teachings and practice more of truth, justice, and regard for the rights of humanity.[2]

A similar evangelical note was being expressed as late as 1910, as in the following statement by William L. Lewis:

And now we feel at liberty to ask the indignant follower of the lowly Nazarene what he and his like have meant by this two thousand years of cant about the Fatherhood of God and the Brotherhood of Man? What kind of brotherhood? A brotherhood in which the brother with a weaker body or a less cunning brain shall be fed on poorer food and wear inferior clothing and live in a less desirable house? Is this the mouse your mountain has brought forth after all these centuries of labor? Nay, gentlemen, you are not in earnest. . . . The world is weary of your pretenses. . . . And now it requests you to step aside and give room to earnest men and sincere women who really believe in, and labor to realize, that doctrine of human brotherhood which you have preached so long in sniffling tones, and which in your hearts you have always despised[3]

James Dombrowski, in his survey of the nineteenth century situation, summarizes the labor case against religion as follows:

Labor leaders criticized religion on four counts: first, that it was conservative, viewing society with its class distinctions as a result of an unalterable edict of Providence; second, that it taught meekness and submission to authority, rather than revolt in the face of oppression and injustice, and offered the rewards of a life in the next world as compensation for the lack of well-being and happiness in this world; third, that its ethical pretensions with respect to brotherhood were steeped in hypocrisy, since it preferred charity instead of economic equality and justice; fourth, that its vested interests and dependence upon the wealthy ruling class made it inevitably an instrument for promoting the ends of the bourgeois group and explained its failure to take the side of the workers in any of the major industrial disputes in the United States.[4]

At the same time that this labor protest was being made, there was developing a liberal and radical movement within Protestantism which has come to be known as "social Christianity" or sometimes as the "social gospel" movement. The appearance of social Christianity cannot be attributed to any one single cause. It involved a rejection of the moral individualism of Protestant fundamentalism. A theological liberalization went hand in hand with a social reorientation. For the most part, this movement did not go much beyond liberalism and reformism. The more radical wing went on to make penetrating criticism of the capitalist system, and became identified with Christian socialism.

Throughout the history of the pre-World War I socialist movement, three types of approach to socialism were interwined without being wholly reconciled. One was the Marxist of Left-wing socialism with its class struggle emphasis and its consciousness of being identified directly with the working class. The other was the ethico-religious or independent socialism that was associated with the Protestant reform. The latter was largely a middle class movement. Its leaders were addressing primarily a middle class audience. A third brand of so-called "grass roots" socialism, under the leadership of mid-western radicals, gained a following among progressive farmers and some labor groups. It was an eclectic socialism of a vaguely religious type, considerably influenced by Utopian and Fabian thought. The "Appeal to Reason", a weekly paper issued from Girard, Kansas, was the organ of this mid-Western type of radicalism, becoming by far the most widely read socialist paper in the United States. From 1900 to 1910 it maintained a circulation of between 300,000 and 500,000.[5] In 1896 the mid-western group founded the Brotherhood of the Cooperative Commonwealth, of which Eugene Debs was national organizer. Its stated purpose was "To usher in—A union of socialists in the world, the Brotherhood of the Cooperative Commonwealth, Mutualism, or the Kingdom of God here and now."

The Development of Religious Socialism

Religious socialism as it developed within the Protestant culture of the United States had a multiple origin.[6] It was influenced by British Fabian thought, by the work of John Ruskin, and by the writings of prominent Christian socialists in England. Most of its force, however, derived from American leadership. Henry George and Edward Bellamy were two of the most influential figures in the development of a popular middle class socialism. Both of them were religious believers, relating their social views closely to their religious outlook. Any history of radicalism in the United States must pay due respect to the interest and political activity which

George's single-tax program aroused. The influence of Bellamy's fantasy *Looking Backward* in stimulating the formation of the socialistic "Nationalist Clubs" is equally well known. Bellamy's socialist message appealed to many Protestant ministers as well as to laymen.

The George and Bellamy influences fed into the "social Christianity" movement which had arisen earlier, partly in response to the challenge of working class agitation and organization.

Reinhold Niebuhr has designated Walter Rauschenbusch as "the real founder of Social Christianity in this country", but this statement is historically inaccurate since Rauschenbusch's most influential writings appeared between the years 1907 and 1917. By that time social Christianity had been established in recognizable form for more than thirty years. If any one person could be said to have been its founder, the honor might go to a Protestant layman, Stephen Colwell. He was a wealthy Philadelphia manufacturer, interested in religion, political economy, and sociology, who was also a trustee of the Princeton Theological Seminary. He published a remarkable book in 1851 called *New Themes for the Protestant Clergy*, in which he raised the question of the relation of religion to the political and economic order. He criticized strongly the bourgeois character of the Church. Colwell himself was not a socialist, having hopes of a Christian reformation of capitalism, but he was by no means out of sympathy with socialism. He stated:

> We look upon the whole socialist movement as one of the greatest events of this age. We believe no man can understand the progress of humanity or its present tendencies who does not make himself, to some extent, acquainted with the teachings of socialism, and does not watch its movements. It is regarded by many, especially by Protestant divines, as a war upon Christianity. This betrays ignorance . . . it is stubborn and wicked conservatism which is rooted to one spot in this world of evil . . . not perceiving that the social, political, and commercial institutions of the present day, founded on and sustained by a selfishness heretofore unequalled, are the great barriers to the progress of Christianity. The works of socialists have exposed this hideous skeleton of selfishness—they have pursued it with unfaltering hatred; and this constitutes our main obligation to them . . .[7]

Colwell's book, followed by several others which he wrote within the space of a few years, was greeted with indifference and with antagonism by most of his religious contemporaries. In 1871, Colwell was instrumental in founding at Princeton the first chair of Christian ethics ever to be established at a Protestant theological seminary in this country, an example that was followed in 1877 by the Union Theological Seminary in New York.

After the Civil War, a number of American clergymen became actively engaged in building up a Christian socialist movement. Jesse H. Jones, a Congregationalist minister, preached his own distinctive brand of Christian communism. He inspired the organization in Boston of the Christian Labor Union which was founded in 1872. This is described as "one of the earliest efforts to bring organized religion into the class struggle on the side of the workers."[8] The Union published two shortlived papers, which espoused a revolutionary program. It endorsed the strikes taking place at that time as well as the 1878 platform of the Socialist Labor Party.

By the end of the 1880's, a number of books on Christian Socialism were being published, testifying to a considerable public interest. One of the most notable was entitled *Socialism from Genesis to Revelation*, written by the Reverend Franklin M. Sprague, who held that capitalism was incompatible with applied Christianity.[9]

One devoted and tireless minister, W. D. P. Bliss, was active for more than forty years in the interests of labor, having joined the Knights of Labor in 1886.[10] Bliss was one of the chief organizers of the Society of Christian Socialists which was founded in 1889. The society, conceiving of itself chiefly as an educational organization, stated that it had a twofold aim. One was "to show that the aim of Socialism is embraced in the aim of Christianity", and the other was "to awaken members of the Christian churches to the fact that the teachings of Jesus Christ lead directly to some specific form or forms of socialism."[11] Bliss and his followers felt themselves to be in harmony with the British Fabian movement, although the right wing Fabians later came close to renouncing socialism even as a long range goal.

A substantial majority of those involved in the religious socialist movement were adverse to a "class struggle" emphasis. They appealed to rich and poor, to owners and workers, to inaugurate an era of "reason and goodwill". Individual reform and change of heart were to be the primary instruments of social regeneration.

A less optimistic and more Marxist view was promulgated by George D. Herron, a Congregationalist minister who has been described as ". . . the most influential and dramatic character in the Christian socialist movement and the intellectual leader of social Christianity during the last decade of the nineteenth century."[12] Herron supported the Socialist Labor Party without becoming a member. He assisted Debs in opening a socialist rally in Chicago in September 1900. His speech on this occasion attempted to unify the essentials of Marxism with Christianity and with the credo of democratic individualism which he claimed would be more fully realized under socialism than under capitalism. Herron wrote that economic propaganda would not be enough to achieve the cooperative commonwealth: "Socialism must become a religion, a spiritual as well as an economic idea. . . . Not a letter of the economic philosophy or historic interpretation need be sacrificed in order for Socialism to avow itself as the historic approach to an ideal reaching away beyond itself."[13] Herron played a leading role as a reconciler of various factions in American socialism, helping to pave the way for the creation in 1901 of the Socialist Party which united various groups of Marxists, Christian socialists, and mid-western progressives in a temporary and unstable coalition.

Other Christian socialists, dissociating themselves from Herron's class struggle emphasis, were in sympathy with the moderate aims of the newly formed Socialist Party. Minister and laymen organized the Christian Socialist Fellowship (later called the Christian Socialist League) in June 1906 for the purpose of giving support to the Socialist Party.[14] Christian Socialists at that time were publishing two weekly papers and a monthly magazine. An increasing number of articles sympathetic to socialism appeared in church publications of many denominations. Walter Rauschenbusch's *Christianity and the Social Crisis*, which appeared in 1907, attained readily a fairly wide audience and was received with a good deal more sympathy than its author had anticipated.

We can look back to the decades stretching from 1870 to 1917 as a special period in United States history during which the interest in socialism on the part of middle class persons identified with the Protestant tradition gradually reached a peak which has not been attained again since that time. While the views expressed by writers within the Christian socialist movement varied, ranging from liberal to radical, it is fair to say that the ideology and values of capitalism were attacked by even the mildest socialists of that day in a relatively forthright manner. It should be remembered, however, that even at its height, the Christian socialist movement reached only a small minority of American Protestants.

The Relations between Religious Socialism and the General Movement

There was a certain amount of mutual hostility and mistrust between persons in the camp of Left-wing or Marxist socialism and those whose views were religious or at least non-Marxist. We cannot say that this hostility was universal. It would also be going too far to say that the mistrust on the part of the Left-wing socialists was based wholly or even primarily on the sense of difference in religious outlook. Left-wing socialists, identified with the working class, were convinced that socialism would be achieved almost wholly through working-class action. They were hostile toward middle-class gradualism and toward the tactics of class collaboration called for by many persons in the Christian socialist movement. For their part, a number of "respectable" middle class socialists in the Bellamy nationalist clubs and in Christian socialist groups wished to make it quite clear that they were not endorsing the "atheism" of the Left-wing, popularly associated with "immorality". Many nationalists held aloof from direct association with people in the working class.

The attitude of Marxists in the Socialist Labor Party toward other varieties of American socialism and toward religious socialism was variable. Daniel DeLeon, later noted for his extreme sectarianism and intolerance of opposition, was himself a recruit from the "nationalist" socialism of Bellamy. Long after he had left the Nationalist movement, he was still ready to write of "the great service rendered by Bellamy to the cause of human progress."[15]

The Workmen's Advocate, organ of the Socialist Labor Party, was sympathetic toward Bliss, the crusading Christian Socialist minister, when Bliss lost his post as an Episcopal minister in 1890. The paper at that time described him as an ". . . . honest man and scientific socialist . . . driven from his pulpit for daring to preach the doctrines of the Carpenter of Nazareth." Nine years later, however, the Socialist Labor Party paper The People published an article which ridiculed Bliss for his preaching of socialism to the rich: "Asking God and landlords and speculators to change their tactics is more absurd than trying to make a hungry lion lay down in peace besides a lamb!"[16]

224

The Socialist Party incorporated a number of American Marxists and left-wing socialists who had withdrawn from the Socialist Labor Party, as well as center and right-wing socialist groups. The question of the stand to be taken with respect to religion by the party and by individual members in their capacity as propagandists for the party became a subject of considerable dispute.[17] The party contained many persons who believed that religious ideology should be demolished, while at the other extreme were Christian socialists who did not want to alienate themselves from the church membership and who strove to give socialism a religious sanction.

The Socialist Party as an organization was committed to the strategy of political action and the seeking of votes, and was quite eager to solicit the support of Protestant ministers. A great many socialists, however, carried on their usual attacks on organized religion during this period. At the Party convention in 1908 it was proposed that the platform include a statement declaring that "religion" was of no official concern to the Party. This proposal was protested by the left wing section and by many in the center. At least one religious radical, Elliott Smith, an Episcopalian minister from Massachusetts, objected to the new policy, so strong was his feeling concerning the reactionary role of church organization. He maintained that Christianity in its present organizational form would have to "go under." Another eloquent plea expressing the common anti-religious attitude is on record in the following convention speech:

> . . . when we talk of educating mankind and when we talk of raising mankind above the level in which he is, then we have got to throw from his arms those crutches that bind him to his slavery, and religion is one of them. Let it be understood that the moment the Socialist Party's whole aim and object is to get votes, we can get them more quickly by trying to please the religionists and those whose only ambition is to pray to God and crush mankind. . . . To spread forth to the world that religion is the individual's affair and that religion has no part in the subjection of the human race, we lie when we say it. (Great applause). The Socialist Party has reached a stage where it has come to the turnpike, and will either have to stand for the truth or declare for opportunism of the barest kind and invite anybody and everybody to give us their vote, irrespective of the importance of the views they hold on economic slavery.[18]

The resolution placating the "religionists" was finally passed by a margin of a single vote when it became tacitly understood that the "materialist attitude toward religion" could still be explained from the lecture platform.

Apparently, anti-religious socialist speakers continued to operate as they had before the resolution of 1908 was passed. We find Walter Rauschenbush, an outstanding exponent of Christian socialism, complaining in 1912 that socialist leaders were permitting some of their speakers to violate the policy of neutrality on the question of religion which had been pledged by the party platform.[19]

The Socialist Party soon passed into the control of the "Right wing", composed largely of middle-class business and professional people and conservative trade unionists.[20] The left wing was expelled in 1919. From that time on the socialist movement in the United States was split into several separate organizations, events being greatly influenced by the Russian Revolution and by the newly mobilized hostility of the entire capitalist world to the emerging socialist nation.

The epoch in world history that began in 1917 coincided with the decline of the progressive and anti-monopoly movement in the United States and also with the decline of the Christian socialist movement. The U. S. Communist Party, organized in 1919, felt itself to be culturally a part of the international communist movement. Its theoretical attitude on religion followed the Marxist tradition.

During the depression decade of the 1930's a strong pro-socialist sentiment developed among the liberal Protestant clergy. At the time that Reinhold Niebuhr was developing his "crisis theology" he was also calling himself a "Christian Marxist."[21] The great majority of socialist clergymen felt much closer to the Socialist Party than to the Communist Party. Little friendly collaboration and cultural interchange between these two segments of American socialist thought took place during this period.[22]

An Abstract of the Past

It appears that the anti-religious attitude that was marked among some socialists and labor spokesmen expressed a strong class resentment of "status quo" religion, a sense of its moral and social irrelevance and a repudiation of the moral pose adopted by the urban churches in their opposition to labor. The attack on this sort of "religion" was bound up with an attack on "religion in general". Support of "religion" and support of "economic slavery" were sometimes conceived as two sides of the same coin. Anti-religious socialists were ready at times to tolerate religious socialists when they appeared to be on the right side of the fence in their social sympathies, but their theology was regarded as a regrettable handicap. The rationalistic antagonism of Marxism to religion in general became fused with the evangelical or moralistic anti-religious antagonism of the militant labor leadership. The arguments against religion reflected a complex of attitudes.

Rauschenbusch expressed the opinion that "Socialist leaders in America have committed an enormous tactical mistake in allowing Socialism to be put in antagonism to Christianity."[23] In fact, the anti-religious hostility could scarcely be described as a rational tactic. It was a strong emotional expression, a repudiation of the claims of special groups to act as self-constituted moral and social authorities. Anti-religious agitation was associated with the democratic independence and the moral self-sufficiency of the working classes who in defying class oppression were also overthrowing the authoritarian sanctification of upper-class power. It was entirely consistent with the democratic protest that the authority of the New Testament Gospels should have been used by the anti-religious groups to sanction the socialist cause.

Many religious socialists, immersed in their middle-class environment, were unable to project themselves into the feelings of those who identified with labor or who were themselves in the ranks of labor. Some were all too ready to misinterpret in a crude manner the nature of the "historical materialism" of socialist theory. Even Walter Rauschenbusch took this position, failing to achieve a full insight into the rational and emotional basis of the Left-wing socialist and labor hostility toward church religion.

The anti-religious emphasis of many American socialists was accompanied by an exaggerated optimism concerning the ability of a politically conscious working class to achieve a socialist victory single handedly in a developed capitalist economy. Such an optimism, which saw single-class victory as achievable in the fairly near future, was able to postpone serious thought about what would be involved in an alternative long-range strategy of coalition and collaboration among persons in various class groups should a more protracted endeavor prove necessary.

A good many of the middle-class socialists of the same period were similarly optimistic, differing from the Left-wing in their opposition to the dualistic class struggle theory of social change. Socialism was to involve a mild struggle, an organized effort for change, chiefly through parliamentary political action, communication and persuasion, aided by a spontaneous heaven-sent increase of good will.

We must bear in mind that the ideological divisions within the pre-World War I socialist movement were not clearcut. By no means all middle class socialists were religious socialists. Some opposed the left wing on matters that had no connection with religion. A policy of racial separatism was supported by a good many persons in the socialist right wing but was actively opposed by the Left. Some of the more realistic religious socialists shared the Left-wing view concerning the extent of opposition that would be encountered among the privileged classes and entrenched interests when it came to making a fundamental change in the economic system. Yet these realists in the religious camp were unwilling to discard reliance on the evangelical and moral method of appeal that cut across class lines, strove for maximum communication, and looked toward the construction of a unifying social movement.

The Present in the Light of the Past

At the present time, the religious controversies within the socialist culture of the past have lost their relevance.

A look at the past reveals an age that was ethically more unsophisticated and more idealistic than our own post-Victorian capitalist culture. Today, in a political atmosphere of moral apathy, nihilism, and nationalism, the emotional boundary between an idealistic active humanism and radical humanistic religion is vague and undefinable. Committed ethical universalists and idealists, religious or not, are an embattled minority.

Today ethical and political communication is proceeding across the lines of theological division. This is true in the Negro liberation and peace movements. Today we have also a Catholic Left-wing which is showing considerable initiative in communicating with various Marxist groups. An American socialist movement of the future will undoubtedly follow the pattern of the intersectarian unity that is developing on all the front lines of progressive social action and thought.

NOTES

1. For a summary impression of this antagonism, see H. Richard Niebuhr, *The Social Sources of Denominationalism,* first published 1929, Living Age Books, N. Y., Meridian Books press.
2. George E. McNeill, *The Labor Movement,* N. Y. 1887, p. 210.
3. William L. Lewis, *Ten Blind Leaders of the Blind,* Chicago, 1910, p. 190.
4. James Dombrowski, *The Early Days of Christian Socialism in America,* N. Y. 1936, ch. 12.
5. Ira Kipnis, *The American Socialist Movement, 1897-1912,* N. Y., 1952, ch. 12.
6. The most useful single source of information on the background of Christian socialism is the book by Dombrowski, cited above.
7. Stephen Colwell, *New Themes for the Protestant Clergy, Philadelphia,* 1851, pp. 359-63.
8. Dombrowski, *op. cit.,* ch. 7, p. 77.
9. Howard H. Quint, *The Forging of American Socialism,* N. Y., 1964, ch. 4 on "The Christian Socialist Crusade".
10. See Dombrowski, *op. cit.* ch. 9; also Quint, *op. cit.*
11. Dombrowski, *op. cit.* ch. 9, p. 99; also Quint, *op. cit.*
12. Dombrowski, *op. cit.* ch. 13, p. 171; also Quint, *op. cit.*
13. Kipnis, *op. cit.,* ch. 13, p. 267.
14. Kipnis,, *op. cit.* ch. 13 pp. 269-70.
15. Cited by Quint, *op. cit.* ch. 3, p. 86.
16. Quint, *op. cit.* ch. 4, pp. 117 and 126.
17. Kipnis, *op. cit.* ch. 13.
18. Socialist Party, *Proceedings of the National Convention,* 1908, p. 204, speech by C. H. Vander Porten. Cited by Kipnis, *op. cit.* ch. 13.
19. Walter Rauschenbusch, *Christianizing the Social Order,* N. Y., 1912, ch. 7, p. 398.
20. Kipnis, *op cit.* ch. 19.
21. Robert Moats Miller, *American Protestantism and Social Issues, 1919-39,* Chapel Hill, 1958, ch. 6.
22. Miller, *op. cit.* ch. 6 and 7.
23. Rauschenbusch, *op. cit.,* p. 398.

THE PUBLISHED WRITINGS OF HARRY FREDERICK WARD:
A BIBLIOGRAPHY°

This bibliography includes, it is hoped, all the published work of Dr. Ward that appeared in books, pamphlets and magazines; no attempt has been made to include translations of his writings, nor letters which appeared in various newspapers. In all cases, for each year, first are listed books, then pamphlets, and then articles, the latter given in chronological order. Separate titles reach the formidable total of 192; of these 20 are books.

1909
1. "Palestine for the Jews," *World Today*, September, XVII, 1062-69

1910
1. Ed., *Social Ministry: An Introduction to the Study and Practice of Social Service;* for the Methodist Federation for Social Service (N.Y., Eaton and Mains; Cincinnati, Jennings & Graham) 326p.
2. "The Religion of Kipling," *Methodist Review*, October, IX, 318-24

1912
1. "Muscatine," *Survey*, June 1, XXVIII, 362-63

1914
1. *The Social Creed of the Churches* (N.Y., Eaton & Mains), 196p. (Reprinted, 1915, Abingdon Press, N.Y.).
2. *Social Service for Young People, What Is It?* (Boston, Social Service Department of the Congregational Churches), 48p.
3. Ed., *A Yearbook of the Church and Social Service in the United States* (N.Y., Fleming H. Revell, Vol. I), 328p.

1915
1. *Social Evangelism* (N.Y., Missionary Education Movement of the U.S. and Canada), 145p.
2. *Poverty and Wealth from the Viewpoint of the Kingdom of God* (N.Y., Methodist Book Center), 135p.
3. "The Church and Social Service, A Selected List [of Readings]", *General Theological Library Bulletin* (Boston), October, VIII, No. 1, 9-13

1916
1. Ed., *A Yearbook of the Church and Social Service in the United States*, (N.Y., Fleming H. Revell, Vol. II), 318p.
2. *The Living Wage: A Religious Necessity*, (Philadelphia, American Baptist Publishing Society), 24p.
3. "Establishing World-Wide Social Justice," *World Outlook*, May, II, 3-4.

1917
1. in collaboration with Sidney A. Weston, *The Bible and Social Living*, edited by Henry H. Meyer, (N.Y., Methodist Book Concern) 196p.

°Prepared by Prof. Robert S. Cohen, with the collaboration of the Editor.

2. *The Labor Movement, from the Standpoint of Religious Values* (N.Y., Sturgis & Walton), 207p.
3. *Social Duties in War Time* (N.Y., Association Press) 168p.
4. with Henry A. Atkinson, *What Every Church Should Know About Its Community* (N.Y., Federal Council of the Churches of Christ in America) 27p. (re-written by S. M. Harrison & W. M. Tippy).
5. *Foreign Missions and Social Service* (N.Y., Board of Foreign Missions of the Methodist Episcopal Church) 8p. September, CIII, 96-100

1918

1. (with Richard H. Edward), *Christianizing Community Life*, (N.Y., Association Press, for Council of North American Student Movements), 180p.
2. *The Christian Demand for Social Reconstruction* (Phila., W. H. Jenkins), 126p.
3. *The Gospel for a Working World* (N.Y., Missionary Education Movement of the U.S. and Canada), 260p.
4. *The Religion of Democracy* (Boston, The Murray Press), 12p.
5. "The Present Task of Christian Ethics," *Union Theological Inaugural Exercises*, 18-27

1919

1. *The New Social Order: Principles and Programs* (N.Y., Macmillan), 393p.
2. *The Opportunity for Religion in the Present World Situation* (N.Y., The Womans Press), 66p.
3. *Social Unrest in the United States* (N.Y., Methodist Federation for Social Service), 15p.
4. "Capital and Labor after the War," *World Outlook*, January, V, 10
5. "The Russian Question," *Social Service Bulletin*, January-February (Methodist Federation for Social Service)
6. "Labor and the New Social Order," *Homiletic Review*, March, LXXVII, 222-30
7. "A Statement by Prof. Harry F. Ward," *Christian Advocate*, April 3, XCIV, No. 14. (This is related to the two items, 8a and 8b, below.)
8. "The Kaiser and Others: The Treatment of International Offenders in the Light of Penal Reform," *World Tomorrow*, November, II, 298-303
8a. "Bolshevism and the Methodist Church: An Account of the Controversy Precipitated by Prof. Ward," *Current Opinion*, June, LXVI, 380-81
8b. G. Taylor, "The Bolshevism of Prof. Ward," *Survey*, March 29, XLI, 920-21

1920

1. "The Social Revolution and Religion," *Christian Century*, April 1, XXXVII, No. 14, 10-13
2. "Why I Believe in Giving Justice," *Bible World*, July, LIV, 348-51
3. "Some Studies in Christian Fellowship," *Churchman*, December 12, XV, 12-18

Bibliography

1921

1. "The Bible and the Proletarian Movement," *Journal of Religion*, May, I, No. 3, 271-81
2. "The Competitive System and the Mind of Jesus," *Christian Century*, June 9, XXXVIII, No. 23, 9-12
3. "The Moral Valuation of our Economic Order," *Journal of Religion*, July, I, N. 4, 416-17
4. "Christianity in the Modern World," *The Nation*, July 13, CXIII, 47-49
5. "The Open Shop Drive," *Christian Work*, July 30, CXI, 142-43
6. "Can the Church Stand Fire?" *The Nation*, August 24, CXIII, 195-98
7. "Which Way Will Methodism Go?" *Methodist Review*, September-October, CIV, 685-695

1922

1. "Dies Turns Philosopher," *Christian Century*, February 16, XXXIX, No. 7, 204-06
2. "West Virginia and the Church," *Churchman*, March 11, CXXV, No. 10, 14-15
3. "The Challenge of West Virginia to the Churches," *Christian Work*, March 18, CXII, No. 11, 339-40
4. "The Function of the Church in Industry," *Annals, American Academy*, September, II, 476-89
5. "Social Science and Religion," *Journal of Religion*, September, II, 476-89

1923

1. *Repression of Civil Liberties in the United States* (1918-1923) (Chicago, Publication, American Sociological Society) 24p.
2. "What the Church is Doing for the Workingman: The Challenge of Religion," *Locomotive Engineers Journal*, January, XXI, 14-17
3. "Our Political Secret Service," *Christian Century*, April 26, XL, 525-27
4. Review of *The Decay of Capitalist Civilization*, by Sidney and Beatrice Webb, *New Student*, June 2, II, No. 18, 8.
5. "Can the Church Influence Public Opinion?" *The Nation*, June 27, CXVI, 739-40
6. "Is the Profit Motive an Economic Necessity?" *Christian Century*, June 28, XL, 810-13
7. "American Christianity and Social Idealism," *American Review*, July-August, I, No. 4, 434-41
8. "Is Profit Christian?" *Christian Century*, December 27, XL, 1681-84

1924

1. *The Profit Motive: Is It Indispensable to Industry?* (N.Y., League for Industrial Democracy), 44p.
2. "Amnesty and the Civil Liberties Union," *The Nation*, March 26, CXVIII, 3064 (Letter to the Editor)
3. "How Can Civilization Be Saved?" *Christian Century*, September 11, XLI, 1176-78
4. "Professor Harry F. Ward in India: An Interview," *Christian Century*, November 13, XLI, 1481

233

1925

1. *Ethical Aspects of Industrialism* (Peking, Peking Leader Press) 88p. A series of lectures, delivered at the National University, Peking.
2. "The Future of the Intellectual Class," *Calcutta Review*, February, XIV, No. 2, 227-43
3. "Will Religion Survive in Russia?" *Christian Century*, February 12, XLII, 215-18
4. "Civil Liberties in Russia," *The Nation*, March 4, CXX, 234-37
5. "Lenin and Gandhi," *World Tomorrow*, April, VIII, No. 4, 111-12
6. "The New Situation in India," *The Nation*, April 29, CXX, 489-90
7. "Gandhi and the Future of India," *Christian Century*, June 4, XLII, 727-29
8. "Will Russia Return to Capitalism?" *The Nation*, July 8, CXXI, 64-67
9. "Chinese Christians and the Shooting in Shanghai," *Christian Century*, July 16, XLII, 918-20
10. "The Meaning of Shanghai," *The Nation*, July 22, CXXI, 108-09
11. "China Learns from the West," *Christian Century*, July 30, XLII, 973-75
12. "What the Chinese Want," *New Republic*, August 26, XLIV, 9-11
13. "Strike! The Students of China Fight for their Country's Freedom," *New Student*, October 3, V, No. 1, 13-15
14. "Race Contacts in the World Today," *World Tomorrow*, November, VIII, 327-29
15. "The White Boomerang in China: The Patronizing Superiority of the West that is Firing China to end 'Special Privilege'", *Asia*, November, XXV, 936-40, 1004-12
16. "The Morality of Capitalism," in *Kirisutokyo Kenkyu* [Studies in the Christian Religion] November, III, No. 1 (Text in Japanese)
17. "War Talk in China," *Christian Century*, November 19, XLII, 1438-40
18. "The Future of Religion," *World Tomorrow*, December, VIII, 372-74
19. "Meaning of Upheaval in China," *Religious Education*, December, XX, 426-29

1926

1. *The New Social Order: Principles and Programs* (N.Y., Macmillan) 384p.
2. *Creative Ideas in the Orient*, (Bloomington, Ill., Public School Publishing Co.) This is reprinted from *American Review*, December, IV, 520-27.
3. "Can China Be Stabilized?" *Christian Century*, January 14, XLIII, 46-48
4. "The Political Puzzle in China," *American Review*, March, IV, 167-76
5. "Free Speech in China," *The Nation*, March 10, CXXII, 253-55
6. "China's Industrial Battlefront," *Christian Century*, March 18, XLIII, 611-13
7. "The Place of Religion in the Industrialization of China," *Chinese Students' Monthly*, April, XXI, No. 6, 12-14
8. "China's Anti-Christian Movement," *Christian Century*, April 15, XLIII, 474-76
9. "The Student Crisis in China and Political Consequences," *Chinese Students' Monthly*, May, XXI, No. 7, 50-52

234

Bibliography

10. "China's Anti-Christian Temper," *Christian Century*, May 13, XLIII, 611-13
11. "Plight of the Japanese Preacher," *Christian Century*, August 19, XLIII, 1034-36
12. "Will China Turn to Force?" *Christian Century*, October 1, XLIII, 1231-33
13. "The Kingdom of Gold," *World Tomorrow*, December, IX, 246-48

1927

1. "Growth of the Soul," *Christian Century*, February 24, XLIV, 239-41
2. "Why Violence?" *World Tomorrow*, March, X, 111-14
3. "Are We Slipping into a Chinese War?" *Christian Century*, May 12, XLIV, 585-87
4. "Free Speech for the Army," *New Republic*, July 13, LI, 194-96
5. "Anglo-American Relations in China," *Christian Century*, September 1, XLIV, 1016-18
6. "China Tests Our Religion," *Nation*, September 21, CXXV, 283-85

1928

1. "Progress or Decadence," in Kirby Page, ed., *Recent Gains in American Civilization* (N.Y., Harcourt, Brace), pp. 277-305; being a reprint of article with same title in *World Tomorrow*, November, XI, 463-66, with some additions.
2. "The Challenge of the Chinese Revolution," *China Outlook*, March 1, I, No. 4, 4-5
3. "Why I Have Found Life Worth Living," *Christian Century*, March 1, XLV, 281-83
4. "Twenty Years of the Social Creed," *Christian Century*, April 19, XLV, 502-04
5. "A Social Strategy for Religion," *Christian Century*, May 3, XLV, 566-68
6. "The Ministry," *Survey*, June 1, LX, 289-90
7. "The Function of Faith in Modern Life," *Christian*, July 12, IV, 532-33

1929

1. *Our Economic Morality and the Ethic of Jesus* (N.Y., Macmillan), 338p.
2. *What Religion Means to Me* (with Harry Emerson Fosdick and others), (Garden City, N.Y., Doubleday).
3. "Perils of Competition for Private Gain," *World Tomorrow*, January, XII, 21-24
4. "Who Commands the Officers' Reserves?" *Nation*, January 2, CXXVIII, 8-10
5. "Religion and Justice," *Christian Century*, February 7, XLVI, 194-96
6. "The Rauschenbusch Memorial," *Religious Education*, April, XXIV, 297-98
7. "Religion and Political Corruption," *Christian Century*, June 12, XLVI, 772-74
8. "Strategy for a New Economic Order," *World Tomorrow*, August, XII, 328-31

1930

1. "Is Jesus Superfluous?" *Journal of Religion*, October, X, 471-86
2. "Stagger Incomes Instead of Jobs," *Christian Century*, November 12, XLVII, 1385-86

1931

1. *Which Way Religion?* (N.Y., Macmillan), 221p.
2. "Jesus' Significance in our Modern Age," *World Tomorrow*, January, XIV, 15-17
3. "The Challenge of Unemployment Relief," *Religious Education*, March, XXVI, 200-05
4. "The Handwriting on the Wall," *Christian Century*, March 4, XLVII, 304-06

1932

1. "Religion Confronts a New World," *Christian Century*, February 3, XLIX
2. "Working for Themselves," *Christian*, May 21, VIII, 445
3. "Pioneers Among the Soviets," *Nation*, June 22, CXXXIV, 696-97
4. "Soviet Russia, Land of Youth," *Nation*, August 3, CXXXV, 103-04
5. "Religion and Anti-Religion in Russia," *Christian*, September 3, VIII, 649-51

1933

1. *In Place of Profit: Social Incentives in the Soviet Union*, (N.Y. & London, Scribner's) 476p.
2. "Preaching and the Industrial Order," in *Preaching and the Social Crisis*, edited by G. B. Oxnam (N.Y., Abingdon Press) pp. 44-62

1934

1. *Fighting to Live* (N.Y., American League Against War & Fascism) 15p.

1935

1. "Methodists Assail Roosevelt," *Literary Digest*, February 16, CIX, 17
2. "Religion and the Economic Crisis," *Friends Intelligencer*, April 6, XLII, No. 14, 213-14 (Abstract of address given at Philadelphia Yearly Meeting)
3. "The Supreme Court and the Aftermath of N.R.A.", *Fight Against War & Fascism*, July, II, No. 9, 3
4. "The Development of Fascism in the United States," *Annals*, American Academy, July, CLXXX, 55-61
5. "The Development of Fascism in the U.S.", *Christian Leader*, October 19, XXXVIII, 1324-27
6. "Judgment Day for Pacifists," *Christian Century*, December 18, LII, 1620-22
7. "Christians and Communists," *Christian Century*, December 25, LII, 1651-53

1936

1. *The Development of Fascism in the United States* (N.Y., American League Against War & Fascism) 7pp.

Bibliography

2. *Spain's Democracy Talks to America: An Interview* [with A. A. MacLeod] (N.Y., American League Against War & Fascism), 18p. Anna Louise Strong took the notes and compiled the material for this publication; it also was published in Toronto
3. "Ethiopia," *Fight Against War & Fascism,* February, III, 7
4. "Liberalism at the Crisis," *Christian Century,* March 25, LIII, 463-65
5. "Greetings on 25th Anniversary," *New Masses,* December 22, XXI, 21

1937
1. *The Fascist International* (N.Y., American League Against War & Fascism) 16p.

1938
1. *Concerted Action for Peace* (N.Y., American League for Peace & Democracy), 12p.
2. *The Neutrality Issue* (N.Y., American League for Peace & Democracy), 8p.
3. "Appeal to Members of the Methodist Federation for Social Service to Boycott Japanese Goods," *Congressional Digest,* April, XVII, 117
4. "The Morals of Reaction," *Christian Century,* November 16, LV, 1395-96

1939
1. "Introduction," to *Russia Without Illusions,* by Pat Sloan (N.Y., Modern Age Books), pp. vii-x
2. "Non-Cooperation and Conference," *Christian Century,* April 12, LVI, 474-76
3. "The International Situation and America's Relation to It," *Radical Religion,* Summer, IV, 22-27
4. "The Dies Committee and Civil Liberties," *Union Review,* December, I, No. 1, 9-11

1940
1. *Democracy and Social Change* (N.Y., Modern Age Books), 299p.
(Dr. Ward's views and actions provoked expressions of administrative displeasure this year from Union Theological Seminary; below are listed three reactions to this:)
1a. "Union Seminary's Ward," *Time,* February 5, XXXV, 38
1b. "Valiant Churchman Takes a Well-Earned Rest," *Christian Century,* February 14, LVII, 205
1c. "Rebuff to Reaction," Dr. Henry Sloane Coffin rebuffs efforts to remove Dr. Ward from Union, *New Masses,* June 18, XXXV, 16
2. "Star Chambers for Teachers [on the Rapp-Coudert investigation of New York Schools]" *New Masses,* December 24, XXXVIII, 11

1941
1. "As Seen by a Churchman and Scientist," *Soviet Russia Today,* January, IX, 16
2. "30th Anniversary Greetings," *New Masses,* February 18, XXXVIII, 26
3. "Debs, Bourne and Reed," *New Masses,* March 4, XXXVIII, 13 (text of address at 30th Anniversary meeting)

237

4. "Why Earl Browder Should Be Free," *New Masses*, March 25, XXXIX, 17
5. "The Crime of Thinking," *New Masses*, April 22, XXXIX, 24 (concerning witch-hunt in N.Y.C. schools)
6. "Christianity, an Ethical Religion," *Union Review*, May, II, 7-9
7. "The Communist Party and the Ballot," *Bill of Rights Review*, Summer, I, 286-92
8. "Two Democracies: Soviet and American," *New Masses*, November 11, XLI, 8
8a. In 1941 Dr. Ward left Union Theological Seminary; a characteristic story was "25 Years of Social Gospel: Prof. Ward of Union Retires," *Newsweek*, June 30, XVII, 46

1942

1. "Protestants and the Anti-Soviet Front," *Protestant*, December (1941)-January, IV, No. 3, 62-69
2. "Religion and Economics: A Bibliography," *Bulletin, General Theological Library*, February, XXXXIV, No. 2
3. "The Anti-Soviet Front and its Objectives," *Protestant*, April-May, IV, No. 5, 35-42
4. "Is Russia Forsaking Communism?" *Christian Century*, October 28, LIX, 1314-16
5. Review of *Victory and After* by Earl Browder, *New Masses*, December 15, XLV, No. 11, 23-27

1943

1. "It Is Time To Fight," *Protestant*, December (1942-January, V, No. 1, 56-61
2. "The Future of the Profit Motive," *Christian Century*, March 31, LX, 389-90
3. "Pulpits in War," *New Masses*, June 15, XLVII, No. 11, 15-17
4. "Reader's Digest Capitalism," *Protestant*, June-July, IV, No. 10, 26-31
5. "The Moral Equivalent of War," *Christian Century*, July 14, LX, 817-19
6. "Soviet Morals and Morality," *New Masses*, November 9, XLIX, 17-18

1944

1. *The Soviet Spirit*, (N.Y., International Publishers), 160pp.
2. "Fascist Trends in American Churches," *Christian Century*, April 19, LXI, 490-92
3. "Official Protestantism and Soviet Aims," *Protestant*, May, V, No. 8, 37-41
4. "So You Are Going to Russia," *Motive*, May, IV, No. 5, 17-19
5. "Vatican Fascism," *Christian Century*, June 12, LXI, 693-95
6. "The Soviet Personality," *New Masses*, November 14, LIII, No. 7, 13-16

1945

1. "Black Markets," *New Masses*, March 27, LIV, No. 13, p.22
2. "What Is Soviet Democracy?" *New Masses*, November 13, LVII, No. 7, 6-8

Bibliography

1946

1. "Whose State Capitalism?" *Protestant,* February, VI, No. 11, 32-39

1947

1. *Soviet Democracy* (N.Y., Soviet Russia Today), 48p.
2. "Our Relations to Russia," *Witness,* February 27, XXX, No. 11, 8-10
3. "Method in Madness," *New Masses,* November 11, LXV, No. 7, 3-6
4. "Faith, Phrases and Facts," *Zion's Herald,* December 17, CXXV, No. 51, 1203-05, 1222-23

1948

1. "Organized Religion, the State and the Economic Order," *Annals, American Academy* . . ., March, CCLVI, 72-83

1950

1. "War or Peace: The Basic Moral Issue," *Soviet Russia Today,* November, XVIII, No. 11, 8-9, 26
2. "The Necessity for Peaceful Co-Existence," *Soviet Russia Today,* December, XVIII, No. 12, 14-15, 27-28

1951

1. "Soviet Deeds Back Soviet Words on Peace," *Soviet Russia Today,* January, XVIII, No. 13, 16-17, 34-35
2. "Concerning Aggression," *Zion's Herald,* May 23, CXXIX, 798-802
3. "Why I Believe in Justice," *Bible World,* July 20, LIV, 348-51
4. "The Case of Dr. Du Bois," *Jewish Life,* July, V, No. 9, 23-25

1952

1. "The U.S.S.R.: A Reliable Partner in Peace," in *Thirty-Five Years of the Soviet State* (N.Y., National Council of American-Soviet Friendship), pp. 11-24
2. "Judgment Has Begun," *Protestant,* January-March, IX, No. 1, 1-16

1953

1. "Professor Ward's Denial," *Christian Century,* August 19, LXX, 943 (A Letter to Editor, denying truthfulness of testimony concerning him offered to the House Un-American Activities Committee)

1956

1. "Congress and Religion," *Social Questions Bulletin,* March, XLVI, No. 3, 10-11
2. "MFSA vs. Congress: The Issues," *Social Questions Bulletin,* Summer, XLVI, No. 6, 1-22

1957

1. "The Federation and Congress," *Social Questions Bulletin,* November, XLVII, No. 8, 34-36

1958

1. "The Soviet Contribution to Mankind's Future," *New World Review,* November, XXVI, No. 10, 37-42

1959

1. *The Story of American-Soviet Relations, 1917-1958* (N.Y., National Council of American-Soviet Friendship), 95p.

1960

1. "Crisis in Cuba," *Social Questions Bulletin*, September, L, No. 7, 29-31

1963

1. *The Harry F. Ward Sampler: A Selection from His Writings, 1914-1963*, edited by Annette T. Rubinstein (Ardsley, N.Y., Methodist Federation for Social Action), 30pp. (Brief excerpts are offered from: *The Church and Social Service*(1914); *The New Social Order*(1919); *Our Economic Morality and the Ethic of Jesus*(1929); *In Place of Profit*(1933); and *Democracy and Social Change*(1940).

1964

1. "What Needs Now To Be Done?", *Social Questions Bulletin*, March, LIV, No. 3, 17-19